Linking Arms Together

Linking Arms Together

AMERICAN INDIAN TREATY VISIONS OF LAW AND PEACE, 1600–1800

Robert A. Williams, Jr.

New York Oxford
OXFORD UNIVERSITY PRESS
1997

Oxford University Press

Oxford New York
Athens Auckland Bangkok Bogota Bombay Buenos Aires
Calcutta Cape Town Dar es Salaam Delhi Florence Hong Kong
Istanbul Karachi Kuala Lumpur Madras Madrid Melbourne
Mexico City Nairobi Paris Singapore Taipei Tokyo Toronto

and associated companies in
Berlin Ibadan

Published by Oxford University Press, Inc.
198 Madison Avenue, New York, New York 10016

Oxford is a registered trademark of Oxford University Press

Library of Congress Cataloging-in-Publication Data
Williams, Robert A., 1955–
Linking arms together : American Indian treaty visions of law and peace, 1600–1800 / Robert A. Williams, Jr.
p. cm.
Includes index.
ISBN 0–19–506591–3
1. Indians of North America—Government relations. 2. Indians of North America—Treaties. 3. Indians of North America—Legal status, laws, etc. I. Title.
E93.W755 1996
323.1'197—dc20 96–23095

1 3 5 7 9 8 6 4 2

Printed in the United States of America
on acid-free paper

FOR RALPH JOHNSON

teacher, mentor, friend

Acknowledgments

Many friends have generously helped me complete this project. My wife, Joy Fischer Williams, deserves special thanks for her support and patience during the past five years while I carried on the task of writing this book. Rennard Strickland in his own subtle but effective way convinced me of the need to write a book on Indian treaties. Vine Deloria, Jr., was most generous in sharing his treaty research with me. James Anaya, Rudy Peritz, and Candice Maze provided thoughtful comments on the manuscript. Christine DeZarn O'Hare assisted me in gathering research materials and preparing the index. I am grateful to them all.

I have benefited from many other types of support in writing this book. At the University of Arizona, I thank especially Michael Cusanovich, vice president for research, and E. Thomas Sullivan, former dean at the College of Law. I also thank Barbara Clelland, Norma Kelly, Kay Clark, Judy Antell, and Rebecca Scheibley for providing invaluable assistance by patiently preparing the manuscript. The John D. and Catherine T. MacArthur Foundation and the National Endowment for the Humanities extended grants that greatly aided in the completion of this book. I gratefully acknowledge their invaluable support.

Tucson, Arizona R. A. W.
September 1996

Contents

Linking Arms Together

We are what we imagine. Our very existence consists in our imagination of ourselves.

N. Scott Momaday, *The Man Made of Words*

There were even stories about the different versions of stories and how they imagined these different versions came to be.

Leslie Marmon Silko, *Storyteller*

Introduction

Paradigms for Behavior

A Response

Soon after completing *The American Indian in Western Legal Thought,*[1] I realized the need to imagine a very different kind of work for my next project. I had set out in that first book to tell the history of the legal ideas that the West brought to the New World to justify the colonization of American Indian peoples. But this, as I knew even then, was only half the story. As the cultural critic Edward Said has written, nearly everywhere in the non-Western world, the coming of the white man brought forth a response.[2]

This book examines the response of North American Indian peoples to the West's "will to empire" over them. In this sense, it *is* very different from my first book, but I also regard it as a complementary study. This book attempts to tell a history of the legal ideas that American Indian peoples sought to apply in their relations with the West during the North American Encounter era.[3]

My realization of the need for such a book was prompted by more than just scholarly interest in the intercultural dynamics of colonial era Indian diplomacy or a subversive desire to uncover the suppressed and long-silenced discourses of resistance to the West's colonial hegemony. As the legal historian G. Edward White has explained, legal scholars tend to pursue a much different type of research paradigm from that of our colleagues in the humanities or social sciences. We practice the strong belief that legal scholarship should be actively directed toward the resolution of contemporary policy issues.[4] Thus, as a legal scholar, I concede that I have immediate concerns in mind when I examine the history of legal thought in the European conquest of the Indian in America, whether it be the legal thought of Indians or that of Europeans.

For nearly a decade now, I have listened closely to the concerns expressed by indigenous tribal peoples in their ongoing decolonization efforts around the world.[5] This global reality of the active resistance of indigenous tribal peoples to continuing Western domination has helped me realize the contemporary relevance of the first responses of North American Indians to the coming of the white man to the New World.

One simple story illustrates the important point that the many different types of self-determination struggles presently carried on by the world's indigenous tribal peoples have a long history behind them. At the 1988 session of the United Nations Human Rights Commission's Working Group on Indigenous Populations in Geneva, Switzerland, an Iroquois diplomat made a special presentation to the Working Group of the *Gus-Wen-Tah,* the Two Row Wampum treaty belt.[6] This sacred treaty belt is part of a long tradition of Iroquois resistance to the West's vision of Indian rights.[7] The *Gus-Wen-Tah* treaty belt was presented centuries ago by the Iroquois to the Western colonizing nations that first came to North America.

The *Gus-Wen-Tah* is comprised of a bed of white wampum shell beads symbolizing the sacredness and purity of the treaty agreement between the two sides. Two parallel rows of purple wampum beads that extend down the length of the belt represent the separate paths traveled by the two sides on the same river. Each side travels in its own vessel: the Indians in a birch bark canoe, representing their laws, customs, and ways, and the whites in a ship, representing their laws, customs, and ways. In presenting the *Gus-Wen-Tah* to solemnize their treaties with the Western colonial powers, the Iroquois would explain its basic underlying vision of law and peace between different peoples as follows: "We shall each travel the river together, side by side, but in our own boat. Neither of us will steer the other's vessel."[8]

In presenting the *Gus-Wen-Tah* to the group charged with the task of drafting the United Nations' Universal Declaration on the Rights of Indigenous Peoples,[9] the Iroquois were renewing a centuries-old indigenous North American legal tradition. They were offering an American Indian vision of the law governing the relations between the different peoples of the world.

Paradigms for Behavior

Those who have observed or participated in the ongoing decolonization efforts of indigenous peoples around the world will be quick to tell you that the reemergence of the Two Row Wampum at the United Nations in Geneva is not an isolated story of the continuing relevance of tribal traditions in the contemporary indigenous rights movement. As intervenors in the international human rights process, in litigation and petitions before the lawmaking bodies of their Western colonizers, in tribal councils and community meetings, and, at times, even in armed conflicts, the world's indigenous tribal peoples assert that their traditions are highly relevant to the determination of their rights in their relations with the West. Like the Two Row Wampum presented to the United Nations Working Group, these indigenous tribal responses embrace visions of law between different peoples opposed to the colonizing legal tradition of the West. These indigenous tribal visions assert that the world's tribal peoples are entitled to the same basic human rights of cultural survival, autonomy, and self-determination recognized as belonging to the peoples from Europe who colonized them.

From the first recorded colonial encounters, tribal visions of law like that represented by the *Gus-Wen-Tah* have sought to provide the paradigms for behavior in the relations between indigenous tribal peoples and the Western settler–societies.[10] These paradigms are imprinted on the historical patterns of tribal resistance to Western colonial domination. They have been long suppressed by the West because they deny the underlying legal legitimacy and moral foundation of the West's continuing colonial hegemony over indigenous tribal peoples.

As this book relates, there was a time when the West had to listen seriously to these indigenous tribal visions of how different peoples might live together in relationships of trust, solidarity, and respect. Throughout the North American Encounter era of the seventeenth and eighteenth centuries, the survival of many of the European colonies in North America depended on their ability to reach accommodation with surrounding Indian tribes. In countless treaties, councils, and negotiations, American Indians insisted upon the relevance of the principles contained in tribal traditions such as the *Gus-Wen-Tah* for ordering the unique and fractious kind of multicultural society that was emerging on the continent. Throughout this period, Europeans secured Indian trade, alliances, and goodwill by adapting themselves to tribal approaches to the problems of achieving law and peace in a multicultural world.

The treaties, councils, and negotiations between Europeans and Indians during the Encounter era reveal a truly unique North American indigenous perspective on the principles and governing paradigms for achieving justice between different peoples. In a rapidly changing world of human diversity and conflict, American Indians sought to apply their traditions to the problems of achieving law and peace on a multicultural frontier. Given the fragmenting nature of our present societal and world order, there are a number of important reasons for trying to develop a better understanding of these American Indian tribal visions of law, peace, and justice between different peoples.

The White Man's Indian Law

A better understanding of American Indian visions of law and peace resituates American Indians from the margins to the center of a history of the legal traditions that have determined Indian tribalism's rights and status in America. As Vine Deloria, Jr., my former colleague at the University of Arizona, once instructed me, a major problem with the way that most non-Indian scholars have discussed the law governing relations between the United States and Indian tribes is that there are no Indians in the story. It is as if the great historical struggles for Indian survival that finally culminate in a U.S. Supreme Court opinion or congressionally enacted statute were fought only by groups of non-Indian lawyers and advocates in the white man's courtrooms and legislatures.

The emphasis of most scholars who have written on the role of law in the relations between Indians and European-derived peoples focuses almost exclusively on the story of "the white man's Indian law."[11] The story builds on a narrative theme, either expressed or implied, that the legal rules and principles adhered to in the course of this country's historical dealings with Indian peoples are the exclusive by-products of the Western legal tradition brought to America from the Old World. These by-products, so the familiar story goes, were then developed here by the courts and policymaking institutions established by the dominant European-derived society into a redemptive force for perpetuating American Indian tribalism's survival. Without the European Law of Nations, without the English common law's recognition of fiduciary duties arising from a guardian-ward relationship, without the elasticity of feudalistic property law concepts to recognize and protect lesser rights of aboriginal occupancy on the land, without the precedent of the King's sovereign prerogatives of centralized control over colonial affairs, and so on—that is, without the white man's Indian law, as this story tells it—the Indian would no longer be among us.

The story of the white man's Indian law as the salvation of the Indian in North America has exercised an unshakable hold on the legal imagination of generations of Indian law scholars. They have told and retold its various chapters in their committed efforts to understand and perpetuate tribalism's survival in the United States. Yet when we closely examine this provocative idea of the white man's Indian law serving as a positive, purposive force in tribalism's persistence in this country, we immediately confront a most difficult conceptual problem. It is the problem that inevitably arises from the very nature of the colonial situation. We are talking, after all, about the legal system of one of the modern world's most efficient colonizing powers. The United States began as a loose and disorganized confederation of thirteen former Atlantic seaboard British colonies, expanding its sovereignty over the vast, prime midsection of North America in less than a century of frontier conquest. In the process, the United States basically eliminated Indian tribalism as a potent political or cultural force on the continent. Given its history, how does this system of colonizing law imposed on the Indian by the United States—this white man's Indian law—manage to transcend the threat it has historically posed to the perpetuation of Indian cultural identity, existence, and sovereignty? How can such a unilaterally imposed system of colonizing law and power ever manage to assist Indian peoples in their decolonization struggles and achieve justice?

We may never be able to develop satisfactory answers to these problematic questions by focusing solely on the story of the white man's Indian law. As Audre Lord, the African-American poet, has tried to teach us, the Master's tools have not been designed to dismantle the Master's house.[12] A deeper, more complex understanding of the decolonizing principles that have enabled tribalism to survive under U.S. law will begin to emerge only when we begin to seriously consider the contributions of American Indians to this struggle.

There is, therefore, an important need for a more complete account of the legal visions American Indian peoples have developed in response to the white man's Indian law. Such accounts do not yet proliferate in the literature of Indian decolonization. It is an immense project that needs to be undertaken: a countermythology of the Indian legal visions that have sustained the decolonization struggles of Indian tribal peoples in the United States.

Such a countermythology of the history of Indian rights in the United States could help us begin to understand the processes of how the white man's Indian law *and* American Indian visions of law have engaged each other throughout the cycles of confrontation and accommodation between Indians and the dominant society over time. This more complete account of the Indian's role in the history of the legal traditions that have determined Indian rights in the United States can only be rendered by dispelling the myths that have grown up around the white man's Indian law. Developing that account requires us to recognize and research the fact that Indian tribalism's continuing survival in America is something other than a gift bestowed by a benign conqueror's courts and legislature.

"A Measured Separatism"

Our failure to account for the role of American Indian traditions in U.S. law holds many important present-day implications for how we understand the rights belonging to Indian peoples in our society. We need desperately to broaden our contemporary conceptual framework for approaching questions of Indian rights to include Indian legal visions and traditions as not only relevant but also absolutely essential to protecting Indian tribalism's survival under U.S. law.[13]

This process of expanding the sources of law with precedential validity for protecting Indian rights requires developing a much better appreciation of the role of Indians in helping to create the beginnings of a multicultural society in North America. During the Encounter era, European colonists could not avoid dealing with Indians or confronting the conceptions of justice that Indians insisted applied to their relations with the strange newcomers to their lands. The importance Europeans attached to their dealings with tribes is evidenced by the large number of well-known European and Anglo-American names appearing in the history of Indian-white relations during the seventeenth- and eighteenth-century Encounter era: George Washington, Benjamin Franklin, Thomas Jefferson, Sir Jeffrey Amherst, and Daniel Boone, to name just a few. That well-known Indian names, such as Pontiac and Tecumseh, are also featured in this opening chapter of the larger national creation epic indicates, as Richard White has explained,[14] that the parameters of American history need significant readjusting.[15] "Colonial and early American historians," White writes, "have made Indians marginal to the periods they describe. They have treated them as curiosities in a world that Indians also helped create."[16]

As I try to show in this book, Indians helped create a legal world during the Encounter era—a world made up of multicultural negotiations, treaties, and diplomatic relations with Europeans. Indian visions of law and peace exercised a profound and direct impact on this world.

During the critical, initial stage of cultural encounter in North America, Indians and whites each became aware of the other's strange and alien customs and traditions. Indian tribes throughout North America drew on their own legal visions in responding to Western colonial assumptions about the diminished rights of "infidels" and "savages" to occupy and control the vast territories of the New World.[17]

What emerged out of this intense and crisis-filled period of initial cultural encounter between American Indian and European-derived peoples is represented in the hundreds of treaties and agreements negotiated during the colonial era. Extraordinary documents in their own right, the records of the colonial period treaty conferences between the European colonies and North American Indian tribes constitute, as Lawrence C. Wroth wrote in his oft-cited 1928 essay on Indian treaties, "a literary type that has been neglected by readers and teachers of early American literature."[18] Surveying the themes and metaphors of this "single original American contribution" to the basic forms of literary expression, Wroth declared that in the treaty literature of the colonial period

> one reads the passion, the greed, and the love of life of hard living men brought into close relationships without parallel conditions in the history of either race to guide its conduct. . . . [A]ll this is in the Indian Treaties, and in dramatic form. I wish that some teacher had poured for me this strong wine instead of the tea from Boston Harbor with which the genuine thirst of my youth was insufficiently slaked, or that some teacher of literature had given me to read these vivid picturesque records instead of saying that the colonial period had nothing to show of literary production except dull sermons, political tracts, prosy essays, and poems of invincible mediocrity.[19]

The "Indian Treaties" of the colonial period, of course, stand for something more than a "neglected literary type." The Encounter era treaty tradition recalls the long-neglected fact in American history that there was a time in our national experience when Indians tried to create a new type of society with Europeans on the multicultural frontiers of colonial North America. Recovering this shared legal world is crucial to the task of reconstructing our contemporary understandings of the sources and nature of the rights belonging to Indian peoples in present-day American society. This process of recovery begins with the Encounter era treaty literature. In this amazing body of literature, we find the primary source documents for the basic principles defining Indian rights in the United States today and for American exceptionalism among the Western settler-states in elevating the sanctity of treaties with indigenous tribal peoples to a rule of law.[20] In countless reiterations, the Encounter era treaty literature affirms the sovereign capacity of Indian tribes to engage in bilateral governmental relations, to exercise power and control over their lands and resources, and to maintain their internal forms of self-government free of outside interference. The unique right belonging only to Indian tribal peoples in U.S. law, the right to what Charles F. Wilkinson has called a degree of measured separatism[21] (the same right found embodied in the message of the *Gus-Wen-Tah*),[22] emerges for the first time in American legal history out of the Encounter era treaty system.

The principles recognized in the Encounter era treaty system regarding tribal peoples' basic human rights stand in sharp contrast to the colonizing legal tradition brought to the New World by the West. That tradition, originating in the medieval Catholic Church-sponsored Crusades to the Holy Lands, provides the historical context for understanding the development of Indian rights under the white man's Indian law. That tradition denies "infidel" and "savage" tribal peoples the same basic human rights of self-determination recognized as belonging to the peoples who colonized them centuries ago.[23] According to this tradition, and the white man's Indian law, indigenous tribal peoples rightfully belong under the superior sovereignty of the Western colonizing nations—even in the postcolonial world of today.[24]

American Indian peoples have always responded to this vision of their rights with resistance. This book, in recognizing that response, proceeds on the assumption that a legal tradition that unquestioningly accepts the legality of the West's colonial conquest and power in the New World is not the best place to search for the origins of those principles that add up to a right of measured separatism belonging to Indian peoples under U.S. law. Rather, this book looks for those origins in Indian legal traditions of the Encounter era, when the West was first required to recognize the novel thought that American Indian tribes are self-determining peoples.

In looking to Indian legal traditions, this book resituates Indians, rather than just their lawyers or those who rule and jurisprudentialize over them, as a dynamic force in the perpetuation of the first principles of Indian tribalism's rights in America. This book, in other words, attempts to rewrite Indians back into Indian law.

Developing a greater appreciation for the contributions of American Indian legal visions to the Indian's persistence opens up new vistas for understanding and explaining how U.S. law works and does not work to ensure the survival and development of Indian tribalism in modern American society. By examining the relation of American Indian legal traditions to the rules and principles protective of the Indian's right of a "measured separatism" generated under U.S. law, it is possible to imagine and theorize new visions of law that can work to ensure Indian cultural survival in the future. Just as significant, understanding how these American Indian legal traditions have worked to help perpetuate Indian tribalism in America might also assist us in beginning to understand how U.S. law is enabled to achieve racial justice more generally.

Law and Peace in a Multicultural World

This, then, is perhaps the most important reason for trying to develop a better understanding of American Indian visions of law and peace. These American Indian treaty visions of law and peace are rich in insights on how we as human beings go about the difficult process of justly structuring relations with strange and different others in a multicultural world. To this extent, there is much to be learned from unearthing the long-neglected history of cross-cultural confrontations, accommodations, and diplomatic negotiations between American Indian peoples and colonizing Europeans found in the Encounter era treaty literature.

The early Encounter era represents a singular time in our North American history with respect to cultural group relations. It was a time of intense crises and confrontation. Radically different peoples were required to negotiate as rough economic, military, and political equals for survival on the land. No one group's narratives occupied a privileged or dominant position in the new type of society that was emerging on the multicultural frontiers of seventeenth- and eighteenth-century North

America. Throughout the treaty literature of the period, numerous and distinct cultural groups, indigenous and European, can be found negotiating with each other at arm's length about the competing visions of peace and justice that would govern their mutual relations. Throughout the Encounter era, these groups, more often than our histories might suggest, agreed to create multicultural alliances of law and peace.

These cross-cultural interactions generated and sustained a rich and dynamic rhetorical archive of discourses and narratives on the problems of achieving justice between different peoples on a multicultural frontier. As this book relates, these different peoples were able to achieve law and peace with each other, at least some of the time, creating the beginnings in North America of the modern world's first multicultural society. Reexamining this unique period of crises and cooperation between different peoples in our North American history may reveal to us the vitally needed metaphors and language of the new legal visions we require for our own emerging multicultural world of human diversity and conflict.

American Indian visions of law and peace contain much useful knowledge about the problems of establishing just paradigms for behavior between different peoples. By retrieving and examining such visions as they were expressed and acted on on the North American colonial frontier, perhaps we too can begin to construct new and fresh approaches to the critical dilemma of justly ordering relations of power and privilege between the different groups of peoples in conflict and confrontation in our world today.

The Language of North American Indian Diplomacy

In short, then, this book imagines the possibility of a critical, organizing role for American Indian visions of law and peace in the emergence of the modern world's first multicultural society on the North American colonial frontier. These visions converge in a distinctive language of multicultural diplomacy that Indians and Europeans used to conduct their treaty relations with each other. This North American indigenous diplomatic language, borrowing from J. G. A. Pocock, functioned paradigmatically to prescribe what the actors within the North American Encounter era treaty system might say and how they might say it.[25]

The methodology employed to identify the general themes and paradigms that governed this North American indigenous language focuses on the treaty literature of the seventeenth and eighteenth centuries. Among the reasons for pursuing this methodology are that our understandings of the role of American Indian visions in the Encounter era treaty system are incomplete and inaccurate, and that by reviving and reconstructing these visions we begin the process of elaborating a new theoretical framework for interpreting Indian rights. More important, this book asks how the ancient treaty visions of law and peace embodied in a tradition such as the *Gus-Wen-Tah* can speak to the challenges we confront in achieving justice in our own multicultural world.

The Problem of Sources

I have outlined several of the reasons for the different emphases in methodology pursued in this book. However, significant limitations arise in dealing with American Indian legal visions and their role in the Encounter era treaty system. One of the most serious obstacles confronting the historian of decolonization generally in pursuing this type of project is the problem of sources.

By virtue of the adversarial nature of the Western legal traditions implemented by the majority society in America, U.S. law has been the locus where that society has so often sought to exercise its power over Indian tribes. There is, therefore, a relatively rich archive of legal resources where opposing indigenous visions of Indian tribalism's rights to survival have been recorded and preserved. Treaties, treaty conferences, legal briefs, written appeals and testimony submitted to the white man's legislatures and political leaders, written court opinions, and executive branch reports are just a few of the sources available to the historian of decolonization.[26] But, at best, these are only partial fragments and signs of indigenous North American legal traditions at work in the history of Indian responses to Western colonial domination. Because the conqueror writes history in the colonial situation,[27] the cultural archives maintained by the conquering society frequently neglect to record or adequately document the many different and distinct visions of law that have contributed to the traditions of resistance forged by the colonized peoples.

Many of the legal visions that sustained Indian tribal resistance in North America have been suppressed or dismissed by the historians of colonization as irrelevant to the catalog of documents that celebrate the triumphs of the conqueror nation. Those sources that are preserved in the conqueror's history often represent mere signs or fragments of a far more complex cultural product and world. Selectively documented as necessary background information to the great triumphs of the conqueror over the conquered people, they suffer from a perverse incompleteness, pervasive bias, and inadequate attention to the indigenous cultural contexts out of which they arise. "There is no document of civilization," Walter Benjamin writes, "which is not at the same time a document of barbarism."[28]

Thus, the historian of decolonization is confronted with a number of difficulties in utilizing the archives of the conqueror's history. Many of the most important stories of tribal resistance and the legal visions and traditions that sustained American Indians in their struggles for survival are simply left unrecounted in the written historical record maintained by the conqueror. The sources that are available for study and analysis are most often partial, inattentive, and biased accounts of Indian resistance to the will of the conqueror, as recorded by the conqueror's scribes.

This book, therefore, cannot help but reflect these inherent limitations in the sources available to it in reconstructing the role of American Indian legal ideas in the Encounter era treaty system. My discussion and analysis in this book are focused primarily on those American Indian visions of law and peace that are most readily retrievable from fragmentary sources available in the documentary record of the conqueror's history. This has meant, inevitably, that the book relates only a highly selective and incomplete group of stories of American Indian response and resistance to Western colonial domination. Nonetheless, such a limited, localized approach, while neglecting the important struggles of a vast number of Indian tribes, does focus attention on those specific visions propounded by tribal peoples that have generated extensive, albeit fragmented, documentation in the conqueror's archives. To the extent that these responses have made significant documented contributions to the archival record of American Indian opposition to the white man's Indian law, they represent defensible beginnings for the historian of decolonization in recovering and reconstructing an understanding of the language of North American Indian visions of law and peace.

These beginnings show that the complex challenges we confront and theorize about today in our multicultural world have confronted American Indian tribal peoples ever since the strange and alien peoples of the Old World came to the New World. They also show that American Indians have responded with imaginative, and sometimes even fruitful, approaches to the immensely difficult problems of achieving justice between different peoples and cultures. These responses have enabled Indian peoples to survive 500 years of territorial invasion, foreign-born plagues, wars of extermination, suppression of their religious beliefs, language, and traditions, and a continent-wide, ethnic cleansing campaign. For anyone at all interested in the history of human resistance to colonial domination and injustice, these particular responses merit careful scrutiny and attention. Ultimately, what I hope this book will show is that our own survival in our multicultural world may well depend on our learning to understand the responses of indigenous tribal peoples to the challenge of achieving justice among different peoples. We must learn what it means to link arms together, according to American Indian treaty visions of law and peace.[29]

1

National Mythologies and American Indians

The National Mythology

The task of developing a more complete understanding of the response of American Indians to the coming of the white man immediately confronts a formidable obstacle: the great American mythos of frontier conquest. The national creation epic of a simple, agrarian, "Anglo" race of conquerors defeating "a fierce race of savages" for control and civilization of an extraordinary wilderness land has long provided us with a catalog of images and stories of who we think we are as a people.[1] The mythos of white conquest has also defined what we think of Indians in our American history. It has functioned, to borrow from the cultural anthropologist Bronislaw Malinowski, as "a warrant, a charter, and often even a practical guide"[2] for most Americans' understanding of American Indians as *obstacles* to their manifest destiny.

The deeply ingrained negative image of the Indian in the national consciousness represents a significant impediment to our acceptance of Indian tribalism's unique response to the coming of the white man to North America. We find it difficult to believe that American Indians responded to European colonial invasion by envisioning the beginnings in North America of the modern world's first multicultural society.

The Indian as Obstacle

The Indian's antagonistic role in the national mythology of western frontier conquest has deep roots in the American experience. As elegantly described in *The Savages of America*, Roy Harvey Pearce's classic study on the American Indian and the European-derived idea of civilization,[3] a clearly identifiable set of themes regarding the tribal Indian's perceived difference emerged within a few short decades of the European invasion of America. These themes comprised the genesis of an important narrative tradition in the American public imagination.[4] In this tradition, tribalism's deficiency and unassimilability set it apart from the superior agrarian civilization European-Americans sought to transplant in America from the Old World. Through this narrative tradition on tribalism's cultural inferiority, European-Americans, according to Pearce, came to understand the Indian, "not as one to be civilized and to be lived with, but rather as one whose nature and whose way of life was an obstacle to civilized progress westward."[5]

Removing tribalism as an obstacle to white civilization's procession westward across North America emerges as the dominant theme of this tradition at an early point in the colonial encounter. The seventeenth-century Puritan leader Cotton Mather spoke with assurance that Providence ultimately intended success for His elect in the New World wilderness, though the Indian admittedly presented a formidable barrier. The "Promised Land," Mather warned, "is all over filled with fiery flying serpents. . . . There are incredible droves of *devils* in our way."[6]

The English promoter of New World colonization, Samuel Purchas, arguing for the benefits of Virginia's settlement by the English, put forward the following argument in favor of his nation's natural right to dispossess the savage tribes of America:

> On the other side considering so good a Country, so bad a people, having little of humanity but shape, ignorant of Civility, of Arts, of Religion; more brutish than the beasts they hunt, more wild and unmanly than that unmanned wild county, which they range rather than inhabit; capitulated also to Satan's tyranny in foolish pieties, mad impieties, wicked idleness, busy and bloody wickedness.[7]

The narrative tradition of tribalism's incompatibility with European-derived civilization generated a richly diverse corpus of texts on both sides of the Atlantic. Thomas Hobbes drew on the tradition in his 1651 study on the fundamentals of government, *Leviathan*.[8] In the state of nature, Hobbes's notorious text declared: "[T]here is no place for Industry . . . no knowledge of the face of the Earth; no account of time; no Arts; no Letters; no society; and which is worst of all; continual fear, and danger of violent death; and the life of man, solitary, poor, nasty, brutish, and short."[9] Hobbes's readers then learned that this abhorred primitive state of nature was more than just a philosophical conceit. Hobbes pointed to "the savage people in many places of America" to illustrate that this state of nature still prevailed in certain parts of the world. The Indians of America, he wrote, "have no government at all; and live at this day in that brutish manner as I said before."[10]

John Locke, in his *Second Treatise of Government*, also relied on the narrative tradition of American Indian cultural inferiority to hypothesize a savage world of peoples without civilization or advanced law.[11] Locke's late seventeenth-century declaration that "in the beginning, all the world was America" illustrates the widely diffused nature of the impact of a century of English colonial activity in the New World on so many aspects of English life and society.[12] In his text's most oft-cited chapter on "Property," Locke turned repeatedly to the narrative tradition of the Indian's deficient social state as a foil to illustrate his central argument that human labor was the basis of individual property according to natural law. The Indians of America, he wrote,

> are rich in land and poor in all the comforts of life; whom nature having furnished as liberally as any other people with materials of plenty, i.e., a fruitful soil, apt to produce in abundance what might serve for good, raiment, and delight, yet for want of improving it by labor have not one-hundredth part of the conveniences we enjoy. And a king of a large and fruitful territory there feeds, lodges, and is clad worse than a day-laborer in England.[13]

The Great American mythos of white frontier conquest located another sustaining source of ideas on American Indian tribalism's cultural inferiority in the writings of the major European legal theorists on the Law of Nations. According to Emmerich Vattel's influential treatise, *The Law of Nations or The Principles of Natural Law* (1758),[14] for example, no individual or community should be permitted to hold great tracts of land left uncultivated. Echoing John Locke's natural law argument on human labor as the basis of property, Vattel declared that the whole earth was designed by God to furnish sustenance for its inhabitants, "but it cannot do this unless cultivated. Every Nation is therefore bound by the natural law to cultivate the land which has fallen to its share."[15] Thus, Vattel castigated those peoples

> who, though living in fertile countries, disdain the cultivation of the soil and . . . in order to avoid labor, seek to live upon their flocks and the fruits of the chase. This might well enough be done in the first age of the world, when the earth produced more than enough, without cultivation, for the small number of its inhabitants. But now that the human race has multiplied so greatly, it could not subsist if every people wished to live after that fashion. Those who still pursue this idle mode of life occupy more land than they would have need of under a system of honest labor, and they may not complain if other more industrious Nations, too confined at home, should come and occupy part of their land.[16]

According to Vattel's reasoning, Spain's conquest of the "civilized Empire of Peru and Mexico" was a "notorious usurpation" because those peoples engaged in large-scale crop agriculture. But, he went on, "the establishment of various colonies upon the continent of North America might, if done within just limits, have been entirely lawful. The peoples of those vast tracts of land roamed over them, rather than inhabited them."[17] Europeans, according to Vattel's reasoning, followed the dictates of natural law and the Law of Nations in dispossessing the "savages" of North America of their uncultivated lands.

Old World texts such as those produced by Hobbes, Locke, Vattel, and others became an important part of the Great American Mythology of Frontier Conquest.[18] Generated from European myths about the deficient qualities of "savage" life in the New World, these texts spoke directly to European-Americans who could point to a venerable narrative tradition to justify the colonization of the Indians and their "waste" lands in America.

The Myth as Policy

Myths have consequences. The narrative tradition of Indian tribalism's cultural inferiority has been deeply impressed upon our understanding of the national experience and the Indian's negative role as part of that experience. Tribal Indians are peoples without civilization, without laws, and without place in the nation created by white Americans out of the frontier wilderness of North America. From the time of the Founding Fathers, the racist premises derived from this tradition have informed the basic framework of our nation's policies toward Indian tribalism and the basic rights of tribal Indians under U.S. law. The acts of genocide and ethnocide perpetrated against Indians under U.S. law have been justified as simply the extension of the West's enlightened reason upon the "savage" Indian-occupied frontiers of the New World.

Commander-in-Chief George Washington relied on the narrative tradition of Indian cultural inferiority in framing his recommendations to Congress on U.S. Indian policy immediately following the Revolutionary War. In a letter to Congress that patiently explained the most expedient strategy for the new nation's acquisition of the western frontier lands from the Indians, General Washington declared:

> I am clear in my opinion, that policy and economy point very strongly to the expediency of being upon good terms with the Indians, and the propriety of purchasing their lands in preference to attempting to drive them by force of arms out of their country; which as we have already experienced is like driving Wild Beasts of the Forest which will return as soon as the pursuit is at an end and fall perhaps on those that are left there; when the gradual extension of our Settlements will as certainly cause the Savage as the Wolf to retire; both being beasts of prey tho' they differ in shape.[19]

Washington's recommendations were readily adopted by Congress as the foundation of the first U.S. Indian policy, an empire-building vision of America grounded upon the comforting, racist assumption that Indian tribalism was a doomed form of cultural existence on the North American continent. The "Savage as the Wolf" would retire westward when confronted by the onslaught of a superior white civilization.

John Quincy Adams, the great American statesman and rhetorician, deployed the narrative tradition of tribalism's cultural inferiority with an unrivaled degree of eloquence, persuasiveness, and skill during his public career.[20] As president of the United States from 1825 to 1829, Adams was confronted with the problem of what to do with those Indian tribes east of the Mississippi River that had refused to fulfill Washington's prophecy of doom. The Cherokees, Chickasaws, Choctaws, Creeks, and Seminoles had maintained their cultural sovereignty despite having been caught for decades in the path of white civilization's progress across the continent. In his 1828 Message to Congress, Adams proposed the need for a "remedy" for such "unfortunate children of nature":

> [I]n appropriating to ourselves their hunting grounds we have brought upon ourselves the obligation of providing them with substinence; and when we have had the same good fortune of teaching them the arts of civilization and the doctrines of Christianity we have unexpectedly found them forming in the midst of ourselves communities claiming to be independent of ours and rivals of sovereignty within the territories of the members of our Union. This state of things requires that a remedy should be provided—a remedy which, while it shall do justice to those unfortunate children of nature, may secure to the members of our confederates their right of sovereignty and soil.[21]

Adams's proposed remedy for the nation's Indian problem drew upon a narrative tradition that had long situated the Indian as an obstacle on the frontiers of America's destiny. Adams proposed removing the remaining tribes east of the Mississippi River across the Father of Waters to an Indian territory out of the way of the intended trajectory of white settlement and civilization. Adams's proposal was soon adopted as a genocidal national policy by his successor, President Andrew Jackson, after the U.S. Congress passed the Indian Removal Act of 1830.[22]

The Myth as Source of Legal Rights

The famous American historian Frederick Jackson Turner announced the closing of the nation's western frontier in 1890. But Turner was really only perpetuating a long-standing narrative tradition concerning the Indian's role in the national experience when he wrote what he regarded as his closing chapter to the American creation epic. "[V]ast forests blocked the way; mountainous ramparts interposed; desolate grass-clad prairies, barren oceans of rolling plains, arid deserts, and a fierce race of savages all had to be met and defeated."[23] The Indian as foil; the savage, lawless contrast to pioneer values; the stubborn red-skinned obstacle to white civilization's dynamic westward march; the vanquished warrior at the end of the trail—these images the American mind calls up from its collective catalog of stories on the Indian in the national experience all originate in the Great American Mythology of Frontier Conquest.

In our own century of combatting racism in all of its forms,[24] the narrative tradition concerning Indian cultural deficiency continues to define what we think of the Indian and Indian rights. Even justices of the U.S. Supreme Court feel no hesitancy in citing the mythology of Indian conquest as a reason to deny Indians justice under U.S. law. In the 1955 landmark case, *Tee-Hit-Ton v. United States,*[25] for example, the tradition was called upon by the Supreme Court to provide the European-derived society that colonized North America with a legal justification for denying constitutional protection for the lands occupied by Indian peoples on the continent from time immemorial. According to Justice Reed's opinion for the Court in *Tee-Hit-Ton:*

> The line of cases adjudicating Indian rights on American soil leads to the conclusion that Indian occupancy, not specifically recognized as ownership by action authorized by Congress, may be extinguished by the Government without compensation. Every American schoolboy knows that the savage tribes of this continent were deprived of their ancestral ranges by force and that, even when the Indians ceded millions of acres by treaty in return for blankets, food and trinkets, it was not a sale but the conquerors' will that deprived them of their land.[26]

The current chief justice of the U.S. Supreme Court, William Rehnquist, has freely drawn upon the narrative tradition of Indian cultural inferiority and Indians as peoples without law in his Indian law jurisprudence.[27] In 1979, Rehnquist, then an associate justice on the Court, wrote the majority opinion in *Oliphant v. Suquamish Tribe* (1979),[28] the modern Court's most important decision on the rights of Indian tribes to control their reservations. Rehnquist's opinion declared that Indian tribes lacked the inherent sovereignty to try and to punish non-Indians for crimes committed within their reservation communities. Quoting from an 1834 congressional report, Rehnquist explained:

> This principle would have been obvious a century ago when most Indian tribes were characterized by a "want of fixed laws [and] of competent tribunals of justice." It should be no less obvious today, even though present-day Indians tribal courts embody dramatic advances over their historical antecedents.[29]

Depictions of Indians as a "fierce race of savages" characterized by a "want of fixed laws" are frequently elaborated in the contemporary culture. Supreme Court decisions, outmoded paradigms of American historical scholarship, dime novels, Hollywood westerns, and myriad other sources all conspire to perpetuate the idea of the American Indian as an unassimilated obstacle in the Great American mythos. Even seemingly benign or superfluously regarded cultural meditations on *Indianness*—the tomahawk chops at sporting events, movies such as *Dances with Wolves,* New Age white male religionists beating drums in solar-powered sweat lodges—flourish in insidious fashion throughout our public discourses because of the continuing vitality of the myth of the *otherness* of the Indian in our national experience.[30]

A Countermythology

The narrative tradition of the Indian as obstacle to the white man's destiny in America makes it difficult for most Americans to conceive of Indians as anything other than a savage, lawless, and unassimilable race of peoples in responding to the coming of Europeans to the New World. But this narrative tradition fails to acknowledge that a countermythology is available to us that would assign a very different role to Indians and Indian ideas in American history. According to this set of counterstories about Indian-white relations in American history, Indians, particularly during the crucial early stages of the Encounter era, did not act as obstacles to white expansion in North America. Quite the opposite, Indians responded as active facilitators of the many multicultural accommodations that Europeans found absolutely essential for survival on a colonial frontier.

The North American Multicultural Frontier

As Francis Jennings writes, beginning with the initial period of significant Indian-white contact in the early seventeenth century and throughout much of the eighteenth century, "Indian *cooperation* was the prime requisite for European penetration and colonization of the North American continent."[31] "Cooperation" is not a word the American public imagination usually calls up from its collective memory to describe Indian-white relations in our national history. We are too habituated to the images of violent and brutal race wars and cutthroat competition for territory between Indians and whites in our history. We have difficulty conceiving of these two different groups of peoples sharing the identity of interests necessary to make any sort of intercultural cooperation possible during any period of our history.

But during the initial period of colonial encounter in North America, white survival and white desires for territorial expansion required negotiating with a large number of formidable American Indian tribes already on the land. In the seventeenth- and eighteenth-century Encounter era, European colonists often found themselves outnumbered and outflanked with a bare foothold on the North American continent. During much of this period, whites in their small colonial settlements were not the dominant power on the continent. They soon learned that their survival, flourishing, and expansion could be better secured through cooperative relationships with surrounding Indian tribes rather than through wars and conflict.[32]

The Great American Mythology of Frontier Conquest has obscured the historical significance of the Indian's important role in facilitating these patterns of accommodation in the early colonial settlement of North America. In eastern North America particularly, where the major European colonial powers concentrated a great deal of their efforts and capital to establish a beachhead for their imperial ambitions in the New World, Indians entered into numerous cooperative relationships with Europeans. The emerging European world trading system of the seventeenth and eighteenth centuries required these types of intercultural relationships of commerce and accommodation to sustain and expand its reach around the globe. Indian tribes sought out these relationships for the valuable trade goods, military alliances, and strategic advantages that encouraged their participation in this absorptive mercantile system.

The map of human settlement in North America after more than a century of European colonial activity on the continent illuminates key aspects of this emerging European world trading system. By the early eighteenth century, virtually all of the major contending European colonizing powers—England, France, and Spain—had staked out their competing claims to territory and spheres of influence in North America. But beyond a few sparsely populated coastal and riverine settlements, actual European presence on the continent was minimal. Relatively large populations of North American indigenous tribal peoples, however, surrounded the periphery of these settlements. The middle ground where Indians and whites encountered each other as rough equals came to define the multicultural frontiers of North America.

Necessity as well as convenience dictated that colonial Europeans learn how to develop economic, political, and military relations with these tribal groups on the frontiers of their tiny settlements. Through such relations, Indian tribes, sometimes willingly, sometimes reluctantly, found themselves quickly absorbed into the larger, emerging system of global colonialism and trade that was being relentlessly driven by Europe's extended imperial rivalries around the globe.

In eastern North America, most of the initial relationships that Europeans developed with Indian tribes were organized around the immensely valuable fur trade of the Eastern Woodlands. Because of the fur trade, the tribes of eastern North America during the Encounter era were often treated in fact, if not wholly regarded in theory, as political, economic, and military equals by their European trading partners. In this unique period of increasing interdependence between the different cultural and racial groups engaged in the commerce and politics of accommodation and conflict that surrounded the trade, Europeans came to regard Indian cooperation as vital to the success of the new type of society that was emerging in Encounter era North America.

The countermythology of American Indians responding as accommodators of, rather than obstacles to, European survival on the North American continent looks to this early period of Indian-white relations for its much differently inflected stories about American history. When we examine diplomatic relations between Indians and Europeans during the seventeenth and eighteenth centuries, we see innumerable instances of different groups of peoples engaged in the difficult process of society building in the context of a multicultural frontier. Certainly, periods of great confict between the different groups struggling for survival on the continent occurred during this period. Most of these groups recognized, however, that their own long-term survival could only be secured by adequately managing this conflict. As in most situations of human conflict, war during the Encounter era was deemed necessary to a group's vital strategic interests only when efforts at negotiation and accommodation with an opposing group finally broke down.

During the early Encounter era in particular, negotiation and accommodation were well-advised initial strategies for both Europeans and Indians to pursue. The positions of all of the different groups of peoples on the continent were highly tenuous. In such a chaotic world, no one group could claim the cultural self-sufficiency out of which a *homogenous* society might emerge and sustain itself. In this world of the Encounter, the interests of both Europeans and Indians could sometimes converge to dictate strategies of mutual cooperation with each other.

From this unique set of conditions emerged the beginnings of a much different type of society: a *heterogeneous* society. This new type of society was composed of different groups of peoples in ongoing or potential situations of social crisis who recognized the need to resolve their conflicts. The modern world system created by European colonialism, in other words, also created the unique conditions for a new type of modern world society. It was a multicultural society, "made up of the conflicting forces which hold it together by tension, and tear it apart as each group seeks eternally to remold it to its advantage."[33]

The Old World's feudal order and structuring of human status were simply incapable of being applied fruitfully in this unique type of New World society. This society was being built from the ground up, along the more heterogeneous and contractual lines characteristic of much of modern Western political thought.[34]

This new type of society beginning to emerge on the multicultural frontiers of North America was intensely competitive and dynamic. It was driven by the invisible hand of forces unleashed when different groups of peoples agree to pursue their own interests in a mutually agreed-upon framework of grudging cooperation created by intense, arm's-length negotiations.

A very different type of cultural landscape thus emerges when we look at the stories that can be generated from a countermythology of Indian-white relations during the Encounter era. By viewing the period as the beginning of efforts of competitive, intersecting, and roughly equal cultural groups to build a workable social order, we see the response of Indians to the European invaders on their lands as part of a much more complex setting. As opposed to simply being barriers to European expansion, Indians assume essential roles as potential allies and facilitators, acting for their own reasons in concert with European colonial powers. As opposed to history simply passing them by in their "savage" social state, Indians are found coping and responding to Europeans with sophistication, resourcefulness, and long-term vision on the complex cultural landscape of the Encounter era frontier.

The stories of this countermythology thus present much different versions of the more familiar American narratives on Indian-white relations in American history. These counterstories recognize that competing European claims to empire in North America during the early Encounter era presented tribes with an especially dangerous situation and a number of difficult challenges. Europeans often desperately needed Indian cooperation for many of their enterprises. At the same time, Europeans carried with them from the Old World their long-held attitudes of cultural superiority to the types of tribal peoples they encountered in the New World. Such racial and cultural attitudes made it easier for Europeans to discount the importance of outright honesty and consistent fair dealing in their relations with the "savage" and "barbarous" peoples of North America. When such dismissive attitudes of Indian inferiority combined with Old World imperial rivalries scripted according to the rules laid down in Machiavelli's *The Prince,* these counterstories tell of a particularly rapacious and unsettling form of mercantile colonialism brought to the New World.[35]

In this countermythology, Indian tribes find themselves simultaneously courted and coerced as potential military and trading partners. Europeans regard Indian tribal territories as open to appropriation and exploitation by a self-proclaimed "superior" race of conquerors. Tribes are manipulated and hired as proxies by one European colonial group to carry on wars against other European colonial rivals and their client tribes. Tribes find themselves attacked without warning for failing to yield to European desires for unbounded empire in North America.

In these stories, Indians respond to the complex, life-and-death challenges of a multicultural frontier in diverse and surprising ways, not anticipated by the mythology of the Indian as an unassimilated, savage *other.* Tribes quickly learn to calculate the advantages of conducting trade and the necessities of establishing good relations with the various contending European powers. The desire for the Old World's manufactured trade goods, perceptions of their own self-interests, and prudence gave tribes more than sufficient encouragement to adapt their own subsistence-oriented economies to commercial dealings with the strange newcomers to their lands. The Indian fur trade with European colonies produced previously unimagined goods for the tribes. Old World factories churned out blankets and strouds, copper pots, metal axes and knives, glass beads, and other merchandise targeted at the Indian trade in North America. Within and among tribes, control of the flows of this valuable European trade determined vital issues of political power and influence. Military alliance with a European colony could produce various forms of tactical advantage and protection for a tribe, including guns and ammunition. Indians came to realize quickly that control of the flows of trade could dramatically alter the balance of power among the groups contending for survival during the North American Encounter era.

In the countermythology of Indians as facilitators of America's multicultural frontier destiny, some unfortunate tribes fail to grasp the enormity of the new forces shaping their world and their survival in it; they find their independence and cultural sovereignty rapidly declining in the face of European pressures. Some tribes did "disappear" during the Encounter era, although perhaps it would be more accurate to say that they removed themselves from the encroaching path of European invasion and allowed themselves to be absorbed into other tribal groupings. But numerous tribes did survive, and some even flourished in this rapidly changing world of the Encounter in North America. Many tribes, contrary to the myth of Indians as hapless foils to the white man's fated destiny in the New World, developed effective strategies for coping with and countering European colonial power.

There are stories of tribes strengthening and consolidating their own internal forms of political organization to achieve greater unity of purpose and action in dealing with Europeans during this time of crisis in their world. There are stories of tribes maximizing what few advantages they possessed relative to the Europeans—superiority in numbers, close proximity to the fur supplies and long-established frontier trading routes, and greater familiarity with the geography and topography of the continent. There are stories of tribes reinvigorating alliances and confederacies or creating new structures of cooperation with other Indian groups to counter European influence and power in a region. Those tribes able to maximize the few advantages they did possess and organize effectively could strengthen and improve their bargaining and tactical positions. These "trading tribes," in fact, were able to incorporate themselves as vital actors within the European colonial system that was inexorably spreading its influence throughout North America.[36] Their stories constitute a narrative tradition of Indian accommodation of Europeans in the countermythology of the American frontier experience.

A Different Set of Stories

The Great American Mythology of Frontier Conquest traditionally ignores these stories of the Indians' facilitative response to Europeans on the colonial frontier. Indians have always been obstacles in the traditional American histories of white expansion on the frontier, never willing and calculating accommodators.

In the countermythology of Indian tribalism's facilitative role in the American frontier experience, however, a much different set of stories is told. Europeans are seen adapting to the cultural landscape of the North American Encounter era frontier in unexpected ways. They are seen placing a high value on the relationships that could be formed with the more effectively organized tribal groups. They recognize clearly that their failure to come to terms of accommodation with the tribes surrounding their settlements could indeed produce conditions of life that were "solitary, poor, nasty, brutish, and short"[37]—at least for themselves in the New World.

The devastation that a well-organized "savage enemy" could inflict on a fledgling colony was demonstrated early and often in the Encounter era. At Jamestown, Virginia, in 1622, the Indian chief, Opechancanough, led the tribes of the Powhatan confederacy in a coordinated attack that claimed the lives of more than a quarter of the 1,240 English colonists settled in the Virginia Tidewater region. A subsequent assault in 1644 took the lives of more than 500 colonists before Virginia finally captured and murdered Opechancanough and subjugated the tribes of the colony.[38] King Philip's War cost the New England colonies 600 lives.[39] The Dutch at New Amsterdam and the French in Canada were also required to fight costly Indian wars in the early, difficult years of their efforts to establish viable colonial settlements.

More often than not, these wars were brought about by the failure of the Europeans to appreciate the advantages of peaceful relations with surrounding tribal peoples. The Yamasee War of 1715–1716, for example, cost the colony of South Carolina the lives of 400 of its citizens. The government and council, in reporting the "deplorable" condition of the colony to the lords proprietors in England, remarked fearfully that South Carolina's defenses had been reduced to "a handful of Men . . . against numerous and Potent Nations, and we have no Allies of any importance."[40] During the Encounter era, Europeans often learned the hard way the importance of avoiding wars and maintaining good relations with at least some groups of Indians.

Besides avoiding debilitating Indian conflicts, Europeans had other reasons for not always treating Indians simply as movable obstacles to their future destiny in America. Maintaining reliable relationships with the powerful tribal groups on their frontiers was essential to the financial success of many of the colonies. The frontier trading tribes controlled the fur supplies and related commerce of the regions bounding the European colonies. They acted as buffers to the expansion and penetration of rival European powers onto that frontier. They could be called on to counter and even war against less cooperative tribes that might be causing difficulties for a colony. Unlike an unknowing Thomas Hobbes, situated an ocean's distance away in the Old World, those Europeans who actually ventured forth into the New World in the seventeenth and eighteenth centuries did not find that the "savage people in many places of *America* . . . have no government at all; and live at this day in that brutish manner."[41] Rather, they told a different story of well-organized tribal peoples with whom they were required to negotiate the terms of their mutual survival and prosperity on the continent.

The Great American Mythology of Frontier Conquest and its accompanying narrative tradition of the Indian as obstacle fail to account for the fact that during the Encounter era certain Indian tribes came to be regarded as significant powers in their own right. These trading tribes were highly regarded as partners in their relations with Europeans. Politically and economically shrewd, their support, as Stephen Cornell has written,

> was often critical in intra-European conflicts. They came to Europeans, but the Europeans, equally, came to them. Thus the trade produced more than furs. Politics and pelts were intertwined; at one time or another, success or failure for the various European powers, whatever the object, depended substantially on Indian alliance.[42]

There are many stories of Europeans on the North American frontier who, despite their ultimate colonial aims and expansionary desires, acknowledged their interdependence with Indians and the need to establish reciprocal relationships of peace and commerce with tribes. Conflict, though an insistent theme in traditional historical treatments of the period, was not always the singular refrain of cultural group relations during the Encounter. Accommodation over the contested terrain of competing visions of the law and political arrangements governing the relations between divergent peoples and cultures in North America is also an important, contrapuntal theme too often overlooked by historians of the American experience.[43]

The web of connections and interdependent relationships of trade and alliance drew certain Indian tribes and European colonial powers close together during the early Encounter era.[44] These multicultural alliances represent a powerful rebuttal of the conflict-ridden image of Indian-white relations derived from the frontier conquest mythology of the Indian as normatively divergent and deficient *other*. Through force in numbers, skill in organization, and adeptness at diplomacy, certain Indian tribes were able to situate themselves in positions of strategic equipoise with Europeans and negotiate various cooperative ventures for mutual advantage. From the position in which Indians and whites originally found themselves on the continent, a rough equivalency of political, military, and economic power and resources encouraged both groups to engage in the difficult process of building, from the ground up, a multicultural society in North America.

Original Positions

According to the countermythology that emerges from the Encounter era, North America during the seventeenth and eighteenth centuries was a unique, multicultural landscape of different, conflicting groups. Understood in this sense, the North American Encounter era can be reimagined as an extended story of cultural group negotiations in selected areas of intercultural cooperation. Adapting John Rawls's famous philosophical construct to the unique conditions that actually existed on the North American multicultural frontier, Indians and Europeans were in an original position of a rough equality on the continent. A new kind of society was emerging from this unique cultural landscape, in which place, class, and social status were largely irrelevant.[45] Both groups approached cultural group negotiations with each other with little knowledge of what each side's future fortunes would be in this radically different and new type of multicultural society. Each negotiated behind a veil of ignorance. Each was similarly situated to propose the principles of justice that should govern the type of society envisioned by their agreements.

These early efforts of Indians engaging with Europeans to build a new type of society during the North American Encounter era have been largely neglected by our national mythology of white frontier conquest. The traditional American mythos draws largely on stories of nineteenth-century European-American frontier conquest. These stories typically portray cultural contact between Indians and whites as sporadic, violent, and precipitating the rapid demise and decimation of tribe after tribe on the western frontier. This later nineteenth-century vantage point accepts the inevitability of white supremacy on the continent simply because that is what we are taught ultimately happened. From such a limiting perspective on history, present-day North America indeed looks like the exclusive creation of a transplanted European-American culture. It is a continent of European-derived settler-states in which only the conquerors made history.[46]

Europeans during the initial period of cultural Encounter with Indians may well have viewed the continent as an untamed wilderness populated by wandering bands of savages. However, there was nothing inevitable about European conquest of North America, at least from the perspective of those Europeans who confronted the challenge of survival in a hostile new land during the first decades of colonization. Any fellow human being can empathize with the sense of dread and despair expressed by the Pilgrim leader William Bradford, who, from the deck of the *Mayflower,* looked across the water at Cape Cod in 1620 and saw only a "hideous and desolate wilderness, full of wild beasts and wild men."[47] The Pilgrims, Bradford recalled, could find "little solace or content" as they looked out on their intended frontier homeland since "the whole country, full of woods and thickets, represented a wild and savage view. If they looked behind them, there was the mighty ocean which they had passed, and was now as a main bar and gulf to separate them from all the civil parts of the world."[48] No wonder that the Pilgrim colonists at Plymouth relied on Indian hospitality, Indian food, and Indian advice for survival during the first years of their fledgling colony.[49] And no wonder that Indians did not see the inevitability of their conquest by these initial and somewhat hapless-seeming bands of European interlopers on their lands.

From the Indian perspective, there were many reasons, some selfish and calculating and some, indeed, stemming from a sense of shared humanity, to try to welcome these desperate strangers with their alien and ill-suited customs into the Indian world. As told in the countermythology of Indians as facilitators of our national destiny, throughout the Encounter era Europeans from a diverse set of cultural backgrounds and Indian tribes from an even more divergent set of cultural groupings found themselves, at times intentionally and at other times unintentionally, engaging in the process of cooperation that created the beginnings of the complex multicultural society that now occupies North America.

Multicultural Jurisgenesis

Law-creation was central to the society being constructed by Indians acting in concert with Europeans on the multicultural frontiers of Encounter era North America. For Europeans, long-held legal notions about the diminished rights of "savage" and "barbarian" peoples were forced to yield to the reality of formidable and well-organized Indian tribes, with their own deeply ingrained traditions of law for governing relations between different peoples. For Indians, accommodation of the strange newcomers to their lands required adapting their long-held traditions to the challenges of survival in their rapidly changing world. From this process of multicultural legal encounter emerged innumerable stories of what Robert Cover has called jurisgenesis—the creation of new legal meanings. Through these meanings, Indian tribes and colonial Europeans sought to define a *nomos*—a normative world. This world was held together by the jurisgenerative force of the common interpretive commitments to a law created and shared by the different peoples of Encounter era North America.[50]

There are many reasons to study these stories of jurisgenesis between Indians and whites at the beginnings of our shared history in America. Again, returning to Professor Jennings:

> With our eyes fixed upon conflict between two sides, and our sympathies fixed upon one of them, we glory in triumphs and fail to see the benefits to be derived from cooperation, or at least accommodation, between those sides. It seems to me that historical scholarship can be most useful in our day by finding ways to avoid political and social conflicts that all-too-predictably become disasters. This cannot be done by smudging the facts; conflicts of interests and ideas must be protrayed faithfully, or necessary adjustments cannot be made reasonably. But means and devices to avoid such conflicts, or to resolve them with minimum damage, must be given their due. The need is to reject the assumption of inevitability.[51]

From the innumerable acts of jurisgenesis that occurred throughout the Encounter era, it is possible to reconstruct the legal norms and values that governed the justice of American Indian and European-American relations on a multicultural frontier. And out of this reconstructive project a much different role emerges for Indians in our national mythos. The countermythology contained in these stories of multicultural jurisgenesis produces a set of stories that reimagines the uniqueness of American institutions as deriving not from the Anglo-American experience of frontier conquest but from the very different national experience of divergent groups of peoples constantly responding and adapting themselves to the challenges of an emerging multicultural society. In these encounters between the different peoples of America during the seventeenth- and eighteenth-century colonial period, we see the difficult beginning efforts at multicultural society building that have long characterized our national experience. The original position of European-Americans and American Indians on the colonial frontier generates the primary documents in the case for American exceptionalism; what is exceptional and unique about our multicultural society is that its beginnings can be traced to a North American indigenous vision of law and peace between the different peoples of the world.

The Language of the Encounter Era Treaty System

The countermythology that emerges from the remapped cultural landscape of the North American Encounter era now begins to reveal to us a very different set of stories about the Indian's role in American history. The new, heterogeneous, "modern" society being generated from the expanding forces of the European world trading system required Indian cooperation. As opposed to being stubborn, "savage" barriers to expansion, Indians now begin to emerge as active, sophisticated facilitators on a multicultural frontier. They are seen negotiating the terms and conditions by which Europeans secured their cooperation in this new type of modern world social system.

I have proposed viewing the unique situation on the North American colonial frontier from the perspective of the original position of the cultural groups negotiating the principles of justice governing their emerging multicultural society. Concededly, the classic philosophical construction of the original position by Rawls hypothesizes a world of isolated individuals without opinions or prejudices negotiating the principles of justice each individual would select for structuring social relations.[52] This was not, however, the *actual* original positions of the individuals who contended for survival on the North American Encounter era frontier. All of these individuals were already active participants in a distinct human culture. As the anthropologist Clifford Geertz has told us, a human nature independent of culture simply cannot exist.

> Men without culture would not be the clever savages of Golding's *Lord of the Flies* thrown back upon the cruel wisdom of their animal instincts; nor would they be the nature's noblemen of Enlightenment primitivism. . . . They would be unworkable monstrosities with very few useful instincts, fewer recognizable sentiments, and no intellect.[53]

In the Encounter era, Indians and whites each brought to their negotiations a clear sense of their identity as individuals belonging to uniquely constituted cultural groups. To be English or Iroquois or French or Huron meant that negotiations with other peoples took place within the particular context of one's own culturally mediated vision of justice. No matter what our position in the world, we, as individuals, are incapable of directing our behavior or organizing our experience without the guidance provided by systems of significant symbols—the symbols produced for us by our culture.[54]

The symbols American Indian tribes and Europeans sought to draw upon in establishing the principles of justice governing their relations with each other on the North American colonial frontier were remarkably diverse, complex, and distinctive cultural products. Each cultural group sought to act on its own long-held cultural traditions in establishing relations with other groups. But in the decentralized channels of North America Encounter era forest diplomacy, not all of these traditions were favorably situated to impress their mark on that unique and rapidly transforming terrain.

European diplomatic traditions may have worked well in the Old World crucible of consolidating nation-states with defined territorial borders under the sovereignty of absolute monarchs. But as the historian Dorothy V. Jones notes, North American Encounter era diplomacy "was not centralized; it was diffuse. It was not conducted by trained diplomats but by anybody and everybody, by orators, civil leaders, village and provincial councils, missionaries, speculators, traditionalists, dissidents, those with authority and those without."[55] The language of diplomacy that developed on the colonial frontier had no use for inflexible idioms that were nonindigenous to the unique conditions that emerged during the North American Encounter era. This language developed its own diplomatic protocols and ceremonies, borrowing and adapting from cultural traditions that, as Jones notes, "were rarely European."[56]

The protocols and ceremonies of this indigenous North American language of diplomacy were rarely European because it was a language grounded in indigenous North American visions of law and peace between different peoples.[57] The hierarchal, feudal symbols of seventeenth- and eighteenth-century European diplomacy simply did not translate well on the North American colonial frontier.

This point is amply demonstrated in the first reported formal treaty ceremony between English colonists and an Indian tribal confederacy in North America.[58] In 1608, Christopher Newport was sent to the Jamestown colony, the first permanent English settlement in North America, with instructions from the Virginia Company in London to perform a coronation of the Indian "emperor" Powhatan. Powhatan controlled the confederacy of tribes in the Tidewater region surrounding Jamestown. The Virginia Company's proposed coronation ceremony, therefore, held important implications for the assertion of English foothold rights in Virginia. As the historian Wesley Craven explained: "By accepting the crown Powhatan might be understood to have conceded the English title, a point of considerable legal importance to the Europeans. While in the offer of it the English gave due recognition, or so presumably it was felt, to the Indians' right in the land."[59] But the Indian emperor had no desire to be subinfeudated as a minor lord to the superior sovereignty of the English crown. When Powhatan was asked to travel to Jamestown for the coronation ceremony, he refused, replying in royal indignation, "I also am a king, and this is my land. . . . [Y]our father is to come to me, not I to him."[60] John Smith's *Map of Virginia,* published in 1612, then described how Newport had to travel 100 miles upriver to Powhatan's village to perform the coronation ceremony:

> All things being fit for the day of his [Powhatan's] coronation, the presents were brought. . . . But a foul trouble there was to make him kneel to receive his crown, he neither knowing the majesty, nor meaning of a crown, nor bending of the knee, endured so many persuasions, examples, and instructions as tired them all. At last, by leaning hard on his shoulders, he a little stooped, and Newport put the crown on his head.[61]

Powhatan's regal conduct indicates that he understood the symbology of bending the knee during this particular kind of ceremony all too well. The European language of diplomacy was ill-suited to the type of intercultural brokering and mediation required for survival on North America's colonial frontiers. European diplomacy operated on principles of hierarchy and centralization of authority.[62] During the early Encounter, Europeans usually found themselves unable to impose these alien principles unilaterally in their negotiations with their tribal trading partners. They had to learn a different language of diplomacy if they were to negotiate successfully with the most powerful Indian tribes of North America.

In eastern North America, Europeans fortuitously found an already existing system of Indian diplomacy with its own distinctive language and ceremonial forms. For most of the European colonies on the eastern half of the continent, given their small numbers and weak tactical position, it was easier to adapt to this ongoing system. Indians simply refused to accept the alien symbols and ceremonies of the European language of diplomacy that demanded their unquestioning subjugation to a monarch an ocean's distance away. For Indians, correspondingly, there was no reason to believe that the ongoing system they relied on to maintain their connections with different groups in pre-Encounter North America could not also be adapted to the process of establishing treaty relationships with the strange and alien newcomers to their world.

Pre-Encounter Indigenous Diplomacy

Tribal oral traditions and the archaeological record point to the existence of numerous diplomatic relationships between Indian peoples in the pre-Encounter period. In fact, several major tribal diplomatic systems were obviously ongoing at the time of the Encounter among the Eastern Woodlands Indians.[63]

Pre-Encounter Indian diplomacy appears to have revolved around an extensive intertribal trading system among the Eastern Woodlands tribes of North America. Pottery, shell beads, and native copper were among the most frequently exchanged goods traded along the ancient networks of extended trails and water routes linking various villages, tribes, and tribal territories in eastern North America. Perishable goods were apparently exchanged as well between tribes. There is even evidence of specialization in the manufacture of indigenous trade goods such as beads and pipes.[64]

These kinds of extended trading connections probably could not have existed or been sustained over time without benefit of tribal diplomacy. Some form of negotiations over issues of safe passage and other privileges is usually necessary to sustain trade between groups. Precise knowledge of precontact Indian diplomacy is very limited because Europeans could not record on paper what they did not see. However, it is evident that Europeans, particularly in the eastern half of North America, were entering a cultural landscape of numerous preexisting trading relationships and alliance patterns between tribes. European explorers were frequently able to rely on Indian informants in coastal areas for intelligence concerning more remote inland regions and their resident tribes. European traders were also able to transport their commodities along existing Indian trade routes, facilitated by various tribes along the way that welcomed the trade as both consumers and rent seekers.[65]

Europeans encountered a large number of highly organized tribal confederacies and smaller, but nonetheless effectively organized, unions of tribes during the early Encounter era as well. Soon after their arrival in 1607, for example, the settlers at Jamestown discovered that virtually all of the tribes on the James and York rivers appeared to be under the control of Powhatan. Powhatan, as paramount chief, administered his "empire" by means of a tributary system that soon earned the respect of the hapless Jamestown colony in its early, desperate years.[66] Captain John Smith once even conceded that the Indians of Virginia possessed a government that "excel[led] many places that would be accounted very civil."[67]

The English quickly learned of other formidable tribal confederacies and unions in the regions of their settlements in Virginia, the Mid-Atlantic, New England, and the Carolinas. Multitribal groupings and alliances were noted and described by Europeans in their earliest recorded meetings with Indians throughout eastern North America. Contact with whites certainly accelerated the formation and strengthening of these unions. But most scholars of the period do not attribute these tribal alliances to contact change only.[68] These multicultural groupings were indigenous to North America at the time of the initial Encounter. Testimony from Indians and non-Indian traders and missionaries who traveled among Indians attests that these aboriginal forms of multitribal organization in eastern North America were brought about by processes similar to those that brought about alliances and union in Europe; different groups of peoples were linked together by intermarriage of chiefly lineages, by conquest, or by the necessities of defensive alliance against other groups.[69]

The business of waging war, in particular, seems to have been as much a stimulus to the development of diplomacy in precontact eastern North America as it was in Old World Europe. As in Europe, war among Indian tribes (according to Indian oral traditions related to Europeans) served as a catalyst to the formation of alliances and treaty making. Scholars of precontact intertribal relations note the widespread and long-established patterns of intertribal warfare among northeastern agricultural Indian peoples in particular. Indians of the Encounter frequently relate tribal traditions in which the fear of reprisals and the desire to end the interminable "mourning wars" launched by one tribe against another to avenge the murder of a kinsperson are major factors in the formation of their confederacies and groupings.

The precontact existence of widespread intertribal diplomatic systems and well-developed treaty-making traditions is strongly suggested throughout the recorded treaty literature of the early Encounter era. Common protocols and rituals circulated among widely divergent tribes that attended the early treaty conferences with Europeans. Indians from one tribe demonstrated a comfortable familiarity with symbols and metaphors used by Indians from other Eastern Woodlands tribal groups during treaty discussions. The treaty literature is replete with Indian speakers detailing ancient diplomatic connections and alliances with other tribes. The evidence clearly demonstrates that although European contact and trade undoubtedly accelerated the pace and evolution of intertribal diplomacy, the Indian peoples of eastern North America had apparently been negotiating treaties and alliances with each other for some time before the arrival of a strange and alien race on their continent.

The Language of Diplomacy on a Multicultural Frontier

The Eastern Woodlands Indian tribes would have confronted a number of complicating challenges in conducting diplomacy among themselves even before the arrival of Europeans on the continent. Within the relatively defined geographical region of eastern North America, bounded by the Mississippi River Basin to the west, the Atlantic Ocean to the east, the Gulf of Mexico to the south, and the Great Lakes region to the north, there was a remarkable diversity among tribes in language, customs, and traditions.

Consider the matter of language, essential to the conduct of diplomacy. Sharing a language, as anthropologists have long recognized, is the first step to living a life in community with others. Peoples who cannot speak with each other cannot agree to make peace. In the words of Edward Sapir, "[L]anguage is a guide to 'social reality.' . . . It powerfully conditions all our thinking about social problems and processes."[70]

If human beings are at the mercy of the particular language that serves as the medium of expression for their society, imagine the difficulty of developing a mutually intelligible language of diplomacy in pre-Encounter indigenous North America. More than 200 distinct forms of mutually unintelligible Indian languages have been identified, and linguists are certain that many more have not been identified.[71]

The great diversity in languages among Eastern Woodlands Indian tribes in North America was complemented by a similar diversity in cultural patterns and traditions. Tribal religions, kinship patterns, burial and warfaring customs, and other aspects of Indian life differed vastly throughout the region.[72]

The question that arises, of course, is, given this diversity of language, customs, and traditions, how did Indians develop their precontact

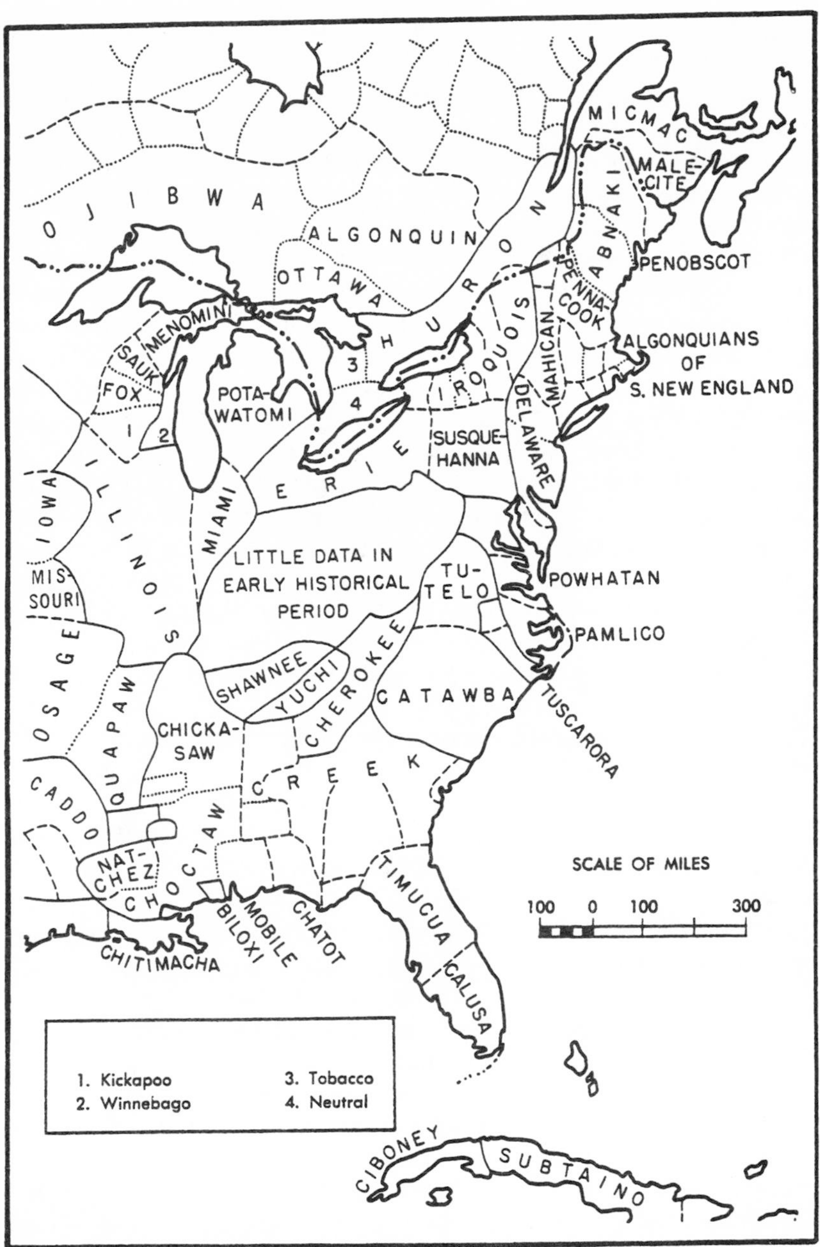

Indian tribes of eastern North America. From Harold E. Driver, *Indians of North America* (2d rev. ed. 1975). (Courtesy of the University of Chicago Press)

systems of diplomacy, which were flexible and effective enough to provide the initial framework for relations with Europeans?

In eastern North America, at least, an amazingly rich and complex specialized "language" of diplomacy had developed among Indian peoples prior to European contact. This shared language among the Eastern Woodlands tribes was spoken in symbols, metaphors, stories, and rituals. It was a language that continuously appropriated, blended, and reconstructed the diverse narrative traditions of the tribal cultures of indigenous North America. This language of law and peace between different peoples can be seen in action in the earliest recorded meetings between Indians and Europeans, as Indian diplomats constantly adapted themselves to the challenges of a rapidly changing multicultural frontier.

Throughout the Encounter era treaty literature, Indians can be witnessed inviting Europeans to make known the "good thoughts" of peace, to smoke the sacred pipe, to clear the path, to bury the hatchet, to link arms together and unite as one people, to eat out of the same bowl together, and to remove the clouds that blind the sun that shines peace on all peoples of the world. These and a host of other intricately related sets of recurring metaphors and sacred Indian rituals are part of a North American indigenous language of law and peace between different peoples that made diplomacy possible and effective on the multicultural frontiers of North America during the Encounter era.

The wide diffusion of this indigenous North American language of diplomacy shows that treaty making was no novelty suddenly thrust upon tribes by foreign invaders seeking new lands, markets, and peoples to exploit. Tribes eagerly sought to incorporate Europeans into their already existing treaty systems and related diplomatic practices and traditions.

The language utilized by tribes in their treaty-making practices and traditions can be best understood as the product of a complex, plural cultural landscape. In the process of cultural-group negotiations, this language of Eastern Woodlands Indian diplomacy appropriated, blended, and reconstructed narratives from many sources. This remarkably adaptive language could be used to conclude wars and make peace, cement military alliances, or secure a valued trade partner among groups with diverse languages, customs, and traditions.

Because so many tribes "spoke" this indigenous North American language of diplomacy, it would perhaps be more accurate to think of it as the product of a plurality of specialized languages, comprehending a variety of paradigms for behavior and action. We can expect that the norms governing relations between different peoples were continually debated in this complex language of North American indigenous multicultural diplomacy. We can imagine that terms and concepts in one tribal treaty-making tradition and its governing paradigms migrated to another, then to another, and so on, to the point where, as J. G. A. Pocock has explained, the processes of change within a language considered as a social instrument can be imagined as beginning.[73] As does any complex language, the language of North American indigenous diplomacy sought to constitute a society. During the Encounter era, that society was the one beginning to emerge from the chaos and crises that characterized the eastern North American multicultural frontier.

If we imagine the language of North American indigenous diplomacy as a fluid medium for translating the intentions and proposals of different Indian tribes engaged in the process of intercultural negotiations, we can begin to understand the difficulties that Europeans would have encountered as they stepped, so to speak, *in medias res* into the Encounter era colonial frontier. In translating this language so that they might be able to employ it in their negotiations with tribes over the terms of their presence on the continent, Europeans were confronted with a much different way of thinking about the world and the way in which relationships between peoples were to be structured in it. We should not be surprised, therefore, if Europeans were imperfect translators of this language. Europeans could not interpret what they did not understand.

Because of these difficulties of translation, however, we confront a number of complex challenges in trying to understand the language Indians used in their treaty diplomacy with Europeans. The primary sources for research on the treaty practices and diplomacy of the major tribal groups of eastern North America are contained in the colonial era records of treaty conferences, negotiations, and agreements. These are a highly selective group of documents, fraught with their own unique set of problems. As Daniel Richter has noted of the colonial era records of Indian-white treaty sessions: "[I]nterpreters' linguistic skills are suspect; clerks frequently tired of long Indian harangues and noted only what they considered to be the high points; and deliberate falsifications sometimes occurred." Yet despite such limitations, the Encounter era treaty literature still represents an invaluable resource for the study of Indian treaty-making traditions and practices that managed to find their way into the historical record. "In no other source," as Richter explains, "did ethnocentric Euro-Americans preserve with less distortion a memoir of Indian thoughts, concerns, and interpretations of events."[74]

Despite the incompleteness of the historical record, the diversity of the tribes that participated in the Encounter era treaty system, and the poor skills of European interpreters, we can discern certain key concepts and terms that frequently recur throughout the treaty literature. Identifying these concepts and terms also makes it possible to discern the patterns of the complex set of paradigms and structures that governed the language of eastern North American Indian diplomacy.

The Puzzles of Translation

The problem of learning how meaning in one system of communication is expressed in another is one of the most difficult tasks we confront in a multicultural world. Solving the "puzzles of translation" that we perceive as separating ourselves from strange, alien sorts of peoples requires what Geertz has called a cultural hermeneutics: a way of "finding out how others, across the sea or down the corridor, organize their significative world."[75] When one reads the treaty literature of the Encounter era, it is immediately apparent that the language of eastern North American Indian diplomacy sought to organize and envision a richly diverse, significative world. Complex sets of symbols, metaphors, ceremonies, and rituals are continuously repeated at major treaty councils throughout the period.

Take, for example, the recurring set of metaphors, ceremonies, and rituals in the Encounter era treaty literature that speak of treaties as sacred texts.[76] Empirically speaking, even a casual reading of the treaty literature confirms that the language of North American Indian diplomacy regarded the negotiating of a treaty as a type of divinely supervised, sacred business.

The sacred language that always accompanies Indian diplomacy in the treaty literature appears in individually recognizable patterns and styles: A peace pipe is smoked and certain words and ideas are expressed at Treaty Council A; the same pattern appears among different tribes at Treaty Council B, held fifty years after Treaty Council A. At Treaty Councils C, D, E, and F—all involving different tribes and different European colonial powers at different times and places on the Encounter era frontier—the pattern appears again. From such recurring, routine instances, a language and its paradigms can be reconstructed and even respoken.[77] We can begin to reimagine American Indian visions of law and peace as spoken in the language of Encounter era Indian diplomacy.

The language of North American Indian diplomacy is remarkably diverse; its idioms and paradigms extend far beyond imagining a treaty as a sacred text. For Eastern Woodlands Indians of the Encounter era, treaties were equally valued for the connections they established and maintained,[78] for the stories of law and peace between different peoples they engendered,[79] for the enduring constitutional bonds of multicultural unity they enforced,[80] and for the relationships of trust they nurtured and sustained.[81] These are the most readily retrievable conceptions of treaties that emerge from the language of Encounter era Indian diplomacy. These indigenous North American visions of multicultural relationships do not exhaust the catalog of ideas and principles Indians sought to apply in their relations with Europeans during the Encounter era. Different Indian tribal goups held differing visions of law, peace, and justice between peoples in the world. In this book I explore several readily identifiable idioms, symbols, and metaphors that proliferate in the treaty literature involving some of the major Indian tribal groupings of eastern North America during the seventeenth and eighteenth centuries. The pathways I follow into these particular American Indian visions of law and peace are connected to one another but through a system that has remained largely unexplained and uncharted by the colonizers' historians. Our explorations of this body of decolonizing knowledge developed by the indigenous tribal peoples of the world have only just begun. Readers will, I hope, forgive me if I sometimes appear lost in this language or wrong in my interpretations or if I fail to generalize beyond the narrow cultural and geographical confines of Encounter era eastern North America and Eastern Woodlands Indian groups. Treaties are also literature,[82] and like all literary texts worthy of serious attention, they seditiously resist essentializing efforts at reduction or summation in the confines of critique.[83] This book simply begins a process of revealing a few of the visions American Indian peoples sought to apply to the complex challenges of achieving law and peace between different peoples on the frontiers of a multicultural world.

2
Treaties as Sacred Texts

The Sacred Pipe

Anthropologists have recognized that although the content of a tradition may change, its structure still persists. If this is so, one way to approach the language of North American Encounter era diplomacy is to look at the traditional rituals practiced by Indians today. These contemporary ceremonies may suggest useful pathways for understanding at least some of the tribal traditions referred to in the treaty literature of the past.[1]

Today, it is still the custom among many Indian peoples in North America to smoke the sacred pipe of peace before any important tribal business commences. According to tradition, a circle is formed, and all are seated, perhaps on a large buffalo skin spread on the floor. The keeper of the pipe slowly takes it out of a bag made of buckskin or some other animal hide or cloth and places it on the ground. Those seated around the circle bow their heads in silence.

At this point in the ceremony, sweet grass is typically rolled into a ball. The keeper holds the ball of grass tightly in front of him and says a prayer. He then raises the ball over his head and passes it to the left, "sunwise" (i.e., clockwise). Each person in the circle repeats the ritual, saying a prayer.

Once the ball of sweet grass has worked its way around the circle, it is placed in a dish and set on fire. According to traditional belief, the heavy smoke of the sweet grass purifies the body and the spirit. As they pass around the smoldering ball, the members of the circle move their hands over it, pulling the smoke toward their nostrils, eyes, mouth, and ears, over their heads, over their whole bodies.

After this purifying ritual, the keeper fills the pipe with tobacco. He holds the pipe in front of him and says a prayer. He rotates the pipe sunwise, pointing it to the east, south, west, and north, then up to the sky and down to the earth. He lights the pipe and passes it to his left. Each person in the circle points it toward all the directions, smokes the pipe, then passes it to the next person in the circle.[2]

The smoking of the pipe as practiced in this sacred manner in contemporary tribal life allows us to retrieve at least a partial understanding of the meanings Indians have attached to a tradition repeatedly referenced in the historical record. We know from anthropological accounts and narratives that the peace pipe has been smoked in this same solemn manner by North American Indian tribes for quite some time. The continuity of the peace pipe tradition is affirmed, for example, in a number of ethnographic texts produced during the late nineteenth and early twentieth centuries. During this period, white researchers recorded the remembrances of a number of Indian elders about the traditions of their tribes before reservation life.

One well-known text in this scholarly genre of Indian traditional knowledge is *The Sacred Pipe: Black Elk's Account of the Seven Rites of the Oglala Sioux.* Black Elk was a Sioux holy man born in 1862 who received his knowledge of Sioux ritual directly from the sage Elk Head, "Keeper of the Sacred Pipe," and other wisemen of his tribe. He was given responsibility for keeping the knowledge of the pipe rituals of his tribe and for preserving the oral tradition by which these rituals had been handed down over time to his people.[3]

According to Black Elk's rendition of the sacred narrative of the pipe, the Sioux were visited "very many winters ago" by a beautiful woman, dressed in white buckskin and bearing a bundle on her back. This *Wakan* (sacred) woman, called White Buffalo Cow Woman by the Sioux, had come with a message of great importance.[4]

The *Wakan* woman entered the lodge of the chief, Standing Hollow Horn, where the Sioux people had gathered to hear her message. She first walked around the lodge sunwise. Standing in front of the chief, she held out her bundle with both hands and declared:

> Behold this and always love it! It is *lela wakan* [very sacred], and you must treat it as such. No impure man should ever be allowed to see it, for within the bundle there is a sacred pipe. With this you will, during the winter to come, send your voices to *Wakan Tanka,* your Father and Grandfather.[5]

The sacred pipe was carved of red stone. "It is the Earth," White Buffalo Cow Woman said: "Grandmother and Mother." She told the

Sioux that every step they take upon the earth should be a prayer since it is sacred. Likewise, every time the pipe is used should be a prayer since it is sacred, like the earth.[6]

A buffalo calf carved in the stone pipe represented all four-legged creatures. From the wooden stem of the pipe hung twelve eagle feathers, representing all winged creatures. "All these peoples, and all the things of the universe are joined to you who smoke the pipe—all send their voices to *Wakan Tanka* the Great Spirit. When you pray with this pipe, you pray for and with everything."[7]

White Buffalo Cow Woman then told Standing Hollow Horn that *Wakan Tanka* had given the sacred pipe as a gift to the Sioux, "so that through it you may have knowledge." This sacred knowledge was to be gained by use of the pipe when one of the people died. As the *Wakan* woman explained:

> It should be for you a sacred day when one of your people dies. You must then keep his soul as I shall teach you, and through this you will gain much power; for if this soul is kept, it will increase in you your concern and love for your neighbor. So long as the person, in his soul, is kept with your people, through him you will be able to send your voice to *Wakan Tanka*.[8]

Black Elk explained the knowledge that was taught by the rite of keeping the soul with the sacred pipe as follows: "It is good to have a reminder of death before us, for it helps us to understand the impermanence of life on this earth, and this understanding may aid us in preparing for our own death. He who is well prepared is he who knows that he is nothing compared with *Wakan Tanka*, who is everything; then he knows that world which is real."[9]

According to the ancient tradition as related by Black Elk, a Sioux keeper of the pipe named High Hollow Horn first performed the rite of keeping of the soul upon the death of a young child in the tribe. As White Buffalo Cow Woman had instructed, High Hollow Horn took the pipe, which

> was then lighted and smoked, and was passed sunwise around the circle. The whole world within the pipe was offered up to *Wakan Tanka*. When the pipe came back to High Hollow Horn, he rubbed sweet grass over it on the west, north, east, and south sides in order to purify it lest any unworthy person might have touched it; turning to the people, he then said: "My relatives, this pipe is *Wakan*. We all know that it cannot lie. No man who has within him any untruth may touch it to his mouth. Further, my relatives, our Father, *Wakan Tanka*, has made his will known to us here on earth, and we must always do that which He wishes if we would walk the sacred path."[10]

Black Elk explained: "It is through this rite that we purify the souls of our dead, and that our love for one another is increased."[11]

The Rite of Making Relatives

Just as for Indians who continue to smoke the pipe today in their ceremonies, for the Sioux Indians, smoking the pipe of peace was serious, sacred business.[12] Pipe rituals were performed as a prelude to the most important occasions in the life of the tribe and its individual members.

According to Black Elk's rendition of his tribe's tradition of the pipe, White Buffalo Cow Woman told the Sioux that, in time, six other sacred pipe rituals would be revealed to them by the Great Spirit.[13] Peace pipe rituals appear throughout the treaty literature involving the Sioux Indians because of the fifth of these seven rituals: the rite of making relatives. As explained by Black Elk:

> In this rite we establish a relationship on earth, which is a reflection of that real relationship which always exists between men and *Wakan Tanka*. As we always love *Wakan Tanka* first, and before all else, so we should also love and establish closer relationships with our fellow men, even if they should be of another nation than ours.[14]

Black Elk related that the rite of the making of relatives was received in a vision by a Sioux holy man, Matohoshila. Traveling to the Southeast, Matohoshila, "exactly as he had seen in his vision," came upon a small patch of corn. He brought this corn back to his people.[15] Matohoshila did not know, however, that the corn belonged to the Ree (or Arikara), a Caddoan-speaking group closely related to the Pawnee nation "with whom the Sioux had long been at war." Because corn was as sacred to the Ree as the pipe was to the Sioux, the Ree sent messengers to the camp of the Sioux "bearing many gifts." According to Black Elk, the Ree wanted their sacred corn back.[16]

The request by the Ree helped Matohoshila understand the significance of his vision from the Great Spirit. He told his people that by holding the rite of the making of relatives with the sacred pipe, "we shall establish a close and lasting relationship with the Ree nation—one that will endure until the end of time, and one that will be an example to all other nations."[17]

In accordance with Matohoshila's vision, the Ree were invited to a council with the Sioux. At this council, Matohoshila filled his pipe and offered it to the Sioux's traditional enemies with the following words:

> I wish you to help me in establishing a rite which for the benefit of all our people, has been given to me in a vision by the Great Spirit. It is his will that we do this. He, who is our Grandfather and Father, has established a relationship with my people the Sioux; it is our duty to make a rite which should extend the relationship to the different people of different nations. May that which we do here be an example to others![18]

Matohoshila conducted the ceremonies of the rite of making relatives precisely according to his vision. He burned sweet grass, made offerings, and said prayers to the six directions. He told the Ree, "In the past, the two-leggeds which *Wakan Tanka* placed upon this land have been enemies, but through this rite there will be peace, and, in the future, through this rite other nations of this island will become as relatives."[19]

The Rees then performed the reciprocal ceremonies of the ritual as instructed by Matohoshila. They sang, "We are all related; We are all one!"[20] After the Ree completed their part of the ritual, Matohoshila rose, raised the pipe, and prayed:

> O *Wakan Tanka,* I raise my hand to you. This day you are standing close to us. I offer You my pipe. . . . On this holy day, we have united into one all that is sacred in the universe. On this day a true relationship has been established. On this day a great peace has been made. . . . [T]hese peoples will walk together that one path which is red and sacred.[21]

After delivering this prayer, Matohoshila turned to the Ree and declared, "[W]e are bound together; we are one!" A great feast, "which lasted through the night," then followed.[22]

Black Elk says at the end of this story that through the ritual of making relatives a threefold peace was established.

> The first peace, which is the most important, is that which comes within the souls of men when they realize their relationship, their oneness, with the universe and all its Powers, and when they realize that at the center of the universe dwells *Wakan Tanka,* and that this center is really everywhere, it is within each of us. This is the real Peace, and the others are but reflections of this. The second peace is that which is made between men. But above all you should understand that there can never be peace between nations until there is first known that true peace which, as I have often said, is within the souls of men.[23]

The Sacred Pipe in the Treaty Literature

The Sioux regarded treaty making as a most serious and sacred business according to their traditions. As the historian and anthropologist Peter John Powell, who studied the Sioux closely during his career, attested: "Any agreement that was signed was a sacred agreement because it was sealed by the smoking of the pipe. It was not signed by chiefs and headmen before the pipe sealed the treaty, making the agreement holy and binding."[24]

The seven divisions of the Sioux occupied most of present-day Minnesota at the beginning of the Encounter era in the seventeenth century. As the fur trade moved into the western Great Lakes region in the early eighteenth century, the Lakota Sioux—Black Elk's group—moved westward, ranging on both sides of the Missouri River in the Dakotas. Though classified as Plains Indians, the cultures of the Sioux are generally regarded by anthropologists as variants of Eastern Woodlands tribal patterns.[25] Controlling the broad zone between the Woodlands and High Plains, the Sioux had frequent dealings with colonial Europeans and the tribes on their eastern flank throughout the early Encounter era.

Some of these dealings involved trade; some were of a hostile nature. Sioux warfare and raiding were the subject of frequent complaints and requests for European protection by Great Lakes region tribes in the treaty literature. But whenever the Sioux proposed a treaty of peace or an alliance with different groups of peoples, the treaty literature records that they smoked the sacred pipe.

In fact, virtually all of the major Woodlands tribal groups of the Mississippi Basin region, from Georgia to the upper reaches of the Great Lakes, attached a sacred significance to the smoking of the pipe of peace during their treaty negotiations.[26] Such widespread diffusion of cultural rituals and practices is characteristic of Indian forest diplomacy at the time of European contact.

For example, the initial contacts between James Oglethorpe of the Georgia colony and the chiefs of the Yamacraw Indians (a mixed band made up mainly of Lower Creeks) focused on the delicate issues related to settlement rights of Georgia's colonists on lands claimed by the Yamacraws.[27] At a 1733 council,[28] the Indians, "their heads adorned with white feathers, in token of peace, and friendship," greeted Oglethorpe with an elaborate procession, followed by the smoking of the pipe.

> They came up to Mr. Oglethorpe and the other gentlemen and waved the white wings they carried in their hands, over their heads, at the same time singing and putting their bodies in antic postures. Afterwards they fixed a lighted pipe of tobacco to the tubes which they held in their hands, and presented it to Mr. Oglethorpe, who having smoked several whiffs they then presented it to the other gentlemen, who observed the same method which Mr. Oglethorpe had done. Then afterwards presented the same pipe to their King and two of their Chiefs, the King and each of the Chiefs smoking four whiffs, blowing the first whiff to the left, the next to the right, the third upwards, and the fourth downwards.

At a 1721 council between the Chickasaw Indians in present-day Mississippi and Virginia's colonial officials, the calumet of peace was presented as a symbol of the Indians' desire to make a firm and lasting peace with the English colony.[29] According to the records of the treaty ceremony, the Indians were brought into the council chamber, where they entered singing, "according to their custom." After this entrance ceremony,

> the Great Man of the Chickasaws carrying in his hand a Calumet of Peace, first presented a parcel of deer skins, which he spread upon the shoulders of the Governor and divers of the council: And then made a speech to the

> Governor importing in substance, that his Nation being at war with the French and wanting arms and ammunition . . . he was sent hither to desire a trade with this colony; after which he presented to the Governor his Calumet of Peace as a token that the Chickasaws desired to live at peace and friendship, with the English of this colony.

The pipe also appears in ceremonies welcoming French traders visiting the villages of various bands of refugee Indians in the Great Lakes region during the 1660s. At a Miami-Mascouten settlement, a French trader was met by a village elder carrying a long-stemmed calumet pipe decorated with feathers. The old man presented the pipe in the traditional manner first to the French traders, then directly to the sun, the earth, and all of the directions. The elder rubbed the head of one of the French traders, then his back, legs, and feet. He spread a buffalo skin on the ground, sat on it with the traders, and commenced to smoke. They ate cornmeal porridge and dried meat, refilled the calumet, and smoked again. The old man blew smoke directly into the faces of the French guests. The apprehensive trader who related this event, no doubt familiar with reports of cannibalism among some of the Great Lakes tribes, likened this purifying ritual to being smoked like drying meat.[30]

Europeans quickly came to appreciate the significance of the pipe in Indian treaty negotiations. In 1765, Alexander Cameron, British colonial agent to the Cherokees in present-day Tennessee and the Carolinas, sensed that tensions between the two groups could soon erupt into a war. Cameron was well acquainted with the Indians' customs. He called a meeting of the Cherokee headmen and asked them to smoke the pipe of peace. When several chiefs declined the offer, Cameron reported that he made them "smoke" it by forcing the calumet into their mouths.[31]

Like Cameron, the early seventeenth-century French Jesuit missionary Father Joseph Francis Lafitau was also a close observer and student of Indian customs.[32] He drew comparisons to classical Roman diplomatic traditions in an effort to illuminate the use of the calumet peace pipe in Indian treaty practices. Lafitau deduced that, like the Caduceus, the Roman god Mercury's winged, serpent-entwined staff, the Indians' peace pipe signaled a diplomatic mission and provided safe conduct.[33]

But as Lafitau recognized, the calumet's symbology served other functions as well in Indian diplomacy. The Indians of North America, the Jesuit explained, had preserved in the diplomatic symbology of the pipe the sacred sense of treaty obligations that European diplomacy had long since abandoned as a nonessential part of its classical heritage:

> [T]he most essential thing, the calumet of peace; it is this pipe, which is I think a veritable altar for the Indians where they offer with all due forms a sacrifice to the sun, a sacrifice which gains for the calumet that respect to which, through a spirit of ancient religions, the sacredness of actions and the inviolable law of nations are attached, in the same way as these things were formerly attached to Mercury's staff.[34]

As Lafitau's description suggests, the respect attached to the peace pipe in Indian diplomacy elevated the temporal agreement represented by a treaty to the realm of a sacred obligation. The calumet was the great sacred token of peace. It was, as described by another early French missionary, Father Jacques Gravier, "the God of peace and of war, the arbiter of life and death. It suffices for one to carry and show it to walk in safety in the midst of enemies who in the hottest fight lay down their weapons when it is displayed."[35] The sacred pipe was smoked at treaty councils attended by virtually all of the major tribal groupings that appear in the Encounter era treaty literature.[36] For many of these tribes, violation of the "law of the Calumet" was regarded as an unpardonable offense,[37] punishable by divine sanction.

The widespread diffusion of the pipe of peace among American Indian tribes reveals several crucial characteristics about Encounter era Indian diplomacy. The language of diplomacy utilized by tribes in their treaty-making practices was the product of a complex, plural cultural landscape. The sacred rituals and symbols of this language circulated as integrative devices on a multicultural frontier. They were adapted from the most important aspects of tribal life and shared with different peoples to construct a conscious framework for conducting treaty negotiations.

In Encounter era Indian diplomacy, the most vital issues of a people's survival—negotiating peace, strategic alliance, commercial trade, the exchange of prisoners, and rights of passage through alien territory—were all facilitated by smoking the pipe of peace. As the language of Indian diplomacy suggests, the peace pipe tradition was able to serve these vital functions because, according to American Indian treaty visions of law and peace, smoking the calumet of peace was a sacred act of commitment that made previously alienated groups regard each other as relatives.[38]

Sacred Texts

The calumet pipe is one of several recurrent symbols and ritual systems dispersed throughout the treaty literature of the Encounter era reflecting the basic understanding of American Indians that a treaty was a sacred undertaking. Indian diplomacy recognized that on a multicultural frontier, the making of peace required an act of commitment between two former enemies. The parties to a treaty had to agree to create and sustain a *nomos,* a normative universe of shared meanings—"a present world constituted by a system of tension between reality and vision."[39] The smoking of the calumet of peace sought to resolve this tension by invoking the larger forces at work in the affairs of human beings. A treaty sanctified by the smoking of the pipe of peace became, in essence, a sacred text, a narrative that committed two different peoples to live according to a shared legal tradition—an American Indian vision of law and peace.

Appreciating the symbolic meanings that Indian peoples attached to treaties as sacred texts provides a basic orienting strategy for understanding the complex language of Encounter era Indian diplomacy. "In Indian diplomatic traditions," Dorothy V. Jones has explained, "treaties were not merely temporal agreements. They were sacred collective obligations, to be broken only under peril of divine displeasure."[40] This empirically based observation that for Indians treaties were sacred texts does not mean that we should expect to see every Indian diplomat negotiate the rate of exchange between English woolen shrouds and Indian beaver pelts by detailed reference to some ancient tribal mourning rite or creation myth. The point is that the treaty literature is rife with Indian *and* non-Indian diplomats who do make such reference. Sacred themes, more so than any other set of references, consistently make their presence felt in the Encounter era treaty literature.

Quaker missionary John Richardson described a 1701 meeting between a group of Conestoga and Shawnee Indians and William Penn, founder and proprietor of the Pennsylvania colony, in which a sense of the sacred was clearly at work.[41] The Pennsylvania Indians had traveled to Penn's country house, Pensbury, to renew their long-standing covenants of amity and peace with Penn, their "loving, good friend and brother." The Indians avowed at this treaty-renewal ceremony that "*they never first broke Covenant with any People*; for, as one of them said, and smote his Hand upon his Head three times, that *they did not make them there in their Heads,* but smiting his Hand three times on his Breast, said, *they made them* (*i.e.* their Covenants) *there in their Hearts.*" After this vow, the Indians then reassembled outside, "to perform their *Cantico or Worship,*" according to Richardson. Sitting around a small fire, "they severally fixed their Eyes." Richardson continued:

> I did not see them move them in all that part of their Worship, while they sang a very melodious Hymn, which affected and tendered the Hearts of many who were Spectators: When they had thus done, they began (as I suppose is their usual manner) to beat upon the Ground with little Sticks . . . till one of the elder Sort sets forth his Hymn; and that being followed by the Company for a few Minutes, and then a Pause; and then the like was done by another, and so by a third, and followed by the Company, as at the first; which seemed exceedingly to affect them and others. Having done, they rose up and danced a little about the Fire, and parted with some shouting like a Triumph or Rejoicing.

The performance of sacred tribal rituals and references to the sacred nature of treaty negotiations proliferate in the treaty literature of the Encounter era. Treaty conferences are routinely opened by Indian speakers who invoke a higher power's sanction and intent in the proceedings. Joseph Brandt, the great Iroquois leader of the Revolutionary era, opened a 1793 meeting with U.S. and British representatives with the solemn declaration: "We are glad to have the meeting, and think it is by the appointment of the Great Spirit."[42] When the Lower Creeks in 1736 explained to Governor Oglethorpe of Georgia their intention to maintain their treaty relationship with the English, they declared that "it is the Great God above that gave us the knowledge to do so."[43]

Entering into diplomatic relations with other peoples was routinely regarded as sacred business by American Indian peoples of the Encounter era. Indians pursued treaty relationships with an earnestness and solemnity of purpose that was readily apparent, even to the most obtuse Europeans. For Indians of the Encounter era, making a sure and lasting peace after the shedding of blood, quelling the desire for revenge, being assured that a military ally would respond quickly to a call for help, and trusting a trading partner over the course of many dealings were the types of weighty concerns, many of them life-and-death matters, that a treaty relationship was designed to address. No wonder that Edmond Atkin, the southern Indian superintendent for Great Britain in the Revolutionary period and a person of long experience in dealing with the tribes, could say of the Indian nations he knew: "[I]n their public treaties no people on earth are more open, explicit, and direct. Nor are they excelled by any in the observance of them."[44] This was because, according to American Indian visions of law and peace, treaties were sacred texts, broken only upon peril of divine sanction.

Gods and Foxholes

"Cultures" as Marshall Sahlins has written, "find gods in foxholes."[45] The seminal anthropological insight that religious beliefs and practice come into play at times of crisis and stress in the social life of a people suggests one obvious reason why Indians relied so heavily on supernatural reserves to secure a treaty and to bind themselves to it.[46] Where the enormity of a task seems beyond ordinary human comprehension and control, or where the uncertainties of an enterprise involve serious risks to life and livelihood, there human beings are most likely to be found calling upon their sacred symbols and religious rites for divine assistance.[47]

The emerging social system of the Encounter era was, after all, extremely fragile and fractious. Aside from divine intervention, the only institution capable of preventing developments on a multicultural frontier from descending into destabilizing chaos and violent and bloody war was diplomacy. To better secure a negotiated peace between radically different peoples, diplomacy collaborated with religion out of necessity in the North American Encounter era.

Throughout their history, human beings, as members of the only symbol-generative species, have routinely called upon religion when negotiating a peace with an avowed enemy. In establishing firm and lasting relationships with others or in agreeing to share in the benefits of common fellowship and mutual trust, humans have invoked gods as added effective means of solemnizing the mutual obligations arising from a treaty agreement.[48] There is nothing unusual, therefore, in a particular group of American Indians performing "their Cantico or worship" or sitting down to smoke a sacred pipe to confirm the sincerity of the promises made in treaty agreements. Anthropologists tell us that such cultural performances are not unexpected forms of group behavior. From the Indians' perspective, calling on a higher power to sanctify a treaty-negotiated relationship of law and peace between different peoples was part of a language of diplomacy that Europeans, as fellow human beings, were expected to understand.

As we have come to understand, the language of North American Encounter era diplomacy regarded a treaty as securing far more than the peace of mind or flow of trade that arose from good relations with a former enemy. As Black Elk's rendition of the Sioux "rite of making relatives" suggests,[49] in North American Indian visions of law and peace between different peoples, the pursuit of treaty relations is a divinely mandated responsibility in and of itself. Treaty making fulfilled what tribal Indians regarded as a sacred obligation to extend their relationships of connection to all of the different peoples of the world. A treaty was therefore far more than just a reassuring way of blunting contradictions and conflicts of interests between societies. Indians understood a treaty as another way of reconstituting a society itself on an unstable and conflict-ridden multicultural frontier.

The modern social sciences recognize that religion typically serves a number of vital, integrative functions for a society. "By the spirits," Sahlins writes, "men represent the secular forces under which they live, and in the rituals of religious cult where the power of society is materialized in the collectivity of worshippers, they affirm their dependence upon this power—which is to say, they affirm the authority of society as constituted."[50] Myths and ritual integrate society, provide it with cohesion, and promote solidarity among its members. The spiritual beliefs said to mirror the structure of society at the same time function to maintain society's continuity.

For Indians of the Encounter era, the universalizing, integrative themes found intricately elaborated in tribal sacred narratives were well suited to the tasks of constructing a society. The performance of such sacred rituals as smoking the pipe of peace habituated the tribal individual to envision the relational potentiality of all peoples and all creation in the universe. When smoked in the context of treaty negotiations, the pipe evoked a vision of a universally conceived society in which different peoples were connected to each other as relatives. In the language of Indian diplomacy, the treaty itself bespoke of a divinely inspired, universal vision of all humankind as one.

By situating the treaty in this larger, sacred narrative context, the language of Indian diplomacy reminded the treaty partners of their moral obligation to realize the cohesion, solidarity, and continuity sanctified by their divinely mandated covenant. Not acting in accordance with the divine command to make relatives with one's former enemies risked a higher power's supreme sanction. God, under this view, is not found in foxholes; rather, we may or may not find ourselves in foxholes because of God's mysterious will.

Understanding the sacred dimensions of treaty relationships helps us to reconstruct the plural roles performed by sacred narratives in the language of Encounter era Indian diplomacy. The frequent occurrence of sacred symbols and rituals in the treaty literature suggests that the paradigms for governing relations between two different peoples were sustained by appeals to supernatural forces. But the sacred character of treaties also suggests their integrative functions in Encounter era forest diplomacy. A treaty can be read as expressive of a vision of a shared world of normative commitments. According to American Indian visions of law and peace, the sacred character of treaties served to mediate crises by blunting contradictions and conflicts between societies. At the same time, the language of Indian diplomacy was adaptive enough to envision a treaty as a supreme act of commitment to create a new type of society—a society of law and peace between different peoples that would emerge on the frontiers of Encounter era North America.

The Wampum Belt Tradition

We can further develop our appreciation of how a treaty created a multicultural *nomos*—a normative universe of different peoples "held together by the force of interpretive commitments, some small and private, others immense and public"[51]—for Indians of the Encounter era by examining another major tribal tradition that circulated widely throughout the language of Encounter era diplomacy. The wampum belt tradition, which figures prominently in the forest diplomacy of seventeenth- and eighteenth-century colonial North America, similarly reflects an Indian understanding of treaties as sacred texts performing a sanctifying and integrative role.

We have already discussed the presentation of the *Gus-Wen-Tah* wampum belt by modern-day Iroquois diplomats at the United Nations Working Group on Indigenous Populations.[52] The wampum belt tradition, like the peace pipe tradition, has a long history of continuous practice by tribes in North America.

Wampum beads woven into belts and strings have been long valued as ritual objects of great spiritual significance among Eastern Woodlands tribes. In fact, wampum appears to have been an already-recognized medium of exchange for gift giving and diplomacy among Woodlands

Indian groups by the time Europeans arrived in force on the continent in the seventeenth and eighteenth centuries.[53]

The wampum beads used in American Indian diplomacy at the time of the European Encounter were cylindrical in shape, made by Atlantic Coast tribes of quahog shells with holes drilled at each end. The wampum belts and strings that were exchanged at treaty conferences were made of beads of one color, typically "black" (actually dark purple) or white or a combination of both colors strung together in graphic patterns. According to common usage among the Eastern Woodlands tribes, black beads typically symbolized death or war (although they could on occasion be used to form a graphic design on a white background symbolizing any number of things). White beads, among other things, could be used to symbolize peace, purity, or life. Red-painted beads were sometimes added to a war belt, which would then be presented to a potential ally to join forces on a military expedition against some common enemy.[54]

Wampum beads were utilized in one of the first recorded treaty conferences between the Iroquois, the most powerful Indian tribal confederacy of the Encounter era, and the French at Three Rivers, Canada, in 1645.[55] We will return to the Three Rivers Council several times throughout this book since many of the major recurring themes, rituals, and symbols associated with the wampum belt treaty tradition are recorded for the first time in the Encounter era treaty literature at this council.

According to the chronicler of the treaty council, the French Jesuit priest Father Barthelemy Vimont, an Iroquois chief named Kiotseaeton approached the French settlement at Three Rivers in a small boat accompanied by two other Iroquois ambassadors and a French hostage. The Iroquois embassy had traveled at the invitation of the French to Three Rivers to discuss an end to the long-running trade war between the confederated Iroquois tribes and the French and their Canadian Indian allies over control of the immensely valuable fur trade of eastern North America.

As described by Vimont, Kiotseaeton, upon landing his boat, stood up in the bow and motioned with his hand for silence. "High in stature" and "almost completely covered with Porcelain [wampum] beads," the "Barbarian" (as Father Vimont described him) cried out:

> My Brothers, I have left my country to come and see you. At last I have reached your land. I was told, on my departure, that I was going to seek death, and that I would never again see my country. But I have willingly exposed myself for the good of peace. I come, therefore, to enter into the designs of the French, of the Hurons, and of the Algonquins. I come to make known to you the thoughts of all my country.

Significantly, the manner in which Kiotseaeton sought to make known the thoughts of his country was through the wampum beads he had worn around his neck on his approach to the French camp.

As explained by Father Vimont, each wampum gift presented by Kiotseaeton told a different story. This use of wampum gifts as a storytelling device was typical of Indian diplomats of the Encounter era.[56] As Father Vimont himself recognized, "It is needless for me to repeat so often that words of importance in this country are presents."

The "words" of Kiotseaeton's wampum presents spoke of the Iroquois' desire to smooth the rapids, calm the lakes, and open the path of peace between the parties. The beads told of the hazards encountered by an Iroquois prisoner released by the French to return to the Iroquois with an offer to open negotiations; they described the Iroquois as an empire of many tribes that had cast their weapons under their feet and now desired peace with the French and their Indian allies.

One of the wampum "collars" presented by Kiotseaeton at Three Rivers spoke of the light of peace—a warming fire that would burn in all of the Iroquois' houses when visited by the French. This wampum gift signified a permanent and lasting peace between the two sides.

Another belt was offered to link the parties together arm in arm in a covenant of peace through the establishment of lasting relationships of reciprocal trade and intercourse. "Even if the lightning were to fall upon us," Kiotseaeton proclaimed while grabbing a Frenchman and an Algonquin by the arms, "it would not separate us, for, if it cuts off the arm that holds you to us, we will at once seize each other by the other arm."

By thus linking arms together, the two sides would join their separate hunting grounds in a great commons, agreeing to engage in mutual trade and exchange of furs and goodwill. All would now eat together and share in each other's bounty. "The road is cleared; there is no longer any danger." A great peace would be established.

Kiotseaeton, the "Barbarian" diplomat, finished his presentation of gifts and treaty terms with a belt that restored the sun and dispelled the clouds that had hidden the message of the good news of peace from the two sides. He promised the French and their allied tribes that he would spend the summer dancing and gaming. A great dance and feast that included all of the parties followed his performance. Upon leaving the French and their allied tribes at Three Rivers, Kiotseaeton declared, "Adieu my brothers; I am one of your relatives. I am going to carry back good news to our country."

Mourning Rituals and Encounter Era Diplomacy

Notably, in 1645, at the time of Kiotseaeton's offer on behalf of his country "to enter into the designs of the French, the Hurons and of the Algonquins," the League of the Five Nations of the Iroquois—the Mohawk, Oneida, Onondaga, Cayuga, and Seneca—had been engaged for nearly a decade in a fierce and bloody war over beaver furs and the connected trade with the French and the Indian tribes of Canada.[57]

Kiotseaeton, certainly aware that the unannounced arrival of an Iroquois chief in seventeenth-century French Canada could precipitate an armed attack, with questions asked later, likely intended his cautious entry at Three Rivers to serve at least a self-preserving function. The plaintive cry for peace sounded from beyond arrow or musket range was part of a diplomatic language known to all forest diplomats who survived for any significant length of time the multicultural encounter that was the seventeenth-century North American colonial frontier. Anthony F. C. Wallace, in his classic book, *The Death and Rebirth of the Seneca,* describes how a typical Indian messenger arriving at an enemy village on the colonial frontier would call out in a loud voice: "Listen to me! I have come to treat for peace with all the nations in these parts."[58]

But an even more important intention is expressed in the "Barbarian" Kiotseaeton's message at Three Rivers. In the traditions of forest diplomacy practiced by the League of the Iroquois, the plaintive cry for peace "at the wood's edge" initiated the ritualized sequences of the Condolence Council. The council, in its bare essence, was an Iroquois ceremony for condoling the loss of dead chiefs and installing new ones to the league's confederated Council of Fifty Chiefs. Condoling or "mourning" rituals were common among a number of Woodlands tribes.[59] Because they embodied the Indian belief that relationships of close connection were sustained by shared sufferings and solidarity in times of crisis, these rituals were a frequent source for the symbols and metaphors used by Indian diplomats in negotiating their multicultural treaty relationships. Recall that the method by which the Sioux negotiated a treaty involved smoking the sacred pipe. As related by Black Elk's rendition of Sioux tradition, the sacred pipe was first smoked according to a mourning ritual.[60]

The Huron Indians of the Canadian eastern Great Lakes region similarly relied on their central mourning ritual, the "Feast of the Dead," to serve a number of vital diplomatic functions. The ritual involved large-scale gift exchanges at the burial of the remains of those who had died since the last Feast of the Dead. Successors to deceased chiefs were also installed and named at the ceremony. As Eric Wolf has explained, the rituals associated with the Huron Feast of the Dead

> served to ensure continuity in the leadership of local descent groups, while at the same time providing occasions for gift exchanges between the chiefs of such groups. They underlined the separate identity and distinctiveness of such groups, while simultaneously establishing links of alliance between them.[61]

The Iroquois Condolence Council Ritual

The Condolence Council, the Iroquois mourning ritual, permeates the protocol of Iroquois Encounter era diplomacy. As William Fenton, the "dean" of Iroquoian ethnography, has written,[62] "Not only are the key parts of the paradigm of condolence performed in some of the earliest treaties, but the negotiations are embellished by the metaphors in which the later ritual is couched."[63]

The basic pattern of the Condolence Council rituals begins traditionally with the arrival of Iroquois messengers from the condoling "Clear-Minded" village. Similar to Kiotseaeton's cautious entry at Three Rivers, the "Clear-Minded" declare their presence and peaceful intentions at the "wood's edge" of the settlement of the "Down-Minded" Mourners of the dead chief.[64]

> [I]t begins with the arrival of the messengers in the vicinity of the foreign council fire. Tradition prescribes that this be a point at which the cleared land around the settlement meets the forest. . . . Whatever precautionary purpose this may have served at a time when the sudden arrival of strangers could spell imminent danger, it also bears out the Iroquoian penchant for effecting a gradual rapprochement between alien groups. Protocol requires that a delegation from the host settlement repair to the spot where the visitors are waiting and perform a welcoming ceremony—itself a council in molecular form. . . . The two groups arrange themselves on opposite sides of a small fire built just for the duration. . . . A speaker for the hosts expresses his side's gratitude that the messengers have arrived safely over the "long forest path." . . . There are many things, he says, that could have caused them to stumble and fall.[65]

Following the greeting at the wood's edge, the Clear-Minded, together with the Mourners, perform the Condolence Council ritual of the three bare words of requickening: the eyes, ears, and throat. A speaker for the Mourners "wipes the eyes" of the weary travelers from the Clear-Minded side with buckskin cloth, so that they will be able to see normally again. He then "clears their ears" of all they have heard that might cause them to alter their messages of peace and condolence. Then, offering a beverage, he "clears the obstructions from their throats" coated with dust from the forest paths so that they will be able to speak normally once again.[66]

After this requickening ritual at the wood's edge, the Mourners lead the Clear-Minded "by the arm"[67] to the village council house, where the condolence ceremony continues. At the village, the Clear-Minded initiate a sequenced exchange of gifts of wampum strings and belts (the "Porcelain beads" around Kiotseaeton's neck)[68] with the Mourners. Each highly prized gift of wampum contains the "words" of a message explained or often sung by the speakers for the Clear-Minded side.[69]

The wampum strings and belts presented to the Mourners usually speak of the hardships encountered by the Clear-Minded in traveling the rivers, rapids, and roads leading to the Mourners' village. A speaker for the Clear-Minded side offers the wampum gifts to the Mourners, telling the stories spoken by the wampum: stories of rekindling the fire "to bind us close''; of grave sorrow for the dead chief; of wiping away any bad blood between the two sides; of sharing the same bowl to eat together; of dispelling the clouds and restoring the sun that shines truth on all peoples.[70] More songs follow this ritualized exchange of wampum to condole the loss of the deceased chief. After the Clear-Minded finish with their side of the ceremony, the Mourners reciprocate by presenting their own gifts of wampum, stories, condolences, and songs to the Clear-Minded.[71]

With completion of these condoling ceremonies, the new Iroquois chief, selected by the clan women of the Mourning village who own the chief's name and title, is installed.[72] This ceremony is followed by a great dance and terminal feast. The society is restored: ''And this will strengthen the house,'' as the Iroquois said.[73]

Throughout the treaty literature, Iroquois diplomats can be witnessed conducting virtually all of their treaty negotiations according to ritual structures adapted from the Condolence Council. The exigencies of forest diplomacy often required certain modifications to the traditional mourning ceremony, but as Fenton has noted, ''[T]he evidence from the treaty documents demonstrates how facile the Iroquois were in accommodating its forms to the particular circumstance.''[74]

Condolence Council rituals were performed by Iroquois diplomats to mourn the deaths of non-Iroquois allies.[75] One of the most elaborately detailed instances was recorded by Cadwallader Colden in 1660, when eight Mohawk chiefs visited Albany to condole a group of English colonists murdered by the French at the frontier settlement of Schenectady. Colden's rendition of the speech accompanying the Indians' presentation of wampum belts contains a wealth of ethnographic detail on the language and vocabulary of Encounter era Iroquois diplomatic customs and traditions:[76]

> Brethren, the Murder of our [English] Brethren at Schenectady by the French grieves us as much, as if it had been done to ourselves. . . . Be not therefore discouraged. We give this Belt *to wipe away your Tears.*
>
> Brethren, we lament the Death of so many of our Brethren, whose Blood has been shed at Schenectady. We don't think that what the French have done can be called a Victory, it is only a farther Proof of their cruel Deceit. . . . We will beset them so closely, that not a Man in Canada shall dare to step out of Doors to cut a Stick of Wood; But now *we gather up our Dead, to bury them,* by this second Belt.
>
> Brethren . . . what has befallen you may happen to us; and therefore *we come to bury our Brethren at Schenectady* with this third Belt.
>
> Great and sudden is the Mischief, as if it had fallen from Heaven upon us. Our Forefathers taught us to go with all Speed to bemoan and lament with our Brethren, when any Disaster or Misfortune happens to any in our Chain. Take this Bill of Vigilance, that you may be more watchful for the future. *We give our Brethren Eye-Water* to make them sharp sighted, giving a fourth Belt.[77]

In addition to the performance of the requickening rites, the chanting of songs of peace derived from the Condolence Council is also a recurrent feature of Iroquois treaty councils. Colonial records indicate that the Condolence Council Eulogy to the Founders of the Confederacy appears to have been sung at the Albany treaty of 1694, at Lancaster in 1744, and at Onondaga in 1756.[78] Other songs from the council appear throughout the treaty literature.[79]

The Deganawidah Epic and the Founding of the League of the Iroquois

The wide diffusion of the council's symbolic patterns and metaphors throughout recorded Iroquois diplomatic history can be explained, at least in part, by the ceremony's reputed origins in the league's sacred founding rituals, as preserved in tribal oral tradition.[80] Much of the tradition of the league's founding is contained in the Deganawidah epic, the "charter myth of the founding of the Great Peace, or the League."[81] As Bronislaw Malinowski has explained, generally such founding epics provide "for cohesion, for local patriotism, for a feeling of union and kinship in the community."[82]

Most versions of the epic agree that Deganawidah was an Iroquois prophet[83] born of a virgin[84] of the Seneca tribe at a time of fierce and debilitating wars, blood feuds, and crises:[85]

> The epic is set in a distant period of incessant warfare among the peoples of the Five Nations. "Everywhere there was peril and everywhere mourning," observes one version. "Feuds with other nations, feuds with brother nations, feuds with sister towns and feuds of families and of clans made every warrior a stealthy man who liked to kill."[86]

Daniel Richter has explained the feuds, peril, and mourning at the heart of the Deganawidah epic as part of "a cultural pattern known as the 'mourning war,' which for the Iroquois, as for many other Native Americans, was a principal means of coping with the death of loved ones."[87] In Woodlands Indian culture, the souls of the dead did not always rest in peace. "Those who had been murdered by men of other nations could find no heaven in the next world until their lust for vengeance had been appeased."[88]

The mourning war thus fulfilled an intensely felt moral and legal obligation shared among most Woodlands tribes to avenge the deaths of murdered relatives.[89] Female kin of a deceased person "would appear at public dances and feasts, weeping inconsolably; if this display did not succeed in arousing the warriors, the women might offer payments or accuse the lagging warrior of cowardice."[90] Men might have disturbing dreams and visions of their murdered kin and request the warriors in the tribe to raid an enemy village for captives.[91] The prisoners captured in these raids would either be executed according to the set rituals of the mourning process or adopted into the grieving family as "an almost literal replacement for the departed."[92]

> Psychologically for the bereaved, socially for the community, and demographically for the population, the captives seized in the mourning wars helped fill the void created by death and replenished the spiritual power of all concerned. But mutual mourning-war raids could all to easily become the endless feuds recalled in the Deganawidah story.[93]

It was through the prophet Deganawidah, according to the epic, that the Great Spirit "in compassion for man, the victim of recurrent wars," first incarnated this message of "Peace and Power," for the Iroquois.[94] Deganawidah's divinely inspired vision of "righteousness, civil authority, and peace" taught the Iroquois to stop hunting, killing, scalping, and cannibalizing one another.[95]

In the epic story, Deganawidah first tells his message of the Great Peace to an Iroquois chief, Hiawatha. Hiawatha had been particularly affected by the death of his daughters. The cycle of death, mourning, and warfare sent him into a rage and he wandered into the forest. There he met Deganawidah, who taught Hiawatha the rituals of condolence accompanying his message of peace. These rituals of peace removed Hiawatha's grief and cleared his mind.[96]

> Offering strings of wampum, Deganawidah spoke several words of condolence: the first dried Hiawatha's weeping eyes, the second opened his ears, the third unstopped his throat, and so on until his sorrow was relieved and his reason restored. These condolence ceremonies were at the core of a new gospel, the Good News of Peace and Power, that would make mourning wars unnecessary. "When men accept it," Deganawidah said of his message, "they will stop killing, and bloodshed will cease from the land."[97]

Hiawatha accepted Deganawidah's message of peace, and the Condolence Ceremonies, which embodied and made effective the Good News of Peace, became, at least in one very strong sense, the reason for the existence of the League of the Iroquois. Together, Deganawidah and Hiawatha carried the "Great Law" to the local chiefs of the Iroquois settlements and urged them to "abandon their feuds, reform their minds, and unite."[98] A "Tree of Peace" was to be planted among the Iroquois, with its "Four White Roots of Peace" extending in cardinal directions and reaching all peoples with the "Good News of Peace and Power."[99]

> I, Deganawidah, and the confederate lords now uproot the tallest pine tree and into the cavity thereby made we cast all weapons of war. . . . We bury them from sight forever and plant again the tree. Thus shall all Great Peace be established and hostilities shall no longer be known between the Five Nations but only peace to a United people.[100]

According to the epic, it was Deganawidah, with Hiawatha as his agent, who thus formed the Iroquois confederacy out of this time of intense chaos and crises and endowed it with its central rites and symbols contained in the Condolence Council ceremonies.

In organizing this Great League of Peace around the Condolence Council, Deganawidah and Hiawatha divided the Grand Council of the Fifty Chiefs of the five Iroquois tribes into two major sides or "moieties": the Elder Brothers—the Mohawks, Onondagas, and Senecas—and Younger Brothers—the Oneidas and Cayugas.[101] These two sides were charged, as Deganawidah had set out, with exchanging the ceremonial gifts and words of condolence upon the death of one of their chiefs. Throughout the Five Nations of the League, according to the epic, the tradition of the Condolence Council supplanted the mourning war as the institution for mourning the dead.

Thus, a vital function of the League Council was, in Daniel Richter's words, "to preserve the Great Peace through ceremonial words of condolence and exchanges of ritual gifts."[102]

> In rites that filled the better part of a day, members of the "clearminded" moiety spoke the words of Condolence to the mourning side and requickened the deceased sachem in the person of a kinsman chosen by the older women of the dead leader's lineage. Thus were kept alive the fifty sachems and metaphorically, the League itself. Condolence rituals, ceremonial gifts, and requickening rites symbolically addressed the same demographic, social and psychological needs served by the mourning war. In these ceremonies could be found the spiritual power that others gained from war. The Good News of Peace and Power, then sought to replace the mourning war with what might be termed the mourning peace.[103]

The Great Peace

For the Iroquois, as for many other eastern North American Indians of the Encounter era, peace was a matter of "good thoughts" between different peoples. It was, for John Phillip Reid, "a feeling as much as a reality."[104] The league and its rituals operated to maintain and renew the connections of peace and goodwill that bound the confederated tribes of the Iroquois together and made them of "one mind."[105]

> In a nutshell that was what the Great Peace was all about, for to Indians of seventeenth and eighteenth-century eastern North America, "peace" was primarily a matter of the mind. Headmen could not force anyone to forgo mourning-war raids, they could only advise, persuade, cajole, and invoke the obligations of kinship.[106]

For the Iroquois, the Great Peace was a divinely understood natural law state of communication, connection, solidarity, and trust between all peoples, linked together in reciprocating relations of trade, friendship, and goodwill. This tradition of the Great Peace in Iroquois legal thought was most perfectly embodied in the symbols and ritualized sequences of the Condolence Council, which served to maintain and renew the good thoughts linking the five tribes of the confederacy to each other. The Deganawidah epic, the Great Peace, and the league's inaugurating rituals contained in the Condolence Council were handed down to subsequent Iroquois generations as part of a fundamental law emerging out of the period of chaos and crises during which the league itself was founded. "The Great Creator from whom we all are descended," Deganawidah proclaimed, "sent me to establish the Great Peace among you. No longer shall you kill one another and nations shall cease warring upon each other. Such things are entirely evil and he, your Maker, forbids it. Peace and comfort are better than war and misery for a nation's welfare."[107]

The Deganawidah epic, "with its wisdom and its poetry, seized the imagination of the Iroquois people, who took to heart the message it conveyed and derived from it a sense of national mission: to make the Tree of Peace *prevail.*"[108] When all nations are brought under the shade of the Tree of Peace, according to Iroquois belief, "[t]he land shall be beautiful, the river shall have no more waves, one may go everywhere without fear."[109]

Thus, the good news of Deganawidah's message envisioned a multicultural community of all peoples on earth, linked together in solidarity under the sheltering branches of the Tree of Great Peace.

> Roots have spread out from the Tree of the Great Peace. . . . If any men of any nation outside of the Five Nations shall show a desire to obey the laws of the Great Peace . . . they may trace the roots to their source . . . and they shall be welcomed to take shelter beneath the Tree of the Long Leaves.[110]

The sacred rituals of the Condolence Council, the Iroquois ceremony for mourning their dead chiefs, thus became part of a diplomatic language that regarded the negotiation of treaties with different peoples as the fulfillment of a divine command to bring all peoples beneath the branches of the Tree of Great Peace. Offering strings of wampum and performing the other rituals of condolence as instructed by the prophet Deganawidah, Iroquois diplomats situated their treaty relations with others in the realm of a transcendent, sacred vision of all humankind as one.

The Good News of Peace

Deganawidah's performance of the Condolence Council, Matohoshila's vision of the rite of making relatives by smoking the pipe, and sacred narratives of events that happened long ago prescribed the political and legal rituals by which once alienated and warring peoples maintained, renewed, and extended the good news of peace to all peoples. These rituals, in turn, constituted a tradition authorized by the divinely inspired knowledge of having been performed before in sacred time.[111] The parties to a treaty, by exchanging wampum according to the ritual sequences of the Condolence Council or by smoking the pipe of peace as instructed by an ancient tribal oral tradition, located their relationship in the realm of tribal sacred narratives. For Indians, these sacred texts constituted a living reality, "believed to have once happened in primeval times, and continuing ever since to influence the world and human destinies."[112]

For American Indian tribes during the Encounter era, peace was a matter of achieving "good thoughts" between different peoples according to a sacred tradition prescribed long ago. The sacred narratives sustaining a treaty relationship operated to maintain and renew the connections of peace and goodwill that had bound the different peoples of the world together since time immemorial. In the language of Indian diplomacy, treaty relations were structured according to sacred texts by which different peoples were enabled to attain one mind, according to a timeless, divine plan for all humankind. From such sacred narratives, we can begin to reconstruct the governing paradigms for behavior according to American Indian treaty visions of law and peace. We turn to several of the most important of these paradigms in the remaining chapters of this book.

3

Treaties as Connections

The Paradigm of Connections

We now have a better understanding of how American Indians of the Encounter era thought about their treaties. In American Indian visions of law and peace, a treaty was a way of satisfying a sacred command to share in the good thoughts of peace with different peoples.

Indians sought out treaty relationships for other reasons, as well. On the North American Encounter era frontier, connection to others was a prerequisite for survival. Indians understood at the most basic level that making connections with others was a life-and-death matter. Given the harsh realities of survival in indigenous North America, those who failed to establish reliable relationships of sharing and reciprocity were confronted with dire prospects. Individuals with no friends or kin alliances in the tribe could find themselves in desperate straits.[1]

The tribal life of most Eastern Woodlands Indians was therefore lived in a complex web of connective, reciprocating relationships. Connection to others improved the chances of overcoming some calamity or disaster that might befall the individual or group. Peaceful relations with other tribes could provide inestimable benefits: trade and subsistence goods that were unavailable or in short supply in the territory, military alliances that extended power and influence, and protection from feared enemies. Making connections with others, whether clan members or "communities at a distance,"[2] was an important paradigm for behavior in American Indian visions of law and peace. For Indians connections were essential to survival.

Indians during the Encounter era were, in every sense of the term, peoples of connections—to each other and also to differing peoples they sought to bring within their alliance through their treaty diplomacy. The language of diplomacy utilized by Indians in negotiating multicultural treaty alliances emerges directly out of this dynamic matrix of relationships characterizing tribal life in indigenous North America.

The Iroquois Kinship System

It is common, as the anthropologist Eric Wolf tells us, to describe indigenous tribal peoples such as those encountered by Europeans in eastern North America during the colonial period as bound together by "kinship." But it is much less common, Wolf notes, to inquire into what precisely kinship *is* for these peoples.[3]

Wolf himself takes an operational view of kinship. He describes it as "a way of committing social labor to the transformation of nature through appeals to filiation and marriage, and to consanguinity and affinity."[4] Kinship, in other words, establishes an individual's rights to the social labor of others in the group. To be related to another in a system of kinship is to expect assistance from that other person and to expect to be asked for and be ready to render assistance as well. Kinship, then, at least according to this view, operates as a form of social insurance within the tribe. Kinship improves the chances that the needs of individual members and the tribe are provided for through articulated patterns of reciprocal obligations and duties.[5]

Whether any tribal group ever consciously intended kinship to work in this precise way, ordering the intricate, sustaining web of social relations in tribal life, is another matter. Clearly, however, Wolf's operational view is reflected in the kinship systems of many North American Indian tribes. Consider, for example, one of the most powerful tribal confederacies in eastern North America during the Encounter era: the Five Nations of the Iroquois. The Iroquois were characterized by a highly elaborate social system of sustaining and reciprocating connections organized around kinship principles.

Each of the Five Nations of the Iroquois—the Mohawks, Seneca, Cayuga, Oneida, and Onondaga—comprised separate villages and longhouse families.[6] Each local Iroquois village settlement had its own chief, whose name was the same as that of his village.[7] Village "families" numbered up to fifty to sixty people and lived in traditional Iroquois longhouses.[8] The Iroquois longhouse was usually organized around a multifamily maternal lineage: an elder woman and her daughters, her unmarried sons, and the husbands and children of her married daughters. These lineages formed the segments of clans, and together these closely connected familial linkages comprised the building blocks of Iroquois culture and society.[9] "Clan members," as explained by the noted Iroquoianist, William Fenton, "behave as if the members of each generation are indeed siblings, or as if they constituted a single maternal family."[10]

As with most North American Indian kinship systems, all of the members of an Iroquois clan traditionally are regarded as being descended from a common ancestor. Eight different clans—Wolf, Bear, Beaver, Turtle, Hawk, Snipe, Deer, and Heron—are distributed throughout the five Iroquois tribes. Men and women of the same clan ought not to marry, and unless "borrowed" or "adopted" by another clan, a child's clan affiliation is determined at birth by his or her mother's clan. If a child's mother, for example, is a Seneca Bear Clan member and father is a Mohawk Wolf Clan member, he or she is a Seneca Bear Clan member regardless of sex.[11]

"Think Independently, Act for Others"

The close connections of kinship sustained by the Iroquois clan system were reinforced by an ethical ideal of autonomous responsibility taught from early childhood in Iroquois culture. Within the clan longhouses, Iroquois children, as Anthony Wallace has described, "were carefully trained to think for themselves but to act for others."[12]

The ethical precept to think independently but act for others was continually given meaning for the individual Iroquois, both inside and outside the longhouse, by the reciprocal connections of kinship between individual clan members. Clan members were expected to maintain good relations with one another through purposive action. The exchange of gifts, sharing in times of crisis or shortage of food supplies, joking, and expressions of goodwill were expected forms of behavior within the Iroquois clan. As members of one large, relatively happy family, clan members were supposed to be in continual communication and contact with each other through frequent feasts, ceremonies, and celebrations.[13]

Clan members, by virtue of their connections under Iroquois law and custom, had a right to call on the generosity of each other. When traveling in a strange Seneca village, for example, an Oneida Iroquois typically would look for lodging or food from other clan members. "What is your clan?" and "What village are your people from?" would most likely be the first questions asked of a visiting Iroquois stranger.[14] "The totem animal of the clan to which the lineage belonged—Deer, Bear, Wolf, Snipe, or whatever it might be—was carved above the door and painted red. In this way directions were easier to give, and the stranger knew where to seek hospitality or aid."[15]

The Iroquois matrilineal clan system served to organize most major aspects of the intricate web of connections and interdependencies characterizing Iroquois tribal life. The women of the Iroquois clans owned and controlled the longhouses where the extended matrilineal families lived, ate, and slept. They also owned and worked the subsistence agricultural fields on the outskirts of the village. These fields, planted with corn, squash, beans, and other staple crops, provided the primary, reliable source of food for the clan longhouse. The clan women determined the distribution of this food supply within the longhouse. They also were responsible for distributing any surplus to other related clan longhouses.[16]

The role of the clans in organizing and sustaining reciprocal relations of kinship, interdependence, and communication in Iroquois culture extended well beyond the related clan longhouses. Each Iroquois village was divided into two moieties, or sides, composed of two or more separate clans, with reciprocating relationships defined according to Iroquois custom and tradition.[17] The moieties are extremely important in the structure of many of the Iroquois ceremonies. It is customary on many ritual occasions for one moiety to "give" the ceremony to another. This theme of reciprocal benefices between two related sides runs through most Iroquois ritual ceremonies. The two moieties literally sit on opposite sides of each other during a longhouse ceremony. They reciprocally condole and bury each other's dead. They play games like lacrosse to ease internal tensions. Many of the ritual acts of Iroquois custom and tradition are conceived and performed based on the notion of one side supporting the other. "Whatever its origin, the moiety principle," as Anthony Wallace notes, "provides a ready tool for the organization of reciprocal behavior on almost any ritual occasion for the Iroquois."[18]

The strong sense of connection and solidarity each Iroquois individual felt toward others in his or her extended network of clan, village, intratribal, and intertribal relationships was reinforced by a set of relational kinship terms derived from the fireside family. These terms—"brother," "grandmother," "grandfather," "nephew," "uncle"—in essence, defined the individual's lines of appeal and responsibility to others arising by virtue of an established relationship of connection.[19] According to Fenton:

> It works this way: as one moves from the lineage to the clan, to the moiety, to the tribe or nation, and thence to the League, the projected use of kinship terms becomes more fictional and the expected behavior more symbolic. The principle that operates throughout this extension is duality or reciprocity. Even one's fictional or symbolic relatives were expected to respond in kind with set speeches of condolence, wampum string or belt or its like, present for present, word for word.[20]

This intricate system of clans, lineages, and moieties aligned together in a web of interdependent relationships provided the Iroquois with a ready-made communicative and connective structure. Kinship maintained the social, political, and military cohesion of the Iroquois multitribal confederacy. Complex relations of reciprocity and solidarity were sustained and developed through the mutual exchange and sharing of gifts, ritual ceremonies, and goodwill among members of the clan, the different clans comprising the moieties, the individual moieties combining into a tribe, and the five different tribes of the Iroquois allying as the Great League of Peace. The Iroquois prescription to think independently, act for others, therefore, entailed the assumption of close kinship connections and purposive action directed toward the benefit of a large host of others—those in the fireside family, your mother's brother (who might be clan chief), your father's kinsmen, your sister's children, the elders of the clan, the kinfolk, and clan members beyond the village or from other Iroquois tribes.[21] For the Iroquois, as with many American Indian peoples, kinship provided the basic principles for a tribal way of life constituted around connections with others.

"The Family Writ Large": Cherokee Clanship

North American Indians, as the anthropologist Harold Driver once noted, exhibit an amazing variety of marital relationships and family structures. Almost all of the principal variations of marriage, family, and kinship patterns known in the entire world are found in North America alone.[22] Yet despite their wide range of variation, most North American Indian tribes share a number of important similarities with the Iroquois in terms of basic kinship functioning. For many North American Indians, the connections of kinship are a vitally important part of what, in fact, constitutes the tribe.

For example, the Cherokees, another of the powerful Woodlands tribal groupings of the Encounter era, relied on their clan system to provide what has been called the "constitutional fabric" for their nation.[23] The Cherokees divided themselves into some fifty different towns spread out in the mountains and river valleys of the southern Appalachian range (in the area today forming the borderlands of North and South Carolina, Georgia, Tennessee, and southwestern Virginia). They spoke three sectional dialects. Sustaining intratribal communication and relations across village and regional boundaries could be quite difficult at times for the Cherokees. Yet as John Philip Reid writes, "[T]he legal and social structure of clanship, while providing less than perfect governmental unity, conjoined the Cherokees into one nation and one people."[24] To the Cherokees, the clan was the "family writ large."[25]

Seven Cherokee clans were organized along matrilineal lines, somewhat similar to the Iroquois. A Cherokee son, for example, belonged to his mother's clan. Upon divorce, children followed the mother, not the father, and if the mother died, her eldest brother claimed her offspring.

But even while the mother was alive, her brother rightfully instructed and disciplined her children, not the biological father.[26]

For the Cherokees, clanship provided order and security in tribal social life. The preeminent Cherokee legal historian, Rennard Strickland, explains that the clan was "the major institution exercising legal powers."[27] The Cherokee clan system divided Cherokee society into easily identifiable groups of connections; an individual would have "brothers," "uncles," "younger brothers," "grandmothers," "father's sisters," "sisters," and so on. These terms had significant meanings to the Cherokee individual. As a white missionary familiar with the tribe once remarked, "A Cherokee can tell you without hesitation what degree of relationship exists between himself and any other individual of the same clan you may see proper to point out."[28]

Clanship terms were important to the Cherokees because they impressed a binding scheme of reciprocal rights and duties upon each relationship a Cherokee might have within the tribe. These terms had, in other words, the force of law among the Cherokee as a people. Suppose a Cherokee on the hunt away from his town stopped to visit another Cherokee town. He knew there were clan relations to welcome him, to defend his rights, and to perform the duties owed a member of the clan. It was this knowledge that sustained feelings of connection and solidarity beyond the borders of each individual Cherokee town. It was this knowledge about the rights and duties of clanship that provided the Cherokees with their "legal cohesiveness" as a people. In Cherokee tribal life, the clan functioned as a consolidating cultural and legal force that united each individual to the tribal nation as a whole.[29]

A Law of Blood

An example of the legal cohesiveness achieved by the clanship system in Cherokee society is found in the Cherokee law of blood feud. The law was simple. The commission and punishment of a homicide were clan responsibilities. "The ghost of the murdered clansman could not pass from the earth until the blood had been revenged."[30] Thus, if a member of the Bird clan was killed by a member of the Paint clan, a surviving member of the Bird clan could avenge the murder and release the ghost of his kin by killing any member of the Paint clan. The slaying of a Paint, any Paint, satisfied the clan's group responsibility for the crime, and under Cherokee law, the matter ended there. Henceforward, all other Paint clan members had to be "indifferent" to the Bird clan's exercise of its right of retaliation. In fact, members of the Paint clan could protect the innocent in their own clan by killing the guilty clan member themselves. That act, under Cherokee law, ended the potential for any cycle of retaliatory killings; the duty of revenge was satisfied by the death of the murderer. One retaliation ended the matter as far as Cherokee law was concerned.[31]

Though grounded in a code of blood revenge, the Cherokee law of homicide functioned as a law of peace. It did so by working to end the cycle of revenge killings that could lead a group into destabilizing chaos and endless war.[32] On the multicultural frontiers of the North American Encounter era, the Cherokee vision of law and peace relied on the connections sustained by clanship as the most reliable method for different peoples to ensure their mutual survival in a world of human diversity and conflict.

Peoples of Connections: The Delaware, Shawnees, and Fox

Intricate patterns of family, clan, kinship, and social organization are characteristic of most of the Encounter era Woodlands tribes studied by anthropologists.[33] The Delawares, for example, an Eastern Algonquian language–speaking group that occupied the Delaware River valley during the early Encounter period, were organized as a tribe into three groupings: Turkey, Wolf, and Turtle. Each of these "phratry" groupings (to use the anthropological term) was made up of twelve named matrilineal lineages. The lineages regulated marriage, fulfilled obligations connected with the ceremonial "family feasts," controlled the inheritance of ritual property, and determined many other important aspects of Delaware tribal life.

A Delaware belonged to his or her mother's phratry, but he or she also had a formulated relationship of connection with the father's phratry. A Delaware with a Turkey mother and a Wolf father, for example, would be called "Turkey and Wolf-child," thus defining his or her various kinship duties within the tribe. Though a member of the Turkey phratry, he or she could be expected to offer ritual assistance to Wolf members at various tribal ceremonies.

Numerous other intricately elaborated connective systems were built upon principles of kinship in indigenous North America. The Shawnees, a central Algonquian language–speaking group, were settled in the Ohio and upper Mississippi River valleys at the time of European contact. They divided themselves into five descent groups, or divisions, whose members patrilineally inherited their affiliation. Each division was conceived as a distinct territorial, political, and ritual unit centering in a town that bore its name. Each of the five divisions had specific responsibilities to the tribe as a whole. The *čalaka* and *Øawikila* divisions, for example, were in charge of political affairs. The tribal chief of the Shawnees traditionally would be from one of these two divisions. Responsibilities for tribal rituals were assigned to the *pekowi* division, war to the *kišpoko,* and medicine to the *mekoče.*

Within each division, the Shawnees further divided themselves into clans. The clans controlled the division's important ceremonies. They also served important integrative functions in the tribal culture. At death, for example, the body of the deceased was dressed, painted, and carried to the grave by attendants belonging to other clans. These attendants were compensated for their services from the deceased's possessions.

Another central Algonquian tribal group, the Fox (who settled in present-day Wisconsin during the time of initial European encounter), developed a complex social organization around at least eight clan groupings. Each clan functioned conceptually as a kind of kin group, controlling a stock of names and a sacred pack that organized clan ceremonies. In theory, each clan was descended from an individual who, seeking a vision, had been blessed by a spirit. A clan took its name from this spirit (e.g., Bear, Fox, or Wolf). The spirit instructed the recipient of the vision in assembling the sacred pack, the significance of the names attached to it, and the appropriate ceremonies. Through the names and the pack, the powers of the ancestral vision extended to all members of the clan.

The Fox developed other methods of extending and consolidating connections within the group. Within each clan were lineages with names based on varieties of the clan spirit eponym. The Bear clan, for example, included Brown Bear and Black Bear lineages. Hereditary ritual positions and political offices were controlled by these lineages.

Two other divisions, symbolized by the colors white and black, existed within the Fox tribe as well. These functioned like moieties, but they were not descent groups. Siblings were simply assigned to either division according to their birth order. A couple's first child, for example, belonged to the division opposite the father's; the next child belonged to the father's division, and so on. This method of assigning membership produced groupings that were approximately equal and cut across all other social groupings in the tribe. Members of each division were expected to joke with their opposites. Games, ceremonies, dances, warfare, and social functions were all organized around these divisions. As noted by Charles Callender, an eminent authority on the Fox, "By structuring group competition within the tribe along lines that divided bands, clans, lineages, and families, the divisions probably inhibited tendencies toward cleavage."[34]

The Good News of Peace

In indigenous North American tribal life, kinship principles established relationships of connection that commenced at birth, were maintained throughout life, and were commemorated at death. Kinship organized tribal ceremonies, the central events of tribal life, and the reciprocal patterns of gifting and exchange that made relationships within the tribe strong and reliable.

The complex web of relationships of connection established by kinship provided the foundations for a tribal social life constituted by a world of connections and shared normative commitments to others.[35] These commitments were articulated through the mutually understood rights and duties recognized as subsisting between the members of the tribe by virtue of a panoply of integrating sets of kinship connections. The continual renewal of these relationships through shared rituals, sacred ceremonies, and the exchange of gifts defined a rich social life for the tribal individual in indigenous North America. It was a life that was shared with others in the fireside family, the clan, the village, and the tribe. It was a life that depended for survival on the quality and quantity of its connections to others in a multicultural world.

The prescription to think independently, act for others, was therefore not just a peculiarly held sentiment of the Iroquois, Cherokees, Delawares, Shawnees, or Fox. The tribal individual's responsibility for establishing and maintaining connections through reciprocity and shared commitments with others was a widely established ethical precept among the indigenous peoples of Encounter era eastern North America. Only through sharing and reciprocity could the individual tribal member ensure his or her survival for any significant length of time in the vast, hostile, and unyielding wilderness that was North America during the Encounter. This, in fact, *was* the good news of peace that the language of North American Encounter era diplomacy sought to communicate to others.

Extending Connections to "Communities at a Distance"

So far, the processes of making connections with others in tribal life have been presented as a more or less local affair. Discussion of the connective processes of indigenous North America has not yet extended beyond the geocultural boundaries of the tribe. A tribe is generally understood as a coherent, culturally distinct group constituted by its own language, common territory, and consciously conceived kinship ties of long-established consanguinity.[36] Establishing connections to "communities at a distance" beyond the tribe and its intricate system of clan and kinship relationships is, anthropologists tell us, a much different type of social process from what we have been discussing so far.[37] On a multicultural frontier, parties usually have no expectations that the "putatively altruistic" exchange transactions that occur within tribal kinship relations will be replicated with strangers.[38] Relations with strangers generally are based on the expectation of violent war or direct material return. When two groups of human beings meet on the frontier boundaries of their tribal societies, they have very few choices confronting them. In Marcel Mauss's words, "[T]hey may move away or in case of mistrust or defiance they may resort to arms; or else they can come to terms."[39]

Diplomacy, of course, is the art of coming to "terms" of accommodation with communities at a distance. For Indians of the Encounter era, those terms, naturally enough, were derived from the complex language of connection by which close relations of reciprocity and interdependence were established and maintained in tribal life. In tribal society, this language, with its kinship terms, ritual ceremonies, and reciprocal patterns of gifting and exchange, connected members of the tribe together as relatives. This language of connection proved most useful for tribal diplomats of the Encounter era assigned the immensely difficult task of communicating the good news of peace to communities at a distance. In fact, the practice of Encounter era Indian diplomacy can best be understood as inscribing the language of connection used within the tribe onto the relations between different peoples on a multicultural frontier.

Kinship Terms of Connection

It is not difficult to understand why Indians of the Encounter era relied on the language of connection used within the tribe as a principal method for negotiating treaties with communities at a distance. From an Indian perspective, this language provided a precise method for fixing understandings of rights and duties in a relationship of connection. Consider, for example, kinship terms. When we find Europeans referred to as brothers, colonial governors as fathers, or other tribes as cousins, uncles, or nephews in the treaty literature, we should recognize that, for Indians, each of these kinship terms had precisely understood meanings.

Kinship terms, for example, defined the politically correct seating arrangements at the 1795 Treaty of Greenville between the United States and the western tribes. "You all know the Wyandots are our uncles, and the Delawares our grandfathers," the famous Shawnee chief Blue Jacket declared in explaining the reason for changing his seat at the council; "it is therefore proper that I should sit next to my grandfathers and uncles."[40]

Kinship terms were used in treaty making for a variety of purposes. Besides determining many of the minor protocols of council diplomacy, kinship terms were used to define the expected forms of behavior among treaty partners. In this sense, these terms could assume legal significance. Sir Edmond Andros, who resumed the governorship of the colony of New York in 1688, discovered this fact in his reunion meeting with the Mohawks of the Iroquois confederacy. The Indians rejoiced at the return of their "Brother" Andros. The governor returned the Mohawks' greeting by calling them his "children."[41]

The distinction between "brothers" and "children" carried significant import in the Iroquois language of diplomacy.[42] "Brothers" was the term used between formal equals in a relationship of connection. Such relations had duties to each other, but brothers did not presume a right to command one another, as one does a child.[43] Thus, the Indians would not simply let the term "children" slip by in the conversation. They responded definitively by handing the governor a belt of wampum to underscore their position that according to the Mohawks' long-established treaty relationship with the colony, they had always been called "Brethren." That fact, in and of itself, had legal significance to the Mohawks. Like the rest of the terms of their treaty with New York, the term "brother," they explained, had been "well kept." Therefore, they admonished the governor, "[L]et that of Brethren continue without any alteration."[44]

"Younger" and "Elder" Brothers

As a system for fixing rights and duties between treaty partners, the terms of kinship provided a convenient and well-known foundational discourse for structuring relationships with communities at a distance. As an added benefit, Indian diplomats could also draw on a variety of interpretive conventions generated by this discourse for added precision in defining the rights and duties of treaty partners. These conventions permitted the relations between the parties to be more accurately calibrated according to the realities of power on a multicultural frontier.

Take, for example, the unadorned title "brother." The role usually defined by this kinship-derived term for equals in a treaty relationship could be slightly adjusted by designating one party "elder brother" and the other party "younger brother."[45] In the language of connection that organized kinship relations in tribal life, an elder brother could be regarded as having special obligations toward a younger brother. So, too, in the language of Indian diplomacy, an elder brother treaty partner could have special obligations toward a less powerful, but still formally equal, younger brother treaty partner.

The Cherokees, in particular, liked to utilize this convention in their treaty discourse with Europeans. And no wonder, since an elder brother had the duty of primary protection of his younger siblings in Cherokee tribal life.[46] Elder brothers therefore had important responsibilities in a treaty relationship. The Cherokee chief, Utossite, lectured Maryland's colonial officials in 1758 at the height of the French and Indian War:

> You are our elder brothers. We hope you will give us such things as the French give their Indians; some silverware to put on our arms, some wampum and some kettles, we do not desire such clothes as white people wear but clothes we do want for we are naked. We do not beg, it is a shame to do so, but we ask of you as younger brothers, we desire you will treat us as such.[47]

For Indians of the Encounter era, the terms derived from tribal kinship systems were indispensable to the conduct of human affairs and, therefore, to the language of Indian diplomacy. Vital connections of trade and military alliance were simply unthinkable unless the groups or individuals were related according to the terms derived from tribal kinship systems.[48]

In American Indian visions of law and peace, kinship terms provided a foundational discourse for the intricate, sustaining web of relationships within tribal life. No wonder, then, that they were seen as so useful in building the vital treaty connections with communities at a distance that were regarded as essential to survival on a multicultural frontier.

"According to the Excellence of the Name"

For Indians of the Encounter era, the terms of fictive kinship—"brother," "uncle," "nephew," "cousin"—defined and fixed the expected forms of behavior among treaty partners. Brothers in a treaty relationship could not order each other around. Uncles had responsibilities toward their nephews. The language of Indian diplomacy could build even further upon this foundational discourse in defining the rights and duties of connection in treaty relationships. Specific names and titles could be assigned to the colonial officials responsible for the execution of a treaty. This common practice, found repeatedly throughout the treaty literature, reflected more than simply the desire to bestow an honorific title upon a particularly important personage; the giving of a name sought to situate the European official within a carefully defined network of connections created by the treaty.

In the treaty literature, the giving of name-titles to European colonial governors and other high-ranking officers could be attended with great ceremony. Witham Marshe's journal of the 1744 Lancaster treaty records the following Iroquois naming ceremony for the governor of Maryland conducted by the Cayuga chief, Gachradodon:

> As the Governor of Maryland has invited us here, to treat about our lands, and brighten the chain of friendship, the united Six Nations think themselves so much obliged to him, that we have come to a resolution, in council, to give the great man, who is proprietor of Maryland, a particular name, by which we may hereafter correspond with him: And as it hath fallen to the Cayugas' lot in council to consider of a proper name for that chiefman, we have agreed to give him the name of Tocary-ho-gon, denoting Precedency, Excellency, or living in the middle, or honorable place, betwixt Asserigoa [the governor of Virginia], and our brother Onas [the governor of Pennsylvania], by whom our treaties may be the better carried on.
>
> As there is a company of great men now assembled, we take this opportunity to publish this matter, that it may be known Tocary-ho-gon is our friend, and that we are ready to honor him, and that by such name he may be always called and known among us; and, we hope, he will ever act towards us, according to the excellence of the name we have now given him, and enjoy a long and happy life.[49]

The familiar-sounding obsequiousness of the diplomat's speech aside, this formal giving of a name could be a highly effective way of impressing upon a colonial official a unique sense of the responsibilities he had taken on by making treaties with Indians. In fact, colonial officials who were particularly successful at upholding treaty relationships, in the Indians' opinion at least, could pass their name-titles on to successors. The Iroquois and the Algonquians, mortal enemies at various periods of the Encounter era, both applied the name *Onontio* to the individual who served as French governor at Quebec. *Onontio* was the Iroquois word for "great mountain" and represented their rendering of the name of Charles de Huault de Montmagny, the first governor and lieutenant general of New France from 1636 to 1648. The name-title *Onontio* was applied to all subsequent French governors because, in the language of Indian diplomacy, *Onontio* was the Frenchman who was responsible for maintaining the French colony's treaty obligations toward the Indians. He was chief ally, protector, supplier of goods, and mediator of their disputes, as his title implied.[50]

Similarly, the governors of Pennsylvania were given the title *Onas* (meaning "pen") by the Iroquois, a narrative tradition that recalled the Great Treaty of 1682 negotiated between the tribe and the colony's original proprietor and governor, William Penn.[51] *Corlaer* was the name given by the Iroquois to the governors of New York, Arent van Curler being the colonial official who had negotiated the first treaty of mutual assistance between the Mohawks and "all the Dutch" (who preceded the English in New York) in 1643.[52]

Thus, according to American Indian treaty visions of law and peace between different peoples, the death or replacement of a leader of one of the treaty partners did not terminate or alter the treaty relationship. These events were taken as opportunities to renew the treaty by passing on the ceremonial title to the newly installed official responsible for upholding the treaty.

Like the fictive kinship terms "brother," "father," or "nephew," which could be assigned to treaty partners, the name-titles given and handed down to colonial officials were part of a language derived from tribal life to make connections with others. They reflected a basic, organizing paradigm of behavior for Indians—a paradigm restated in a number of different and ingenious ways by Encounter era Indian diplomats. In American Indian visions of law and peace, a relationship of connection established rights and duties in individuals and groups. The terms of connection given to those in the relationship defined these rights and duties. In the language of Indian diplomacy, these terms took on legal significance, defining obligations "according to the excellence of the name" given a treaty partner.[53]

The "Usual Ceremonies"

The language of Indian diplomacy possessed a variety of tools that could be used to broaden and strengthen the foundations for treaty relationships. Besides the terms of connection derived from tribal kinship systems and assigned name-titles, Indians of the Encounter era also relied extensively on tribal rituals to establish and maintain diplomatic connections with others. According to American Indian visions of law and peace, rituals were indispensable to the vital human process of linking groups together in wider social formations and committing potential social partners to common goals and objectives.[54]

Indian diplomats freely borrowed from the rich language of connection organized around the various rituals of tribal life as a vital part of the process of negotiating treaties. Pipe rituals, for example, are performed routinely throughout the treaty literature by Indian diplomats. In tribal life, smoking the pipe of peace connects individuals to each other through a knowledge of the truth revealed by this sacred rite.[55] In the connective processes of Indian diplomacy, the sacred pipe performs this same essential function. It removes the obstacles to communication that prevent different peoples from seeing the truth revealed by the good news of peace and uniting as one.

At an eighteenth-century treaty council,[56] the Cherokee diplomat Ouconastota indicated the reasons why Indians performed "the usual ceremonies" of smoking the calumet of peace at a treaty conference as follows: "We have done smoking, we will proceed on our talk, our thoughts are straight and this is a clear time of day."[57] At another meeting, this time with Virginia's governor and council, the Cherokee chief, Skiagusta, explained the use of the pipe in Cherokee diplomacy similarly. "After all in the room smoked," the treaty minutes report, "the Cherokee chief then smoked himself. He then laid down the pipe on a table in front of him, and declared that he had come to talk on behalf of his nation, and that he would speak with a straight Heart nothing but Truth." Skiagusta told the governor and council the "truth" that had been revealed to him by smoking the pipe: "the power above" had ordered that the English and the Cherokee should be friends. "All quarrels are now ceased so as never to revive," he said; "the hatchet buried, never to be raised again." It had been dark "a great while," the chief said, "but was now light." He hoped now that "all obstacles are removed."[58]

Other tribes shared in this practice of smoking the sacred pipe of peace to clear the channels of communication between the two sides of a treaty. A Shawnee speaker sounded much like the Cherokee diplomats when he announced at a late eighteenth-century treaty conference with the United States:

> We have heard your words. . . . [W]e thank God that you have been preserved in peace, and that we bring our pipes together. The people of all the different nations here salute you. They rejoice to hear your words. . . . We shall, for the present, take our pipes, and retire to our encampments, where we shall deliberately consider your speech and return you an answer.[59]

In American Indian visions of law and peace, the "usual ceremonies" of smoking the sacred pipe enabled treaty partners to speak truthfully and to listen to each other closely, just as relatives would. Indian diplomats adapted other important rituals from tribal life to perform this vitally regarded function of clearing the channels of communication between the two sides negotiating a treaty. Requickening rites, derived from tribal mourning ceremonies, for example, were frequently performed by Indian diplomats to facilitate open and undistorted dialogue at a treaty council. The Chippewa chief Mash-i-pi-nash-i-wish performed a requickening ritual to open the channel of communication at the 1795 Treaty of Greenville with U.S. General Anthony Wayne.

> You see all your brothers assembled here in consequence of your message last winter. . . . You remember, brother, I then told you, that I would withdraw the dark cloud from your eyes, that you might know us again. You see I have done so, for you now behold us all clearly. At the same time, I told you I would open both your ears, and my own, that we might hear each other clearly. Our ears are opened accordingly, and we hear and understand accurately. I now speak to you with a pure heart. This white wampum testifies our sincerity and unanimity in sentiment. I now put your heart in its right place.[60]

Rituals, precisely because of their communicative power, were used for all types of purposes connected with the task of achieving mutual understandings between treaty partners. Tribal gifting rituals, for example, were freely incorporated into the various communicative processes of Indian treaty making.[61] An important message not accompanied by a gift, in the language of Indian diplomacy, was not even worth listening to. A Dutch merchant made the mistake of traveling to an Iroquois village in 1633 without any gifts. The chief of the village was incensed. "He told us that we were not worth anything," the Dutchman's narrative relates, "because we did not bring him a present."[62]

Wampum gifts were particularly valued as a medium of diplomacy during the Encounter era. An Iroquois speaker once told New York's colonial officials: "[Y]ou may know our words are of no weight unless accompanied with wampum."[63]

Fenton has explained some of the many communicative uses of wampum found in the treaty literature: "Strings and belts of wampum served to affirm messages, to stress the import and truth of what was being said and to convey the nature of the message."[64] In the language of Indian diplomacy, to accept a wampum gift indicated that the message conveyed by the "words" of the wampum had been understood and accepted. The receiving party usually would be expected to reciprocate with wampum as well, present for present, word for word, thus sustaining the connection created by the gift.[65]

In Indian diplomacy, the ritualized presentation of wampum gifts could open the path of peace and convince a treaty partner of the sincerity of purpose behind a proposed treaty relationship. We witness the use of wampum gifting rituals in Indian diplomacy in an early seventeenth-century description of an Iroquois diplomat's return home from Canada, where a treaty had been tentatively negotiated with a group of French-allied Indians.

> In the evening, the savages suspended a band of seawan [wampum] that the chief had brought with him from the French savages as a sign of peace and that the French savages were to come in confidence to them, and he sang: "*Ho scheme jo ho schem I atsiehoewe atsihoewe,*" after which all the savages shouted three times: "*Netho, netho, netho!*" and after that another band of seawan was suspended and he sang then: "*Katon, katon, katon, katon!*" and all the savages shouted as loud as they could: *Hy, hy, hy!*" After long deliberation, they made peace for four years, and soon after everyone returned to his home.[66]

Emblematic designs were commonly woven into wampum belts to send a particular message of friendship to a treaty partner. The Historical Society of Pennsylvania holds in its collection one of the great wampum belts that survived the Encounter era, the famous Penn Treaty Belt. The belt depicts two figures holding hands. The Delaware Indians are said to have given William Penn this wampum gift to record their famous treaty negotiated soon after Penn's arrival in the New World in 1682. According to the historian Donald Kent, it was at this council that the Great Quaker was given his Delaware name, *Miquon,* meaning "feather," "quill," or "pen," which was later rendered as *Onas,* its Iroquois equivalent.[67]

Even the simple knots tied on a wampum string could deliver an important message expressing the desire to sustain or renew connections with a treaty partner. A Cherokee speaker at a 1763 council with South Carolina presented the English with a wampum string with three knots, according to the usual ritual gifting forms. The speaker explained that the middle knot on the string represented Fort Prince-George, South Carolina's frontier trading post, which served as the crucial nexus between the speaker's town of Chota and Charlestown, where the English lived. Chota was represented by a knot at one end of the string, and Charlestown by the other end knot on the string.[68]

Other ritual gifts besides wampum were used to transmit important messages between treaty partners. At a 1721 council with the governor of Virginia and other colonial officials, "one of the Great Men" of the

Penn's Treaty with the Indians, by Benjamin West, 1771. (Courtesy of the Pennsylvania Academy of Fine Arts)

Chickasaw Indians made a proposal to the Virginia colony to supply his people with guns in their war with the French. His request was accompanied by the ritual presentation of deer skins and the sacred calumet of peace as gifts for his English treaty partners.

> The said Indians were brought into the Council Chamber, where they entered singing, according to their Custom; And the Great Man of the Chickasaws carrying in his hand a Calumet [pipe] of Peace, first presented a parcel of Deer Skins, which he spread upon the Shoulders of the Governor and divers of the Council; And then made a speech to the Governor, importing in substance, that his Nation being at war with the French and wanting Arms and Ammunition, with which the English of South Carolina were unable to supply them by reason of their having but few Horses for Carriage; he was sent hither to desire a Trade with this Colony; after which he

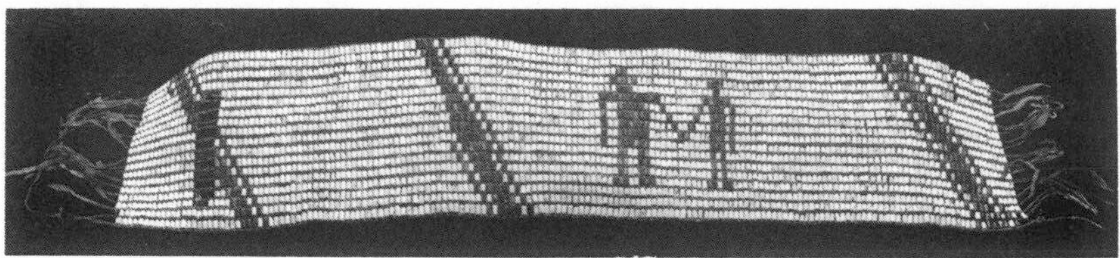

Penn Treaty Belt. (Courtesy of The Historical Society of Pennsylvania)

> presented to the Governor his Calumet of Peace as a token that the Chickasaws desired to live at Peace and friendship with the English of this Colony.[69]

Wampum belts and strings, calumet pipes, furs, and other valued gifts were routinely exchanged at the treaty conferences of the Encounter era. In the language of Indian diplomacy, the giving and receiving of such gifts involved far more than simply a disguised exchange of material goods. According to American Indian treaty visions of law and peace, reciprocal gift giving established solidarity with others by opening the channels of communication and connection that made relationships strong and reliable. Gifts literally carried the message of the good news of peace.[70]

In Encounter era Woodlands Indian diplomacy, ritualized gift exchanges thus became peace treaties[71] or at least a part of the language used to communicate the message that a relationship of law and peace was desired with a potential treaty partner. Like the rituals of smoking the pipe and the mourning ceremonies performed so frequently according to the language of connection used by Woodlands tribes in their daily lives, ritualized gift giving created expectations of cooperation, solidarity, and reciprocity with others. In American Indian visions of law and peace, these rituals established and maintained connection and communication between parties who dealt with each other as relatives under a treaty.

Creek Treaty Rituals

In Indian diplomacy, the language of connection organized around the rituals of tribal life was used as a primary medium for signaling peaceful intentions and the desire to establish and maintain relations with communities at a distance. We should not lose sight, however, of the deeper meanings of these connective rituals for Indians of the Encounter era. For most tribes, such rituals were expressive of a larger vision that might not be fully apparent to a European treaty partner.

Consider, for example, the distinctive set of ritual ceremonies routinely performed by Lower Creek diplomats with the colonial officials of Georgia throughout the Encounter era. Usually a procession would initiate a typical treaty council by the Lower Creeks. A member or members of the Creek embassy would carry eagle wands (long tubes with white eagle feathers attached) and sing and dance to a "warrior's song." Upon finishing the procession, the Creek delegates would stand before the Georgia officials they had come to visit and present the white feathers as gifts. This ritual presentation generally involved stroking the arms of a treaty partner with the white feathers in a fanlike motion. Then the usual ceremonies of smoking the pipe would be performed.[72]

These rituals are performed throughout the treaty literature involving the Lower Creeks. Eagle feathers, for instance, were presented to the King of England in 1734 by Tomochici, leader of the Lower Creek town that had permitted James Oglethorpe and his Georgia colony to settle on tribal lands. Oglethorpe sent the chief to England to "excite curiosity, inspire confidence in the Georgia leadership, and attract new financial support and settlers to the colony."[73]

The chief's trip to England was a smashing success. The nine-member delegation was one of the largest groups of Indians to ever visit England, and the meeting with the king was widely reported and noted. We are fortunate to possess several carefully detailed, complementary accounts of the meeting.[74] The Earl of Egmont, one of the Georgia colony's principal London backers, noted the meeting in his journal: "[T]he King gave audience to the Indians in great form."[75] Charlotte Clayton, Viscountess Sunden, Queen's Mistress of the Robes, received a letter from Dr. Alured Clarke describing the meeting.[76] Even the *Gentlemen's Magazine* reported the event to a curious London public.[77]

From the various accounts, we know that Tomochici and his party were well received in Kensington Palace by King George: "[T]hey made their obeisance, and performed all the ceremony with great decency and exactness."[78] Tomochici made the following speech upon presenting his gift of eagle feathers to the king:

> These are the Feathers of the Eagle, which is the swiftest of Birds, and who flieth all round our Nations. These Feathers are a Sign of Peace in our Land, and have been carried from Town to Town there; and we have brought them over to leave with you, O Great King, as a sign of everlasting peace.[79]

Upon finishing this speech, he laid the "emblems of peace . . . very submissively upon the skins" of the English. This "token of his entering into firm alliance" was followed "with a few sentences more," and the audience was concluded.[80] Tomochici was reported "well satisfied" with the speech he had made but regretted the fact that he and his delegation had not been permitted the time to perform a complete treaty ceremony for the king. According to Lord Egmont's report of the royal audience, Tomochici "wished his People had been allowed to dance their War dance, which was the highest compliment they could make."[81]

The larger vision animating the performance of these treaty rituals can be located in the diplomatic history of the Lower Creeks. Inhabiting what is now Alabama, the "polyglot" Creeks were divided into some thirty autonomous towns. The ten or so Lower Creek towns, located along a fifty-mile stretch of the Chattahoochee River, figure most prominently in the early Encounter era treaty literature of the Georgia colony. Among the most influential of these Lower Creek towns were the "war town" of Cussita and the "peace town" of Pallachicola[82] (Tomochici's original village).

At a 1735 council in Savannah, a delegation of Lower Creeks told the story of how these two towns joined together in a league of peace. According to the story, the "Cussitaws"

> came into the white Path again, and they saw a smoke where there was a town, and now again believed they had found the people they had so long travelled to see. It is the place the present Pallachucolla people dwell in. . . .
>
> The Cussitaws were always bloody minded, but the Pallachucolla people made them black drink as a token of Friendship, and told them their hearts were white, and they must have white hearts, and lay down their bloody Tomihawks, and give their bodies in token that they should be white. Thus they strove for the Tomihawk, but the Pallachucolla people by fair persuasions gained it from them and carried it under their cabin. The Pallachucolla people told them their captain [village chief] should all be one with their people, and gave them white Feathers. That ever since they have lived together and shall always live together, and bear it in remembrance.[83]

In the language of forest diplomacy spoken by Tomochici, the ritualized presentation of white feathers represented "a sign of everlasting peace" between different peoples on a multicultural frontier. But we should not lose sight of the deeper meanings this ritual gift of eagle feathers held for the Lower Creeks. According to their American Indian treaty vision of law and peace, the giving of white eagle feathers recalled a founding act of connection by which two differing groups had sought to assure their survival in a world of human diversity and conflict. The Lower Creeks incorporated this founding act of their own connective alliance into the ritual language of their diplomacy, so that communities at a distance might come to know that by a gift of white feathers, they "should all be one" on the multicultural frontiers of Encounter era North America.[84]

The Sinews of Diplomacy

Europeans, with their attitudes of cultural superiority, regarded the drawn-out naming ceremonies, rituals, and gift giving that Indians routinely performed at treaty councils as time-consuming diversions from the conduct of vital matters of trade, diplomacy, and survival on the colonial frontier. The European scribes who produced the voluminous treaty literature of the Encounter era rarely commented on the visions that animated their Indian treaty partners in giving a tribal name to a colonial official, smoking the calumet of peace, or presenting a gift of eagle feathers. For Europeans, these were the "usual ceremonies" that had to be tolerated if one wanted to do business with the strange and alien-seeming tribal peoples of North America. But for Indians, the relationships established by both sides according to this language of connection constituted what has been called the "sinews" of their diplomacy.[85] In American Indian visions of law and peace, the connections sustained by kinship terms, name-titles, and rituals were what held treaty relationships together. They made survival more assured on a multicultural frontier.

For Woodlands Indian groups of the Encounter, the very meaning of a treaty relationship was contained in the language of a tribal life spoken through kinship terms, name-titles, and the performance of sacred ceremonies and gifting rituals. In American Indian treaty visions of law and peace, this language of connection provided a foundational discourse for sustaining the good news of peace that was realized between treaty partners. In a world of human diversity and conflict, connection to others was a prerequisite for survival.

4

Treaties as Stories

A Special Kind of Story

For Indians, the language of connection that sustained tribal life provided a foundational discourse for treaty relationships with communities at a distance. But the diversity of peoples on the multicultural frontiers of Encounter era North America frequently required Indian diplomats to supplement this language. Particularly when negotiating with strange and alien-seeming European peoples, Indians had to narrate more precisely what they meant by their vision of treaty partners behaving as relatives toward each other.

The records of treaty councils and negotiations relate the remarkable creativity of Encounter era Indian diplomats who would gesture, dance, sing songs, use metaphors, and weave extended stories to explain their visions of a treaty relationship. The variety of narrative devices used by Indian diplomats in the treaty literature, in fact, suggests that only the best storytellers in a tribe were sent to negotiate multicultural alliances during the Encounter era.

Stories are told throughout the treaty literature of the seventeenth and eighteenth centuries. There are long stories, short stories, stories told through songs and dances, stories of sorrow and shared sufferings, stories of burying the hatchet and of rejoicing, stories about connections made, broken, and renewed, and stories that envision all humankind as one people united under a Great Tree of Peace. Stories play a central role in the language of Indian diplomacy. In American Indian treaty visions of law and peace, a treaty itself was a special kind of story: a way of imagining a world of human solidarity where we regard others as our relatives.

The Importance of Stories

Many of the most important works by contemporary critical race and feminist legal scholars advocate the usefulness of stories in helping us to make connections with strange others in a world of human diversity and conflict. Storytelling, in fact, has become an important part of the methodology used by these scholars to analyze the legal relations between different groups in our multicultural society.[1] In a *Michigan Law Review* symposium issue devoted exclusively to legal storytelling,[2] Richard Delgado, a leading critical race theorist, explains how stories connect us to the experiences of others.[3] "Stories," writes Delgado, "are the oldest, most primordial meeting ground in human experience. Their allure will often provide the most effective means of overcoming otherness, of forming a new collectivity based on the shared story."[4] In the same symposium issue, Mari Matsuda tells us that stories can connect us through their legal meanings. Stories, she says, "are a means of obtaining the knowledge we need to create just legal structure" in a multicultural world.[5] Listening seriously to the legal meanings of stories told by others can help us imagine the possibility of "human social progress" and a "just world free of existing conditions of domination."[6]

Indians of the Encounter era would find much they could agree with in the works of these contemporary legal scholars. The language of Indian forest diplomacy reflected a clear appreciation of the importance of stories in imagining the possibility of connections, including legal connections, with others.

Then again, storytelling has always held a particularly important place in American Indian life. In a tribal culture, as the literary critic Arnold Krupat has recognized, "to be known as a storyteller is to be known as one who participates, in a communally sanctioned manner, in sustaining the group."[7]

Stories and storytellers are regarded as vitally important in the life of most American Indian tribal communities. The traditional tales and myths passed down among the people, as well as the day-to-day narratives of the things that happen in the life of the tribe, are told to make things happen.[8] Stories are told in tribal life to educate and direct young ones, to maintain the cohesiveness of the group, and to pass on traditional knowledge about the Creator, the seasons, the earth, plants, life, death, and every other subject that is important to the perpetuation of the tribe. Indians have long practiced the belief that stories have the power to sustain the many important connections of tribal life.

Because stories were so important in sustaining the many connections of tribal life, it is not surprising to find that Indians used stories in negotiating treaties with communities at a distance. Storytelling, in fact, was essential to the myriad processes of Indian multicultural diplomacy in the Encounter era. Stories were told by tribal diplomats to establish the communicative processes regarded as absolutely necessary to a successful treaty relationship. Stories were told to educate a treaty partner about the norms of behavior expected of those in a relationship of connection. Indian diplomats could even tell stories that served as jurisgenerative devices,[9] transmitting and sustaining the legal meanings of the good news of peace shared by different peoples on a multicultural frontier. The use of stories in Indian diplomacy reflected a basic paradigm of American Indian visions of law and peace: Stories could enable once alienated groups to imagine themselves as connected in a world of human diversity and conflict.

"A Path Is Now Open"

Stories abound in the treaty literature. They are told for a variety of purposes. Indians of the Encounter era, in fact, believed that the best way to commence a treaty relationship was by telling a story.

The typical Indian treaty council, for example, routinely included a brief story told by a tribal diplomat about "opening the path of peace," or "clearing the road," between the two sides. In Indian diplomacy, these types of stories sought to establish the communicative processes that Indians regarded as a vital prerequisite to a successful relationship of connection. At a 1768 council convened by the English to negotiate a peace treaty between the Cherokees and the Iroquois confederacy ("ancient" and "implacable" enemies, according to Sir William Johnson, the British colonial superintendent of Indian affairs for the northern half of the continent), the "distinguished" Cherokee chief, Ouconastota, stood up, ritually "raised" his wampum belts and calumet of peace, and told the following story about his people's desire for an open path of peace with the Iroquois:

> Brothers: With this Belt we clear and open the road removing all things out of it that may hurt us. It was not us that stopped it but our Elder Brothers the English and French who in their dispute felled a great Tree across it in the path, but as the tree is now rotten the path is now open.[10]

Ouconastota then proposed the terms of a treaty between his people and the Iroquois by further improvising on the theme of opening the path of peace.

> Sachems and Chiefs, you have heard what we had to say we beg you to agree to it, and that you will send some of your people with us to open the Path between your Towns and Chotte [Chota—the Cherokee town that exercised the greatest degree of political leadership in the nation],[11] that all

> our doors may once more be opened, so that we may be at peace and pass and repass as their occasions require without being in danger of being scratched or wounded by the Briars along the road.[12]

The famous Cherokee diplomat Attakullakulla (the Little Carpenter, his name reflecting his skill in negotiating treaties) drew on the same thematic device of the open path of peace at the 1763 Augusta council.[13] His treaty story told of how "all people here will remove blocks that may obstruct the path" to and from his country. With the path clear, according to Attakullakulla, the different peoples assembled at Augusta would be able to establish a close relationship of connection by their treaty. He personally promised "to keep clear this path in future" and expressed his hope that all those who agreed to the treaty "will do the same."[14]

The Cherokees were not the only tribe whose diplomats told treaty stories built upon the theme of opening the path of peace. At the 1795 Treaty of Greenville,[15] a Pottowatami chief told a sacred story to General Anthony Wayne about the path of peace established by his people's treaty relationship with the United States:

> The Master of Life had pity on me, when he permitted me to come and take you first by the hand. . . . When I got this belt from the Americans, they told me the roads were open and clear, and that no obstructions should prevent our coming to see you. . . . I hope it will remain free of bushes and thorns as long as Americans and Indians live.[16]

Kiotseaeton, the Mohawk Iroquois diplomat who led the 1645 treaty negotiations at Three Rivers with the French and their allied Canadian tribes,[17] used wampum belts to tell a remarkable series of stories about opening the path of peace. He had traveled to Three Rivers, he said, to announce "that the thought of their people killed in war no longer affected them; that they cast their weapons under their feet." But the path to the French was full of obstacles. He first had to pass, he said, "near the place where the Algonquins massacred us last Spring."[18]

He tried to go by quickly when he came upon the site of this horrible crime against his fellow countrymen. Kiotseaeton knew that his grief for his murdered kin could make him forget the purpose of his mission of peace. He tried in earnest not to see the blood of his people that had been shed on that spot of ground. "I turned away my eyes for fear of exciting my anger," he said. Then, striking the earth and listening, Kiotseaeton heard the voice of his forefathers, "massacred by the Algonquins" last spring. Fortunately, the old ones, knowing Kiotseaeton's torment and seeing that his heart was capable of seeking revenge, "called out to him, in a loving voice":[19]

> My Grandson, my grandson, be good; do not get angry. Think no longer of us for there is no means of withdrawing us from death. Think of the living—that is of importance, save those who still live from the sword and fire that pursue them; one living man is better than many dead ones.[20]

Only after Kiotseaeton heard the calming words spoken by his own murdered kinsmen telling him to save and value the living was he able to pass by that place of death on the path of peace leading to the fortress of the French.

Kiotseaeton drew upon a rich store of narrative devices to continue his story of opening the path of peace with the French. He followed up his story of forgiveness for the murder of his kinsmen with another wampum gift. This belt had been used "to clear the river, and to drive away the enemy's canoes." Kiotseaeton, according to Father Vimont's account, "made use of a thousand gestures" in telling his treaty story, "as if he collected the waves and had caused a calm, from Quebec to the Iroquois country." He smoothed the rapids, waterfalls, and strong currents on the rivers connecting the Iroquois country to the French. "I thought that I would perish in those boiling waters," he mourned. "This is to appease them." With his hands and arms, "he smoothed and arrested the torrents."[21]

Other wampum gifts were used "to produce a profound calm on the great Lake Saint Louys" that had to be crossed to reach the Iroquois territory, "to make it smooth as ice, to appease the winds, and to allay the anger of the waves." Father Vimont described how Kiotseaeton, "after having by his gestures rendered the route easy," tied a wampum belt on the arm of a Frenchman. Thus connected, he then pulled the Frenchman "straight across the square" to illustrate the ease with which French canoes could now go to the Iroquois country.[22]

With another belt, Kiotseaeton "performed the whole journey that had to be made on land." With his arms, he "felled trees," "lopped off branches," "pushed back the bushes," "put earth in the deepest holes." When finished, he said, "[T]here is the road, quite smooth and quite straight." He dramatized even further, bending toward the ground to see whether there were any more thorns or bushes or any mounds that might block the path. Seeing none, he proclaimed: "It is all finished. We can see the smoke of our villages, from Quebec to the extremity of our country. All obstacles are removed."[23]

"We Are What We Imagine"

As the preeminent American Indian storyteller of our generation, N. Scott Momaday, has written, "We are what we imagine. Our very existence consists in our imagination of ourselves."[24] In American Indian visions of law and peace, differing peoples come to imagine themselves as connected through stories. Indians of the Encounter era believed strongly that stories could clear the channels of communication and dialogue that opened the path of peace on a multicultural frontier. They believed that through stories, we can imagine ourselves as connected to communities at a distance. In such a world of human solidarity, according to the language of Indian diplomacy, all obstacles to law and peace between different peoples are removed.

Stories That Educate

Stories were used for many other purposes in Indian diplomacy besides opening the path of peace between the two sides in a treaty relationship. Stories could also be used to educate a treaty partner about the expected norms of behavior between peoples in a treaty relationship. A headman of the Lower Creeks told a story to the English at a 1763 South Carolina council: "When we were young men the governor of Charles-Town always spoke good and friendly to us, and told us that the path should be straight and white to the nation; and it is our desire it should so continue, and to let the governors see our good intentions." The English, however, according to the Creek headman, were not acting like very good treaty partners; they were not keeping the path open. In the chief's words: "It seems you keep your talk very private, but there is nothing to be hid from we red people."[25]

Indian diplomats could draw on different types of storytelling techniques to educate a derelict treaty partner about appropriate behavior in a treaty relationship. At a mid-seventeenth-century council, a Long Island chief chastised the Dutch by telling a story using a bundle of sticks. "Sixteen chiefs were there at this Long Island," according to David Pieterszoon DeVries, the Dutchman who heard and recorded the chief's story.[26]

> We sat within a ring. There was one among them who had a small bundle of sticks, and was the best speaker, who began his oratory in Indian. He told how we first came upon their coast; that we sometimes had no victuals; they gave us their Turkish beans and Turkish wheat, they helped us with oysters and fish to eat, and now for a reward we had killed their people.[27]

After this moving narrative of Dutch ingratitude, the chief laid down one of the sticks from his bundle. "This was one point," reads DeVries's narrative of the chief's speech. The chief, however, was not finished with the story. He reminded the Dutch that at the beginning of their voyaging, they had left behind colonists to start a settlement. "The Indians," said the chief, "had preserved these people like the apple of their eye." They had even given up their daughters "to sleep with." "There roved many an Indian who was begotten by a Swanneker [their name for the Dutch]." Yet despite these strong connections and an unbroken tradition of friendship, the Dutch had become so villainous "as to kill their own beloved" in an unprovoked attack on the chief's tribe.[28]

The chief laid down another stick after this part of his story, but DeVries had heard enough. "This laying down of sticks began to be tedious to me," the Dutchman related, "as I saw that he had many still in his hand." He told the chief that he knew of all these things that had happened to the Indians of Long Island. "They had been done unwittingly," however. In any event, it could all be cleared up in the traditional Indian way, as DeVries understood it. He told the Indians to go to the governor, who "would give them presents for peace."[29]

In Indian diplomacy, stories could be told for a number of educative purposes: to state a grievance, to reinforce a long-standing set of values shared by treaty partners, and to elaborate the norms of behavior expected of those in a relationship of connection. In American Indian visions of law and peace, the telling of a story sought to build and sustain a common life, a life lived in solidarity with different peoples on a multicultural frontier.[30] Through their treaty stories, American Indian diplomats of the Encounter era sought to educate the strange and alien-seeming newcomers to their world as to what was meant by treaty partners behaving as relatives toward each other.

That a European in the early seventeenth century might find the educative processes of Indian storytelling tedious is not, therefore, surprising. As newcomers to the vast, hostile wilderness that was the North American Encounter era frontier, European-Americans were only beginning to learn that a treaty relationship, in the language of Indian diplomacy, was built slowly and laboriously, stick by stick, story by story.

Tokhrahenehiaron's Story

Stories that sought to educate a treaty partner about the norms, values, and expectations that governed a relationship of law and peace performed multiple functions in Indian diplomacy. These types of stories contained cautionary prescriptions for avoiding conflict with a tribal treaty partner. But through their educative power, these stories performed important integrative functions as well; they provided a means of overcoming otherness, "of forming a new collectivity based on the shared story."[31] In American Indian visions of law and peace, stories that educated others sought to transcend the differences that separate different peoples in a world of human diversity and conflict.

Kiotseaeton, at the Three Rivers Treaty Council in 1645, provides one of the most remarkable demonstrations in the treaty literature of the power of the stories told by Indian diplomats to educate others about their people's norms, values, and expectations and thereby connect strange others to this experience of the world. Of the many stories told by this master Indian diplomat/storyteller at Three Rivers, none exercised a more profound effect on his French listeners than the sad tale of Tokhrahenehiaron, an Iroquois captive who had been allowed to return home to Iroquoia by the French governor, *Onontio* (Huault de Montmagny).

According to Kiotseaeton's story, Tokhrahenehiaron had been sent back by *Onontio* to Iroquoia with a message and valuable gifts to signal a French desire for a treaty of peace. The problem was that after so graciously releasing Tokhrahenehiaron "out of the fire and away from the teeth of the Algonquins" (ritual cannibalizers of their captives), the Great *Onontio* had sent the Iroquois prisoner home without an appropriate escort or assistance. As Kiotseaeton explained, if Tokhrahenehiaron had died along the way, the French might wrongly have assumed that their peace initiative had been rebuffed by the Iroquois. The all-important channel of communication delivering the good news of peace to Iroquoia would never have been established. "If his canoe had been upset; if the winds had caused it to be submerged; if he had been drowned," Kiotseaeton "complained gracefully" to the governor, "you would have waited long for the return of the poor lost man, and you would have accused us of a fault which you yourselves would have committed."[32]

After "gracefully" lodging his complaint to the French governor about his countryman's poor treatment, Kiotseaeton proceeded to dramatize the more appropriate Iroquois way of sending prisoners home when carrying news of peace proposals and valuable gifts. He tied one of his wampum belts around Guillaume Cousture, a Frenchman who had been captured by the Iroquois and was now being delivered by Kiotseaeton to *Onontio*. The Iroquois diplomat then instructed the governor as follows:

> It is this collar which brings you back this prisoner. I would not have said to him, while he was still in our country: "Go, my Nephew; take a Canoe and return to Quebec." My mind would not have been at rest; I would always have thought over and over again to myself, "Is he not lost?" In truth, I would have had no sense, had I acted in that way. He whom you have sent back had all the difficulties in the world, on his journey.[33]

By tying his wampum gift to the arm of Cousture, Kiotseaeton was delivering a very important message to the French. In Iroquois diplomacy, an invitation to attend a treaty council was made with wampum; it was "that which stretches a person's arm."[34] During the course of a treaty council, the presentation of wampum represented the "words" that carried the message of the connections desired between the two sides.[35] At Three Rivers, the wampum tied to the French prisoner Cousture told a story of the type of connections the Iroquois desired with the French and their allied tribes. If the two peoples were to enter into an alliance of peace and friendship according to an American Indian vision of law and peace, the type of treatment Tokhrahenehiaron received from the French must never happen again. They must take each other by the arm and act as if they were relatives.

To dramatize this vital point of the negotiations even further, Kiotseaeton acted out his countryman's harrowing unescorted journey home from Canada "in so pathetic a manner," according to the Jesuit Vimont, "that there is no merryandrew [i.e., clown] in France so ingenious as that Barbarian."[36] "He took a stick, and placed it on his head like a bundle; then he carried it from one end of the square to the other, representing what that prisoner had done in the rapids and the current of the water."[37] This was lodging a diplomatic complaint Indian-style through storytelling. Kiotseaeton demonstrated how Tokhrahenehiaron had to portage his canoe and his baggage full of French presents alone, "piece by piece," at the nonnavigable parts of streams. He went "backward and forward" to show the journeys, windings, and turnings of the prisoner. "He ran against a stone." "He receded more than he advanced in his canoe; because alone he could not maintain it against the current." He lost courage on his journey and then he regained his strength. Father Vimont summed up Kiotseaeton's impressive performance of the story of Tokhrahenehiaron's harrowing voyage home as follows: "In a word, I have never seen anything better done than this acting."[38] The "Barbarian," according to Vimont, even reprised the major points of his dramatic presentation to the derelict French governor:

> "Again" (said he), "if you had helped him to pass the rapids and the bad roads, and then if, while stopping and smoking, you had looked after him from afar, you would have greatly consoled us. But I know not where your thoughts were, to send a man back quite alone amid so many dangers. I did not do that. Come, my nephew, I said to him whom you see before your eyes [Cousture]; follow me, I wish to bring thee to thy own county, at the risk of my life."[39]

Stories were told for a variety of purposes in Encounter era Indian diplomacy. Kiotseaeton's lesson that a treaty relationship with the Iroquois required commitment and appropriate efforts aimed at opening the channels of communication between the two sides was not lost on the French; Kiotseaeton and his two fellow Iroquois ambassadors were sent home by the governor to Iroquoia with "two young French lads . . . to help them to take back their canoes and their presents."[40] Kiotseaeton's story of Tokhrahenehiaron, however, also had a far more meaningful purpose than simply educating the French in the commonsense protocols of forest diplomacy with the Iroquois. His treaty story sought to evoke a more committed and appropriate sense of connection to the sufferings endured by a fellow human being abandoned by the French on the frontiers of Encounter era North America.

The Use of the Imagination

In his book, *Contingency, Irony, and Solidarity,*[41] the contemporary North American philosopher Richard Rorty has stressed the importance of the imagination in achieving law and peace among different peoples in a multicultural and multiracial world. Rorty's vision of a "liberal utopia" of moral progress "in the direction of greater human solidarity" is achieved through "the ability to see more and more traditional differences (tribe, religion, race, customs, and the like) as unimportant when compared with similarities with respect to pain and humiliation—the ability to think of others as included in the range of us."[42] In Rorty's vision of a liberal utopia, human solidarity is seen

> not as a fact to be recognized by clearing away "prejudice" . . . but rather, as a goal to be achieved. It is to be achieved not by inquiry but by imagination, the imaginative ability to see strange people as fellow sufferers. Solidarity is not discovered by reflection but created.[43]

Rorty goes on to observe that the process of coming to see and understand other human beings as "one of us" rather than as "them" is a matter of detailed description of what unfamiliar people are like and redescription of what we ourselves are like. This, writes Rorty, is much less a task for philosophical theory than for genres such as ethnography and other narrative forms that connect "the present with the past, on the one hand, and with utopian futures, on the other."[44]

As any comprehensive ethnography or narrative of the Encounter era reveals, North American Indians never fully realized the liberal utopia of human solidarity and elimination of human suffering envisioned by Rorty. Indians, according to the familiar accounts, were engaged in frequent and violent wars against many of their neighbors with whom they could not or would not make peace. Their lives, from a European point of view at least, could be described as "nasty, brutish and short."[45] But Indians of the Encounter era also recognized that there were times when their chances for survival in their world could be significantly enhanced by telling stories. They recognized that stories, as acts of the imagination, enable us to be more sensitive to the pain of others, to see and understand other human beings as "one of us," rather than as "them." Such increased sensitivity, as Rorty notes, "makes it more difficult to marginalize people different from ourselves by thinking, 'They do not feel it as we would,' or 'There must always be suffering, so why not let *them* suffer?'"[46]

The use of stories to invoke the imaginative capacity in others to see themselves as connected in a world of human solidarity is wondrously illustrated throughout the treaty literature. Indian diplomats used metaphors, gestures, songs, dances, and other storytelling devices to enable their potential treaty partners to imagine a world in which the differences of "tribe, religion, race, customs, and the like" could be transcended.[47] Like the contemporary philosopher Rorty, these "barbarian" storytellers recognized that connection with others can only be achieved by increased sensitivity to their sufferings as fellow human beings. This goal, as they sought to educate their treaty partners, could best be achieved by acts of the imagination, evoked by the power of telling stories.

Stories That Create Legal Meanings

"No set of legal institutions or prescriptions," Robert Cover once wrote, "exists apart from the narratives that locate it and give it meaning."[48] "For every constitution there is an epic, for each decalogue a scripture. Once understood in the context of the narratives that give it meaning, law becomes not merely a system of rules to be observed, but a world in which we live."[49] In American Indian visions of law and peace, a treaty imagined a world of human solidarity and trust. For Indians of the Encounter era, storytelling was a favored method for transmitting the legal meanings entailed by this vision of a treaty relationship. Stories, to borrow from the language of contemporary critical legal scholarship, were used in Indian diplomacy "to create just legal structure between treaty partners,"[50] a world of shared normative commitments.

The transformative potential of a shared story to create legal meanings between different peoples is suggested throughout the treaty literature. One of the more remarkable instances in which a single story transcended boundaries of time and distance to create binding obligations between treaty partners emerges from the minutes of the 1792 Buffalo Creek Treaty Council. There, a speaker for the Western Indians north of the Ohio River related the extended series of negotiations that had occurred between his confederated group of tribes spread out across the western frontier and the Iroquois confederacy in New York. The speaker for the Western Indians related how an Iroquois diplomat, some four years earlier, had come to his country with a pipe of peace, a proposal for alliance, and a story.[51]

Long ago, according to the story told by the Iroquois diplomat, the Indians were "the eldest people" in North America "and all of one color." Now, however, "there is a white people on this island." To better protect their mutual interests, the Iroquois speaker urged all Indians to "combine ourselves together." This message of multitribal unity was being carried to the Western Indians so that the minds of all the Indians "may be one."[52]

Now, some four years after that Iroquois speaker delivered this message, the Western Indians were using the occasion of the Buffalo Creek Treaty Council to present a large bunch of wampum "from each of the nations north of the Ohio." This wampum gift was proof that the Western tribes had received and considered the meanings of this very important Iroquois story. They further professed that the pipe sent by the Iroquois with this story passed through all of their nations: "[A]ll smoked it, both women and children." This sacred pipe was now being returned to the Iroquois, and the Western Indians asked that it be smoked by the Iroquois chiefs.[53]

One of the Iroquois speakers present at Buffalo Creek took this pipe and repeated the original story that had accompanied its journey on the Indian frontier:

> Brothers: Listen. . . . Our forefathers have handed down to us, that we are one people, of one color, on this island, and ought to be of one mind, and . . . become as one people in peace and friendship . . . but let us attend to our own concerns, and brighten the chain of friendship with our nations; and as our minds are one, let us consider future posterity.[54]

Having repeated the original story that had accompanied the pipe as it traveled among the tribes north of the Ohio, the Indian diplomat verified the legal meanings of the acts of those who had "smoked it." "Now Brothers," the Iroquois speaker declared, "you present us the pipe," the same pipe that the Iroquois had sent four years ago. "[Y]ou say your head chiefs all smoked out of it, and returning it to us again, all took it, and smoked out of it ourselves, in friendship. Now, as we are thus combined together, we are able to lift a heavy burden."[55]

It may seem remarkable that the simple act of smoking a pipe could sustain the difficult and extended processes of forming a pan-Indian alliance on the multicultural frontiers of Encounter era North America. There had been no face-to-face negotiations between the different tribes that announced their alliance at Buffalo Creek in 1792. There were no signed documents or memoirs of understanding between the parties that signified an intent to be bound by the Iroquois' treaty proposal. The language of Indian diplomacy, however, rendered such procedural paraphernalia so familiar to European diplomacy irrelevant. No text had to be signed or legal intentions even stated. In American Indian visions of law and peace between different peoples, the pipe itself was a sacred, therefore legal, text.[56] As a jurisgenerative (i.e., law-creating) narrative device, its use generated a set of distinctive legal meanings according to the language of Indian diplomacy.[57] Any Indians who "smoked" the pipe accepted the treaty sealed by this sacred act as a binding legal obligation. They bound themselves as well to all other Indians who had smoked the pipe and who had thereby participated in the legal story it told. As explained by Cover, "[T]he transformation of interpretation into legal meaning begins when someone accepts the demands of interpretation and through the personal act of commitment affirms the position taken."[58] Through the jurisgenerative device of the sacred pipe, a world of shared normative commitments had been created and sustained on the multicultural frontiers of Encounter era North America. In the language of Indian diplomacy, through such shared stories of law and peace achieved by different peoples in a world of human diversity and conflict, "we are thus combined together, we are able to lift a heavy burden."

Stories as Jurisgenerative Devices

This idea that the jurisgenerative power of stories enabled human beings to achieve connection—in the language of Indian diplomacy, to combine together and lift a heavy burden—is reflected throughout the tribal life of various Eastern Woodlands Indian cultures. The mourning rituals found in different patterns among tribal peoples of eastern North America, for example, are all expressions of the idea that the sharing of sufferings with others is a jurisgenerative act. Mourning rituals are performed by the different groups within the tribe to fulfill a divine command to renew their connections of law and peace. The reciprocal performance of these rituals generated a set of legal meanings that bound together the members of the tribal society through mutual obligations of solidarity and trust. Indians of the Encounter era believed strongly that mourning rituals were a most effective means for transmitting the good news of peace to different groups in a hostile world.[59]

Given the connective, jurisgenerative functions of mourning ritual patterns within tribal life, it is not surprising to find Indian forest diplomats draw so frequently on them in the treaty literature. In Encounter era Indian diplomacy, mourning ritual stories were used to enable once-alienated groups to enter into a binding treaty relationship of law and peace.

Returning to the Treaty of Greenville in 1795, we find Tarke, chief of the Wyandots, using the forms of a tribal mourning ritual to construct a series of narratives. These connected stories spoke of his tribe's intent to enter into a binding treaty relationship with the United States. The recent wars between the Americans and the tribes of the Ohio Valley had claimed many lives on both sides. "I view you lying in a gore of blood," Tarke told General Anthony Wayne; "it is me, an Indian who caused it." The Wyandot chief blamed the English "for giving the tomahawk to his people," which "yet remains in your head."[60] Tarke proceeded to make an offer of peace by telling the following story of condolence:

> Elder Brother: I now take the tomahawk out of your head; but, with so much care, that you shall not feel a pain or injury. I will now tear a big tree up by the roots, and throw the hatchet into the cavity which they occupied, where the waters will wash it away where it can never be found. Now I have buried the hatchet, and I expect that none of my color will ever again find it out.[61]

The Wyandot diplomat then conducted a mourning ritual for the Americans who had been killed by his people in previous battles "in order to clear away an old grief. . . . Listen! I now wipe your body clean from all blood with this white soft linen [white wampum], and I do it with as much tenderness as I am capable of."[62] Tarke proceeded to wipe the tears from the eyes and open the ears of the Americans. He opened their throats, so that "whatever the Great Spirit may think proper for you to swallow, may go down without any obstruction." By these ritual stories of condolence, he placed their hearts "in proper position" so that whatever the Wyandots spoke would be received directly and without diversion, and whatever the Americans spoke would now come "with truth and ease" from their hearts. With the channels of communication and connection now cleared by the performance of these requickening rites and their accompanying narratives, the Wyandot chief presented a blue and white string of wampum to the Americans. He asked forgiveness for past transgressions that occurred during war and the forsaking of revenge for those who had fallen in battle:

> Brother: Listen to us, all Indians; who now speak to you! The bones which lie scattered of your ancient warriors, who fell in defence of the present cause we gather all together, and bury them now; and place this white board over them, that they may never again be seen by our posterity.[63]

Stories, metaphors, and other narrative devices adapted from tribal mourning rituals proliferate in the treaty literature of the Encounter era. Kiotseaeton, the great seventeenth-century Indian storyteller/diplomat, used mourning ritual patterns to tell a story with important legal meanings at Three Rivers. "All obstacles are removed," he announced, after clearing the path of peace between the Iroquois country and New France.[64] Now, he said, the French would always find fires lighted in all of the Iroquois houses. Wood would be cut and waiting for them. The warming fire that welcomed them to the Iroquois country would never go out. Even in their own homes far removed from Iroquoia, the French would see the welcoming light of these fires.[65]

A welcoming fire continually burning bright was a recurrent narrative theme in Iroquois political and legal traditions. Its legal meanings in Iroquois treaty visions can be traced back directly to the Deganawidah epic. In proclaiming the Great Peace, Deganawidah proscribed that a welcoming fire must always be kept burning bright in the Iroquois country. Wood always had to be kept ready at hand to keep its light from diminishing. In this way, according to the lawgiver, all nations that desired to follow the roots of the Tree of Peace could be led by the council fire smoke to Iroquoia to receive the good news of peace.[66]

In the Iroquois mourning ritual ceremony, the Condolence Council, the restoration of the fire symbolically renews the confederacy, allowing those brought to grief by death to resume their duties on the League Council of Chiefs. According to one version of the condolence ceremony, the members of the Clear-Minded side recite as follows:

> Now continue to listen, for when a person is brought to grief, and such is your condition, the sticks of wood from your fire are scattered caused by death, so we . . . brothers, will gather up the sticks of wood and rekindle the fire, and the smoke shall rise and pierce the sky, so that all nations of the

> confederacy may see the smoke, and when a person is in great grief caused by the death of some of our rulers, the head is bowed down in deep sorrow. We therefore cause you to stand up again, our uncles and surround the council fire again and resume your duties.[67]

In the Iroquois vision of law and peace, the story of the fire renewed and kept burning bright imagined a world where all barriers to communication and connection between communities at a distance have been removed. By forgiving the murder of his kinsmen, clearing the rivers, smoothing the rapids, calming the lakes, and removing all obstructions, even the tiniest thorns, Kiotseaeton revealed this same welcoming fire of peace to the French and their allied tribes. By its light, the Iroquois signified their intent to sustain lasting peace and goodwill between their nations according to the legal meanings generated by the sacred narrative of the Condolence Council.[68]

Such mourning ritual stories as wiping away blood, placing the white board over fallen warriors, and keeping the fire burning bright were adapted by Encounter era Indian diplomats so that communities at a distance could enter into a binding treaty relationship of solidarity and trust with each other. In American Indian visions of law and peace, treaties, as stories, were jurisgenerative devices, transmitting and sustaining the legal meanings of a relationship of close connection between different peoples on a multicultural frontier.

Imagining a World of Human Solidarity

The language of Encounter era Indian diplomacy sought to connect different peoples through a variety of complex storytelling methods. Stories of the open path of peace, narrative devices such as sticks and sacred pipes, and mourning ritual stories were seen as "effective means of overcoming otherness, of forming a new collectivity based on the shared story."[69] We now have, therefore, a better understanding of why Indian diplomats had to be such good storytellers. On the multicultural frontiers of the North American Encounter era, they had to tell a special kind of story, a story that imagined a world of human solidarity achieved according to an American Indian treaty vision of law and peace.

5

Treaties as Constitutions

Values, Customs, and Traditions

The language of North American indigenous diplomacy generated many different ways of envisioning a treaty. Treaties as sacred texts enabled different peoples to attain "one mind" according to a timeless divine plan for all humankind.[1] Treaties as connections made survival more assured on a multicultural frontier.[2] Treaties told as stories enabled treaty partners to imagine a world of human solidarity.[3] Understanding these different ways of envisioning a treaty makes it possible for us to discern several of the important constitutional principles that Woodlands Indian groups believed governed their multicultural treaty relationships with European-Americans during the Encounter era.

It may seem odd to most Americans to speak of an Indian treaty negotiated during the colonial period of our nation's history as a "constitutional" text. In the traditional national mythology,[4] discussions of constitutional texts normally revolve around the U.S. Constitution of 1787. Agreed upon by a group of European-descended men usually called the Founders, the Constitution, so we are taught, set out the unique forms and institutions of joint action agreed upon by "We, the people of the United States."[5]

If, however, we think of a constitution—not in the traditional American sense of one basic, written document of law but rather as the British use the term—as encompassing a whole body of values, customary practices, and traditions basic to the polity, we can begin to reconstruct a much different set of indigenous constitutional principles generated by American Indian treaty visions of law and peace for the emerging multicultural society of Encounter era eastern North America.[6] For Indians of the Encounter era, treaties, as sacred texts, required treaty partners to accept a set of constitutional values reflecting their shared humanity under their covenant. Treaties, as constitutionalized connections, gave rise to customary bonds that treaty partners could rely on in times of need or crisis. Treaties told as stories sought to sustain a constitutional tradition of human solidarity between different peoples. When understood as multicultural constitutions, treaties reflected a basic paradigm of a truly indigenous North American vision of law and peace; as fellow human beings in a world of diversity and conflict, we are under an obligation to link arms together.

Treaties as Sacred Covenants

We have come to better understand that a treaty was a sacred text for Indians of the Encounter era. Treaties bound different peoples, in the language of Woodlands Indian diplomacy, to attain one mind in agreement with a timeless divine plan for all humankind.[7] As a matter of constitutional principle, therefore, treaties were seen by Indians as divinely mandated covenants of law and peace between peoples. A treaty required treaty partners to acknowledge their shared humanity and to act upon a set of constitutional values reflecting the unity of interests generated by their agreement.

The basic foundational principle that a treaty enabled different peoples to transcend their differences and unite together is, in fact, one of the most frequently voiced themes of Encounter era Indian diplomacy. We sense this basic principle of multicultural unity informing the treaty relationships proposed by the Chippewa chief Mash-i-pi-nash-i-wish at the Treaty of Greenville in 1795 between the Western Indians and the United States.

> Listen! The Great Spirit above hears us, and I trust we shall not endeavor to deceive each other. I expect what we are about to do shall never be forgotten as long as we exist. When I show you this belt, I point out to you your children at one end of it, and mine at the other. . . . I now feel that we will assist you to the utmost of our power to do what is right. Remember, we have taken the Great Spirit to witness our present actions; we will make a new world, and leave nothing on it to incommode our children.[8]

This vision of a treaty requiring different peoples to recognize their shared humanity according to a divinely mandated plan of multicultural unity recurs throughout the treaty literature. Chekilly, a Creek chief, reminded the Georgia colonists in 1735 that their shared humanity with his people was the basis of their treaty relationship: "I am sensible that there is one who has made us all and though some have more knowledge than others, the great and strong must become dirt."[9] A Seminole chief delivered a virtually identical message to the U.S. treaty commissioners at a 1793 council: "The man above made us all, and we are one people. I speak to you as having one father and one mother. . . . I take you by the hand, as you have taken me, and I hope we shall both keep fast hold in peace and friendship."[10] At another late eighteenth-century treaty council with the United States, the Cherokee chief, The Little Nephew, explained this basic constitutional principle of multicultural unity:

> Our great father above made us both; and if he was to take it into his head that the whites had injured the reds, he would certainly punish them for it: because he made both red and white; and it is his wish that they should live together under a white cloud, without darkness. It is our desire to live in peace and friendship with oldest brother.[11]

It is not difficult to discern the origins of this principle recognizing the shared humanity of the different peoples in a treaty relationship. In American Indian visions of law and peace, treaties fulfilled a divine command for all peoples to unite as one. This obligation could only be satisfied if the two parties agreed to a sacred covenant to attain "one mind."[12] As multicultural constitutions, treaties thus reflected a set of values that sought to realize this divinely inspired vision of human solidarity. In the language of Encounter era Indian diplomacy, by agreeing to a treaty with different peoples, "we will make a new world, and leave nothing on it to incommode our children."[13]

Constitutional Rituals

This indigenous North American Indian vision of a treaty as a sacred covenant informed by constitutional values embracing multicultural unity was reinforced by the sacred ritual acts performed at so many Encounter era treaty councils. These "usual ceremonies," generally regarded as time-consuming diversions by Europeans, made it possible, according to the values informing American Indian visions of law and peace, for treaty partners to accept and embrace the divinely revealed truth of their oneness and shared humanity. For Indians, smoking the pipe of peace, exchanging white eagle feathers, or performing a tribal condoling ceremony before the commencement of treaty negotiations sanctified the proceedings and enabled treaty partners to establish and maintain a close and lasting relationship of law and peace.[14] These rituals were acts of constitutional creation and renewal by different peoples bound together by a sacred covenant of peace.

The idea that a treaty council required the performance of specified ritual acts to have constitutional legitimacy was made apparent to the treaty commissioners from the colony of Pennsylvania at a meeting with the Ohio Indians at Carlisle in 1753. Held on the eve of the French and Indian War, the very success of this important treaty council, at which Benjamin Franklin, a leader in the Pennsylvania colonial assembly, was one of three commissioners, came to depend on the proper performance of the sacred rituals of mourning by which Indians traditionally shared their sufferings with each other.

With French forces poised to invade the Ohio country, the Pennsylvanians eagerly desired information about the movements of the French and the attitudes of the tribes on their frontiers regarding which side they might ally with in the event of war. The Western tribes attending this conference, with their long-established trade connections and patterns of land sales to the English colonies, had reasons to be concerned as well. The French and allied tribes seemed certain to invade their territories, and they needed guns that only the English could supply to defend themselves from the French and Indian onslaught.[15]

Unfortunately, Franklin and his fellow commissioners had arrived for this critical meeting without any gifts for the condoling ceremonies that customarily attended such Indian gatherings. Having assembled the "most considerable persons" of the Iroquois confederacy—Delawares, "Shawonees" (Shawnees), "Twightwees" (Miamis), and "Owendaets" (Wyandots)—the commissioners were told by the Indians that they simply could not commence negotiations without the gifts of condolence that were an integral part of the treaty ceremonies. As the commissioners' report succinctly explained:

> The *Twightwees* and *Delawares* having had several of their great Men cut off [killed] by the *French* and their *Indians*, and all the Chiefs of the *Owendaets* being lately dead, it became necessary to condole their Loss; and no Business could be begun, agreeable to the *Indian* Customs, till the Condolences were passed; and as these could not be made, with the usual Ceremonies, for want of the Goods, which were not arrived, and it was uncertain when they would, the Commissioners were put to some difficulties.[16]

Anxious to commence the council business, the commissioners applied to Scarouady, an Oneida Iroquois chief and "a person of Great weight" among the tribes present at Carlisle. The Pennsylvanians sought out his opinion as to whether the "usual" condolence ceremonies could be dispensed with by presenting "[l]ists of the particular Goods intended to be given with Assurances of their Delivery as soon as they could come."[17]

The commissioners reported that although the Oneida chief appeared "pleased" with the idea, he still let it be "frankly" known that the rituals could not be satisfied by this attempt at innovation on the part of the Pennsylvanians. The goods had to be delivered first. According to Scarouady, "The Indians could not proceed to Business while the Blood remained on their Garments, and . . . the Condolences could not be accepted unless the Goods, intended to cover the Graves, were actually spread on the ground before them."[18]

After receiving this news of the steadfastness of the Indians regarding their customs, the commissioners dispatched a message back East to "hasten" the delivery of the condolence gifts, "since everything must stop till the goods came."[19] Five days later, when the merchandise finally did arrive, Scarouady delivered the following speech opening the conference on behalf of all of the assembled tribes:

> You have, like a true and affectionate Brother, comforted us in our affliction. You have wiped away the Blood from our Seats, and set them again in order. You have wrapped up the Bones of our Warriors, and covered the Graves of our wise Men; and wiped the Tears from our Eyes, and the Eyes of our Women and Children; So that we now see the Sun, and all Things are become pleasant to our sight. We shall not fail to acquaint our several Nations with your Kindness. We shall take Care that it be always remembered by us; and believe it will be attended with suitable Returns of Love and Affection.[20]

In the language of forest diplomacy spoken by Woodlands Indians of the Encounter era, the Pennsylvanians' presentation of gifts fulfilled their constitutionally proscribed role as the Clear-Minded condolers to the Indian Mourners. Revealing the "sun" cleared the minds of the Indians so that they could see the sky. This sharing of sufferings joined the two sides together as one, as the Great Spirit had mandated for all humankind. Having performed the sacred rituals of condolence, a larger constitutional principle of their treaty relationship could now be recognized by the two sides: the divinely revealed truth that all peoples should be united as one.[21]

As Benjamin Franklin and his fellow Pennsylvanians came to understand, the rituals of Encounter era Indian diplomacy could not simply be supplanted by ad hoc European innovations. For Indians, ceremonies such as the Condolence Council were essential to the conduct of treaty negotiations. A treaty simply was not a treaty to Indians unless it was consecrated and reinforced by the constitutional rituals of an American Indian vision of law and peace.

"We Are One People"

Because a treaty was regarded as a sacred text that commanded all peoples to unite as one, certain constitutional principles were invariably made a part of the treaty relationships Indians entered into with European-Americans. The unity of interests created by a treaty mandated recognition of the fundamental shared humanity between the different peoples in the relationship. The constitutional rituals performed by treaty partners enabled the two sides to realize the divinely revealed truth of their oneness. American Indian multicultural constitutionalism regarded these fundamental principles as a vital part of every treaty relationship. Treaty partners were required to accept the basic values of multicultural unity reflected by their entering into a sacred covenant of law and peace with each other. In the language of Indian diplomacy, "The man above made us all, and we are one people."

The Practice of Connection

In North American indigenous diplomacy, treaties were sacred texts that enabled treaty partners to fulfill a divinely mandated plan of multicultural unity. Indians of the Encounter era also had very practical reasons for making treaties with communities at a distance. Treaties established connections that helped assure survival on a multicultural frontier. The customary bonds of unity created by a treaty could be relied on, at least as far as Indians were concerned, in times of need or crisis.[22] Treaty partners, therefore, as a matter of constitutional principle, were bound to protect each other's interests.

Indian diplomats interpreted this basic constitutional principle broadly: it called for certain types of normative acts and practices directed toward one's treaty partners in a number of different contexts. At a minimum, for instance, treaty partners were expected to provide food and hospitality to each other. As the Miami chief Le Gris explained to General Anthony Wayne at the Treaty of Greenville:

> When brothers meet, they always experience pleasure. As it is a cool day, we would hope you would give us a little drink; you promised to treat us well, and we expect to be treated as warriors; we wish you to give your brother a glass of wine. I hope you are pleased with this visit of your brothers. You have some things of which we have not yet had any; we would like some mutton and pork occasionally.[23]

As European-Americans came to discover, Indians relied on their treaty partners to provide far more than food or drink as a customary matter. Given their relationship of close connection, the different peoples connected by a treaty were customarily expected to aid each other in times of wars, crises, or threats. A Choctaw "king" who visited Savannah, Georgia, in 1734 to request aid explained his expectations clearly: "We are surrounded with white people and the French are building forts which we do not like. We have come to see who are our friends and whose protection we may rely on."[24]

Those who failed to uphold the customary bonds of unity created by a treaty risked breaching the sacred covenant of peace created by their alliance. In 1756, as the French and Indian War raged on the frontier, the Cherokee chief Culloughculla spoke bluntly to the Virginia commissioners about the failure of the English to live up to their treaty obligations with the tribe. The chief explained that he had recently returned from England, where he had met the "Great King." The King of England acknowledged the Cherokees as his children, "as well as the English," according to Culloughculla's report, and desired "that we might continue Brethren for ever."[25] But the Cherokees were very worried about the state of their treaty relationship with their brothers, the English. French-allied Indians were committing "horrid murders" on the frontier inhabitants of Virginia. The Cherokees, operating under the obligations of blood feud imposed by their symbolic kinship with the English,[26] were more than willing to help "prevent such massacres" by attacking the French.[27] But, Culloughculla explained, the English had to live up to their reciprocating treaty commitments before the Cherokees could go on the warpath against their common enemy.

> We have had frequent Promises from the Governor of South Carolina, to build us a fort; and it was stipulated at a Treaty held at Saludy last summer, when we signed a release for our lands to the Great King George. But we do not find, that Governor has yet made the least Preparations towards performing his engagement. The king, our Father, told me, that we should mutually assist each other, and therefore, as we are acquainted with the manner of building forts, and had not the necessary materials, we thought ourselves justifiable in making our application to Governor Glen, who, I must again repeat it has forfeited his word. I have a Hatchet ready, but we hope our Friends will not expect us to take it up, till we have a place of safety for our wives and children, When they are secured, we will immediately send a great number of warriors to be employed by your Governor, where he shall think proper.[28]

The Cherokee chief then dutifully explained the consequences of the failure of the English to live up to their treaty responsibilities: "[I]f no steps are taken for our security, the French will extinguish the Friendly Fire between us."[29]

Indians regarded the duty to provide aid and assistance to a treaty partner, like all of the customary bonds of a treaty relationship, as a constitutional obligation. Changes in circumstance or the original bargaining positions of the parties were therefore irrelevant as far as Indians were concerned. Throughout the treaty literature, Indians can be found trying to educate their European-American treaty partners that the duty to provide aid and assistance under a treaty did not change simply because one party became weaker over time in the relationship. If anything, because a treaty connected the two sides together as relatives, the treaty partner who grew stronger over time was under an increased obligation to protect its weaker partner.

The Nanticoke Indians carefully explained in a 1759 council the nature of the continuing obligations of "brotherly" assistance owed them by Governor Horatio Sharpe under their long-standing treaty with the Maryland colony:

> [A]s we love to travel the roads and other places to seek the support of life and as you are our Brother therefore [we] beg and hope you will not suffer us to be trodden down quite for we are as a child just beginning to walk[;] we are so reduced and diminished and are as nothing. . . . When there were great numbers of us Indians and but few white people in this nation we enjoyed our privileges, profits, and customs in quiet but it is quite the contrary now[;] then [we] were not deprived of our freedom and customs for we had the whole nation once under our jurisdiction but now there is but a spot laid out for us not enough for bread for us Indians. . . . [I]f you our trusty Brother suffers us thus to be evilly treated we shall soon be quite destroyed and totally pushed out of this nation, but hope you our Brother will never suffer us thus to be treated.[30]

As the Nanticokes' remonstrance to Maryland's governor illustrates, the different peoples connected by a treaty were expected to abide steadfastly by the sacred principles of multicultural unity sustaining their original agreement. A treaty, as far as Indians were concerned, was entered into precisely to enhance the chance of survival should some calamity or disaster befall the tribe. The constitutionalized connections created by a treaty were a form of assurance and security that could be steadfastly relied on in times of crisis or need as a matter of customary practice.

Constitutionalized Connections

In American Indian visions of law and peace, a treaty connected different peoples through constitutional bonds of multicultural unity. To fulfill these bonds, the parties to a treaty adopted various practices that were expected of close relatives. They customarily were expected to share their resources, provide aid and assistance, and protect each other from harm no matter what circumstances might befall one of them. As a matter of constitutional principle, treaty partners were obligated to provide for each other's needs. In the language of Indian diplomacy, the bonds of unity we establish with communities at a distance assure us "who are our friends and whose protection we may rely on" in a hostile and chaotic world.

"What Do You Want Us to Do?"

The constitutional principle that treaty partners, by virtue of their unique relationship of connection, were customarily obligated to provide for each other's needs and protect each other's interests is amply illustrated by the Encounter era alliance between the French and the Algonquian Indians in the Great Lakes region. The French called this territory on the far frontiers of their colonial empire in North America the *pays d'en haut* (upper country). As Richard White explains in his award-winning book, *The Middle Ground: Indians, Empires, and Republics in the Great Lakes Region, 1650–1815,*[31] the *pays d'en haut* was where ethnically diverse groups of "French" Canadian colonists and polyglot Algonquian-speaking Indians sought to construct a common, mutually comprehensible world in Encounter era North America. This world of the "middle ground," as White calls it, "was not an Eden, and it should not be romanticized. Indeed, it could be a violent and sometimes horrifying place. But in this world the older worlds of Algonquians and of various Europeans overlapped, and their mixture created new systems of meaning and exchange."[32] The middle ground was a product of the chaos and warfare on North America's Encounter era multicultural frontiers. Iroquois efforts to acquire furs for the Dutch in the middle decades of the seventeenth century led to a series of fierce attacks on the beaver territories occupied by the tribes on the Iroquois' western frontiers. The Iroquois—supplied with guns first by the Dutch and then by the English who supplanted the Dutch in the 1660s—decimated these tribes in the early decades of what historians call the Beaver Wars, lasting roughly from the 1650s until the turn of the century.[33] The Iroquois-fueled diaspora created a number of refugee centers between the western Great Lakes and the Mississippi River; multitribal villages emerged from these concentrations of Iroquoian-speaking Huron and Petun groups, Winnebagos (who were Siouan), and Algonquian speakers—Ottawas, Potawatomis, Fox, Sauks, Kickapoos, Miamis, Illinois, and others.

There were very few years when famine was not a pressing concern for this fragmented world of village refugees. In its efforts to attract Algonquian furs to Montreal, France had to overcome Algonquian fears about making the long and dangerous journey across Iroquois-patrolled territory along the Ottawa River. For the Algonquians, particularly, hunting beaver for the French was a luxury that few in their world could afford. As one early eighteenth-century French chronicler recorded: "As the savages give everything to their mouths, they preferred to devote themselves to hunting such wild beasts as could furnish subsistence for their families rather than seek beavers."[34]

For the French, encouraging these tribes to participate in the fur trade was essential to their imperial ambitions on the continent. If the beaver territories of the tribes bordering the Iroquois' western frontiers were lost to the Confederacy of the Five Nations, Canada's furs would most certainly be drained off in that direction to Albany. England, as the Iroquois' sponsor, would then effectively control the trade and therefore the future of the continent.[35] The French thus learned to utilize their potential as military allies to the tribes of the *pays d'en haut* as a lure for the trade: Trade with the French assured the Algonquians protection from attacks by the Iroquois. For both the Algonquians and the French, establishing and maintaining strong connections with each other were the only means for both groups to ensure their survival for any significant length of time on the multicultural frontiers of Encounter era North America.[36]

French trade, and the power that accompanied that trade, thus provided the raison d'etre for the French-Algonquian alliance. The French-Algonquian treaty literature, however, reveals that French was not the language of diplomacy used in the *pays d'en haut*. The French-Algonquian alliance was governed almost exclusively by a language more generally reflective of an Algonquian cultural vision of law and peace between different peoples.

All major aspects of the alliance, for instance, were negotiated through the medium of ritual gift exchange. As the French Intendant Jacques Duchesneau recognized of the Indians: "These tribes never transact any business without making presents to illustrate and confirm their words."[37] The Algonquians condoled the deaths of the French with furs and wampum, and the French were expected to reciprocate by condoling the dead of the Indians with trade goods. Other ritual forms, uniquely Indian in their origins, proliferate in the French-Algonquian treaty literature. Calumets were smoked before the transaction of any important business; peace was made in council by calming the waters, removing the fallen trees, smoothing the land, and opening the path between the two sides.[38] Murderers were surrendered to *Onontio*, the governor of New France, "to whom he will grant pardon in the customary manner."[39]

The terms of kinship and name-titles used in the alliance were all derived from the language of Indian forest diplomacy. The French, as the stronger treaty partner, were expected to act as if they were the "father" of the Algonquians. This meant that as a matter of customary practice, the French were expected to be benevolent; they were obligated to renew the alliance by providing for the *besoins*, or needs, of the Algonquians. As the Algonquians saw it, they deserved to have those goods that the French possessed but did not themselves immediately need.[40] This constitutional obligation was explained to the French court by New France's colonial officials in 1730: "You know, mon seigneur, that all the nations of Canada regard the governor as their father, which in consequence, following their ideas, he ought at all times to give them what they need to feed themselves, clothe themselves, and hunt."[41]

Following the Algonquians' ideas of a treaty relationship cost the French dearly throughout the Encounter era. "The presents that were doled out annually by the French," as Wilbur R. Jacobs, a preeminent historian of the Encounter era has remarked, "were a tremendous burden on the government—in times of peace as well as war."[42] But whereas *Onontio* was obligated to provide trade goods as a matter of constitutional principle to satisfy the needs of his Algonquian children, the Algonquians in turn were constitutionally obligated to provide for the unique needs of their French treaty partners. As good and satisfied children, they were expected to obey and aid the French in times of crisis and wars with their colonial rivals, the British and British-allied Indians. As the Sauk leader, Weasel, once told his people, the Indians must always show their gratitude to the French

> for all they were doing to help them. They came from a long way off and endured many difficulties and much misery to bring them the things they need. Not only that but they were good enough to take an interest in reconciling them with the people they warred against and but for that their villages would soon be reduced to nothing. And if they would think about all that, they would be at a loss as to how to show their gratitude to the French for all the trouble they take for them.[43]

As the French learned in their relations with the Indians of the *pays d'en haut,* violating their customary bonds with the Algonquians could seriously jeopardize their chances of survival on the North American Encounter era frontier. The tribes of the *pays d'en haut* did not hesitate to threaten to abandon the relationship if the French stopped acting like a benevolent father (i.e., if the French stopped fulfilling their needs). The Potawatomi chief Onanghese once railed at French colonial officials for trying to prohibit French traders from coming to the Indians' villages. The Algonquians, Onanghese let it be known, were not about to be told by the French that they now had to travel all the way to Montreal to obtain their *besoins,* which would violate one of the most important constitutional principles of their treaty relationship with the French. "Father," Onanghese explained,

> since we want powder, iron, and every other necessary which you were formally in the habit of sending us, what do you expect us to do? . . . Thus, having in our country none of the articles we require and which you, last year, promised we should be furnished with, and not want. . . . I promise you, if the French quit us; this Father, is the last time we shall come talk with you.[44]

For a substantial period of time during the Encounter era, the French and the Algonquians found themselves obligated to each other by virtue of a unique set of constitutional principles generated by their treaty relationship. Reflecting an American Indian vision of law and peace, these principles established bonds of multicultural unity that required different peoples to take care of each other's needs as a matter of customary practice.[45]

"We and You May All Be One"

Indians of the Encounter era employed a number of customary practices to reinforce their vision of treaties as constitutionalized connections.

These practices were intended to renew and strengthen the bonds of unity created by a treaty, bonds that made survival more assured on a multicultural frontier.

Many Encounter era Indian tribes, for example, used a customary vocabulary of evocative metaphors and gestures to describe their vision of the constitutional principles regulating their treaty relationships with Europeans. At a 1654 treaty conference with New Sweden's colonists, the Delaware Sachem chief Naaman stroked his arm with long sweeping gestures upon accepting the customary presents from the Swedes. According to the treaty minutes, the chief followed up this "sign of particular good friendship" by declaring to the colonists:

> [W]e should hereafter keep a very fast friendship, that if they had hitherto been as one body and one heart. . . . [T]herewith [he] struck himself on his breast, so should they hereafter be as one head with us, [and] at this [he] grasped about his head and twisted around with his hands, as though he wanted to tie a fast knot.[46]

Chief Naaman had not quite exhausted his Delaware vocabulary of treaty metaphors to describe his constitutional vision of the close bond of connection created by his people's treaty with the Swedes. To further reinforce his message, the Delaware Sachem drew on a simile, declaring that "just as a calabash is a round growth, without a fissure or cut, so should we hereafter also be like one head with us." Henceforth, Naaman stated, the two peoples would rely on each other for safety and protection; each would warn the other of dangers and threats, bringing the message even in "the dark midnight."[47]

Naaman was drawing on a constitutional vocabulary encountered frequently in the treaty literature featuring Delaware groups. The constitutional metaphor of "one body, one heart" was used by Sassoonan, head chief of the Schuylkill Delawares, at a treaty council in 1738. Describing the evolving nature of the treaty relationship that had been sustained over the years by his tribe with the English of Pennsylvania, Sassoonan explained that

> it was formerly said that the English and Indians should be as one body or one People half the one and half the other, but they were now to be alas one heart, not divided into halves but entirely the same without any distinction. That their hearts should be equally open on both sides to each other, clear without spot like the Sun in a fair day without a cloud from rising to setting.[48]

The customary practice of using the same set of terms to sustain a treaty relationship over time was widely diffused on the North American colonial frontier. The Muskogean-speaking Creek Indians, spread out over fifty villages in the present-day southeastern United States, elaborated their basic constitutional vision of a treaty through a customary language that spoke of two peoples connected by bonds of multicultural unity. At a 1734 council, for instance, a "king" from the Upper Creeks, after informing Georgia's colonial officials that his party had traveled a long way to Savannah, expressed the hope that a firm peace may be made so that "we and you may be all one."[49] Nearly a quarter century later, the Creek speaker, Stumpee, brought this same message of perpetual union to Savannah: "[T]hus we often tell our people, we deign them to hold you fast by the hands as the surest means to continue secure in their Present Happiness."[50] Eight years later, another Creek chief, needing to explain the constitutional principle that the unity of interests created by a treaty had to be cultivated over time, used the following illustrative metaphor: "In our Nation friendship is compared to a Grape Vine, which tho' Slender and Weak when Young, grows stronger as it grows Older."[51]

"That Justice Should Be Done to Every Person"

Throughout the treaty literature, Indian diplomats reiterated a variety of related metaphors and gestures to elaborate their vision of the constitutional principles governing their treaty relationships with Europeans. This customary practice of using the same set of terms to describe the bonds of connection created by a treaty relationship reflected a more general principle of American Indian multicultural constitutionalism. In American Indian visions of law and peace, treaty partners were under a constitutional obligation to continually renew the bonds that made their mutual survival more assured on the North American Encounter era frontier.

Two meetings held in Philadelphia more than twenty years apart between the Conestoga Indians and Pennsylvania colonial officials provide one of the most compelling illustrations in the treaty literature of how the language of Indian diplomacy could draw on a set of customary terms to renew the constitutionalized connections created by a treaty relationship. The first of these meetings occurred in 1712, more than a decade after the departure of William Penn, who had negotiated the initial treaty relationship between the Conestoga tribe and the Pennsylvania colony.[52] At this 1712 meeting, a group of Conestoga chiefs explained to those now in charge of the colony their understanding of the constitutional principles that had been incorporated into their original treaty agreement with Governor Penn:

> [T]he Proprietor, Govr. Penn had at his first Coming amongst them made an agreement with them that they should always Live as friends and Brothers, and be as one Body, one heart, one mind, and as one Eye and Ear; that what the one saw the other should see, and what the one heard the other should hear, and that there should be nothing but Love and friendship between them and us forever.[53]

After this speech the Indians presented a small bundle of furs, stating that they had always abided by this agreement "[a]nd should constantly observe it in all respects."[54]

In the second meeting, some two decades later in 1735, the Conestoga chiefs once again appeared before the Pennsylvania council, now headed by William Penn's son, Thomas, to renew their ancient treaty with the colony. Civility, a Conestoga speaker, made a speech that once again outlined his people's original understanding of their treaty with the senior Penn. In that first treaty, Civility explained, Governor Penn had agreed to purchase the Indians' lands before allowing any "white people" to possess them. But the sale of these lands, according to the legal meanings the Indians attached to their treaty relationship with Pennsylvania, was not intended to separate the two peoples. For the Indians, allowing the white people to possess their lands formed the basis of a continuing constitutional relationship of multicultural unity. As Civility explained to Pennsylvania's colonial officials, when the Indians gave their lands to Penn, they told him that "he and they should live on those Lands like Brethren, in Love and Friendship together, whereby they became all as one People and one Nation, joined together so strongly that nothing should ever disunite them, but that they should continue one People for ever."[55] Civility then restated the customary terms that had been used in the Conestogas' original treaty with the colony:

> [O]ne chief Article then agreed on between William Penn and the Indians was, that if any Mischief or Hurt should befall either, they should assist one another, and constantly have their Eyes open to watch for each other's Safety, and their Ears open that if any News were brought from any Country that might give uneasiness to either, they should carefully inform each other of what they heard.
>
> That it was further agreed between William Penn and the Indians, that each should bear a share in the other's Misfortunes. That this Country, though it Might be filled with People of different Nations, yet Care should be taken that Justice should be done to every Person, and no Mischief happen without Satisfaction being given when it was necessary.[56]

Civility finished his speech by laying down three bundles of skins "to bind their Words." He declared that "they were now come hither to see William Penn's Sons, to take them by the hand and renew with them the League of Friendship made with their Father."[57]

Constitutional Renewal

As illustrated by Civility's speech recalling the customary terms of his tribe's ancient treaty with William Penn, Indians of the Encounter era believed that treaty partners were obligated to renew the bonds of connection created by their relationship. Renewal, in fact, was regarded as a continuing constitutional obligation of treaty partners.

This constitutional obligation of renewal generated a number of customary practices that Indians of the Encounter era followed as a matter of principle in their treaty making with Europeans. Because the connections established by a treaty continually had to be kept strong, treaty partners, for example, were expected to meet regularly with each other in council. As one Indian speaker tried to explain to his English treaty partners: "[Y]ou may say that Love & Affection may be strong in absence as when present but we say not. . . . Nothing more revives and enlivens affection than frequent conferences."[58]

Indians, as well, customarily bound their future generations to a treaty relationship. As the Creek speaker Stumpee stated to Georgia's colonial officials at the 1757 Savannah conference:

> You have delcared to us that it is your earnest desire to live in the strictest union with us, we cannot but approve these good dispositions. We know that treaties have been made for this purpose by our Fathers and agreed to by many of our Old Men yet living. We are sensible that these treaties are binding not only upon those who signed them but upon our whole people and their posterity. Yet it would be well that they are renewed and confirmed in our days, that the yound men may be witnesses to them and transmit a knowledge of them to their children.[59]

The constitutional obligation of renewal also meant that treaty partners were expected to seek forgiveness for breaches or acts of bad faith toward a treaty partner. Because both parties were under the constitutional duty (a duty that was in their own self-interest to maintain) to renew the sacred bonds between their peoples, forgiveness was an expected customary practice between treaty partners. Sir William Johnson, the Crown's superintendent for Indian affairs, described to the Lords of Trade in a 1756 report that a Delaware chief had confessed to him that some of his people had been "deceived and deluded" by the French and their allied Indians "to join them in their late hostilities" against the English. The chief, Johnson reported, "expressed his sorrow and repentance for what had passed, and asked pardon with all the marks of a sincere contrition." In the most solemn manner, the chief then renewed the treaty of "peace, friendship, and alliance" with the English, promising "as a convincing proof of their returning to their duty and fidelity to his Majesty" that his people would return all of their English prisoners seized during the recent conflict.[60]

Treaty partners, because of the duty of renewal attached to their relationship, were likewise expected to grant forgiveness to each other. Taminy Buck, a Shawnee chief, at a 1748 treaty council with Pennsylvania officials, for example, invoked a constitutional tradition of renewal in asking for forgiveness for breaches of his tribe's treaty with the colony:

> We the *Shawonese* [Shawnee] sensible of our ungrateful returns for the many favors we have been all along receiving from our Brethren the *English*, ever since we first made the Chain of Friendship, came along the road with our eyes looking down to the earth, and have not taken them from thence till this morning, when you were pleased to chastise us, and then pardon us. We have been a foolish People, and acted wrong, tho' the sun shone bright, and shew's us very clearly what was our duty. We are sorry for what we have done, and promise better behavior for the future. We produce to you a certificate of the renewal of our friendship in the year 1739 by the Proprietor and Governor. Be pleased to sign it afresh, that it may appear to the world we are now admitted into your friendship, and all former crimes are buried, and entirely forgot.[61]

In Indian diplomacy, the customary bonds created by a treaty relationship were relied on, as a matter of constitutional practice, in times of need or crisis. This principle meant that the relationship of multicultural unity created between treaty partners should be continually reaffirmed and strengthened. The customary terms used to describe the connections maintained by a treaty, the frequent conferences, the binding of future generations, and the forgiveness of past transgressions were seen as acts of renewal between treaty partners. They sustained the sacred bonds that, as a matter of constitutional principle, could be relied on for survival in a hostile and chaos-filled world.

Stories of Linking Arms Together

As we have come to understand, Indian diplomats recognized that making connections with others was a most difficult process. Successful treaty making required the use of great acts of the imagination so that the two sides could come to see themselves as related in their needs and sufferings as fellow human beings. This is why, in Indian diplomacy, a treaty was told as a special kind of story, a way of imagining a world of human solidarity where we regard others as our relatives.[62]

This vision of treaties as stories generated a number of vital principles that Indians sought to apply in their treaty relationships with European-Americans during the Encounter era. In indigenous North American forest diplomacy, for example, treaty partners were obligated, as a matter of constitutional principle, to perpetuate the story of human solidarity sustained over time through their relationship. For Indians of the Encounter era, a treaty, told and retold as a story over time, was envisioned as part of a constitutional tradition of law and peace acheived between different peoples in a hostile and chaotic world.

One of the most famous Indian-white treaty relationships of the Encounter era, for instance, the Iroquois Covenant Chain, can be understood as the telling of one story in the perpetuation of an ancient constitutional tradition of human solidarity achieved by the Iroquois in immemorial time. Through this tradition, the Iroquois fulfilled the law-giver Deganwidah's sacred command issued at the founding of their ancient confederacy: to make the Tree of Peace prevail.[63]

The Iroquois have been prominent actors in many of the stories of North American forest diplomacy told throughout this book. This is because the Iroquois confederacy of tribes played a central role in so many of the major stories told during the seventeenth and eighteenth centuries.

Historians and chroniclers of the colonial period once routinely referred to the Iroquois as the Romans of the Western World.[64] They are still given a unique place in the history of the Encounter era by contemporary American ethnohistorians. "What antiquity was to European diplomacy," Dorothy V. Jones writes in *The Handbook of North American Indians*, "the Iroquois . . . were to the diplomacy that developed in colonial North America after the coming of the Europeans. Here was the fundamental source for imagery, both visual and verbal."[65]

Many tribes and tribal groups contributed to the diffuse system of treaty relations between Woodlands Indians groups and Europeans on the North American colonial frontier. No tribe, however, more profoundly influenced the substance and form of the Encounter era treaty-making tradition than the Iroquois. In the words of Elisabeth Tooker, a preeminent Iroquoianist:

> [O]ther individuals, both Indian and White, often found their fate rested on an Iroquois decision, and whole peoples also were to learn that their destinies were similarly determined. No nation was exempt. As both France and England knew, their contest for control of the North American continent ultimately would be decided by the choice the Iroquois made between them.[66]

The League of the Iroquois, originally comprising the Mohawks, Oneidas, Onondagas, Cayugas, and Senecas (the Tuscaroras entered as the sixth confederated tribe in the eighteenth century), was one of the largest tribal groups in eastern North America. The league nations possessed an ability to muster up to as many as 2,000 warriors during the colonial period, making their confederacy one of the most significant military powers on the continent.[67]

Geographically, the Iroquois controlled one of the most strategically vital regions in colonial North America. The league's traditional territories were situated in what is now upper New York State along the southern side of the St. Lawrence River and Lake Ontario. To their north and west on the opposite side of the St. Lawrence was French Canada; to their immediate south and east were Great Britain's Atlantic seaboard colonies. Their advantageous position on the major transmontane and riverine highways of the greater Appalachian frontier provided them easy access to the widely dispersed supplies of valuable beaver furs that dominated the North American colonial trade. Situated squarely between the competing imperial ambitions of France and England on the continent and rivaling both countries militarily by sheer force of numbers, the Iroquois tribes were valued and courted as allies by these two European colonial rivals throughout the Encounter era. Of all of the Indian tribes of North America, the Iroquois were listened to most seriously by these Europeans.

Numbers and location are not the entire story in explaining the Iroquois' preeminence of place in the treaty literature. Other tribes and tribal groups were capable of fielding decisive numbers of warriors in battle against a European army and its Indian proxies. Several Indian tribes were nearly equally well situated along the major trade routes of the colonial frontier. In fact, although the Iroquois excelled at the hit-and-run guerilla tactics of colonial era forest warfare, their confederacy was never organized to sustain an extended military campaign against an enemy very far from their home territory. The idea of an army of occupation was as alien to them as it was integral to the imperial administration of ancient Rome. In terms of actual territory seized and held over an extended period of time, the Iroquois were, in point of fact, no "Romans of the West."

The truth is that the plaintive appeal of an Iroquois speaker to the English to protect his people from "destruction" at the hands of an enemy tribe of the French represents one of the more frequently recurring events encountered in the treaty literature.[68] Although such appeals were at the very core of the diplomatic strategy and tactics of the Iroquois, the Iroquois nonetheless suffered debilitating losses throughout their centurylong Beaver Wars with the French and the allied tribes of Canada.

If numbers and location alone, therefore, cannot fully explain how the Iroquois earned their reputation as "Romans of the Western World," how do we account for the Iroquois' dominant influence on the intercultural diplomacy of the Encounter era? One place to start is with the ancient multicultural constitutional tradition the Iroquois sought to perpetuate on the frontiers of Encounter era North America.

The Tradition of the Great Peace

According to traditional accounts, the Lawgiver Deganawidah, as founder of the League of the Haudenosaunee (the Iroquois' own name for their confederacy), had bound together the five separate Iroquois tribes into one united group of peoples in ancient time.[69] In performing this unprecedented act of multitribal unity, Deganawidah offered the following words:

> We therefore bind ourselves together by taking hold of each other's hands firmly and forming a circle so strong that if a tree shall fall prostrate upon it, it could neither shake nor break it, and thus our people and our grandchildren shall remain in the circle in security, peace and happiness.[70]

As told by the Deganawidah epic, "by taking hold of each other's hands firmly," the Iroquois created a treaty alliance of perpetual solidarity, the law of the Great Peace spoken of in their constitutional tradition. As a matter of constitutional principle, each of the Five Nations could rely on the Great Peace established by this treaty relationship as a source of "security, peace and happiness" in a dangerous, hostile world.

For the Iroquois, the joining of hands described by the Deganawidah epic represented the inaugural act of a constitutional tradition of law and peace sustained by their treaty alliance. No wonder, then, that we witness Iroquois diplomats throughout the treaty literature attempting to extend this tradition in their relations with other peoples.[71] "What was agreed upon, it joins their arms," in fact, was the phrase used generally in Iroquois diplomatic discourse to confirm a treaty with different peoples.[72]

One of the most significant efforts by the Iroquois to perpetuate this constitutional tradition occurred at the Three Rivers Treaty Council of 1645, which we have studied closely at different points throughout this book.[73] There, Kiotseaeton, the great Iroquois diplomat/storyteller, sought to form an alliance with the French and their allied tribes by presenting a treaty belt that would, in his words, "bind the two sides very closely together."[74] In explaining the "words" of this wampum belt, described "as extraordinarily beautiful" by Father Vimont, Kiotseaeton

> took hold of a Frenchman, placed his arm within his, and with his other arm he clasped that of an Algonquin. Having thus joined himself to them, "Here," he said, "is the knot that binds us. . . . Even if the lighting were to fall upon us, it could not separate us, for, if it cuts off the arm that holds you to us, we will at once seize each other by the other arm."[75]

Having linked arms with the French and their allied Algonquian tribes, Kiotseaeton further dramatized the belt's message of peace and solidarity, "and thereupon he turned around, and caught the Frenchman and the Algonquian by their two other arms—holding them so closely that he seemed unwilling ever to leave them."[76]

Kiotseaeton's linking arms together with the French and the Algonquian Indians was an imaginative way of retelling the same basic story of Deganawidah's founding act of Iroquois multitribal unity. By joining the Iroquois with the French and their allied tribes of Canada, Kiotseaeton perpetuated an ancient constitutional traditional of human solidarity achieved between different peoples on the multicultural frontiers of the Encounter era.

The Covenant Chain

Understood from this traditional perspective, the Iroquois Covenant Chain, the most famous multicultural treaty system of the Encounter era, was simply the retelling of the Deganawidah epic by Iroquois diplomats through the medium of the league's unique treaty relationship with the English colonies of North America. The Covenant Chain was the name given to the complex system of treaties and agreements regulating trade and military obligations between the Five Nations, a varying number of lesser tributary tribes of the Atlantic Coast region, and several of the mid-Atlantic English seaboard colonies. Under the "silver chain of friendship" maintained by this multiple alliance system, the Iroquois managed the Indian side of the Chain, while New York was the lead colony on the English side of the Chain. The New England colonies, Pennsylvania, Maryland, and Virginia, however, also had to contend with the Iroquois through the Chain.[77]

English colonial officials universally regarded the Iroquois Covenant Chain as the single most important indigenous political, military, and economic institution on the continent. Through it, as the English clearly recognized, the Five Nations of the Iroquois confederacy maintained an effective capability of tipping the balance of power in North America. Only the Iroquois "empire" stood between England's weakly defended colonies on the Atlantic seaboard and France's desires to assert its hegemony over the North American continent. The Board of Trade and Plantations in a report to the House of Commons in 1702 recognized England's strategic interests in "preserving the friendship of the Five Nations of Indians, which are a barrier between his Majesty's Plantations and [the French] in Canada, by treating them kindly, and showing them a force constantly maintained in New York, ready to protect them upon all occasions."[78] The Iroquois, of course, would not have disagreed with this characterization of the Chain. According to their American Indian vision of law and peace, the Covenant Chain told an important story of how two different peoples had established a valuable treaty relationship that both could rely on to protect their interests in survival in a multicultural North America.

The Chain as a Story of Multicultural Law and Peace

For the Iroquois, the Chain, as a treaty, told a special kind of story, a way of imagining a world of human solidarity achieved through treaty making with different peoples. The Chain figures prominently for the first time in the treaty literature at a conference held in 1677 at the conclusion of King Philip's War (in which King Philip, or Metacom, led New England's Indian tribes against Massachusetts and Connecticut to prevent further territorial encroachments onto tribal lands). The treaty conference was sponsored by New York's colonial governor, Edmund Andros, who had intervened in New England's Indian war by arming the Mohawks of the Iroquois Confederacy "to strike a decisive blow against King Philip and his allies."[79] The conference was held at the insistence of New England's Puritan colonies so that they could "deal with the tribes themselves, face to face (under Andros's chaperonage), and . . . each of the parties would be responsible for its own obligations."[80] As Jennings notes, "Such proceedings fitted well into Puritan notions of covenanting";[81] the same, of course, could be said of the Indians. It was probably at this conference that the Iroquois first entered into the formal Covenant Chain alliance linking the Five Nations to the English.[82]

The Chain, told as a story of law and peace achieved between the Iroquois and English over time through their treaty relationship, appears throughout the treaty literature of the next century. In a 1689 speech before New York colonial officials, the Mohawk Sachem chief Tahaiadoris told the story of the Chain's evolution and demarcated its geographic sweep in colonial North America as follows:

> Brethren: You are come here to this prefixed place [Albany] which is by the Christians appointed to be the house of Treaty for all public business with us the Five Nations, and do Return you many thanks for your Renovation of the Covenant chain which is not of iron now as it was formerly, but of Pure Silver, in which Chain are included all their Majesty's Subjects from the Sinnekes [Senecas'] Country quite to the Eastward as far as any Christian Subjects of our great king lives and from thence Southward all along New England quite to Virginia.[83]

At the Treaty of Lancaster in 1744, the Iroquois speaker Canasatego told his lengthy story of the Chain's origins. He began his story with the arrival "One Hundred Years Ago" of the Dutch, who brought valuable trade goods to the Iroquois: "Awls, Knives, Hatchets, Guns, and many other Particulars."

> We saw what sort of People they were, we were so well pleased with them, that we tied their Ship to the Bushes on the Shore; and afterwards, liking them still better the longer they staid with us, and thinking the Bushes to slender, we removed the Rope, and tied it to the Trees; and as the Trees were liable to be blown down by high Winds, or to decay of themselves, we, from the Affection we bore them, again removed the Rope, and tied it to a strong and big Rock (*here the Interpreter said, They mean the* Oneida *Country*) and not content with this, for its further Security we removed the Rope to the Big Mountain (*here the Interpreter says they mean the* Onandago *Country*) and there we tied it very fast, and rolled Wampum about it; to make it still more secure, we stood upon the Wampum, and sat down upon it, to defend it, and to prevent any Hurt coming to it, and did our best Endeavors that it might remain uninjured for ever. During all this Time the New-comers, the *Dutch*, acknowledged our Right to the Lands, and solicited us, from Time to Time, to grant them Parts of our Country,, and to enter into League and Covenant with us, and to become one People with us.[84]

Canasatego next related what had happened to this covenant after the English "came into the country" in the 1660s and supplanted Dutch rule. The English "became one People with the Dutch," and the English governor, upon learning of the "great friendship" that existed between the Iroquois and the Dutch, "desired to make as strong a League, and to be upon as good terms with [them] as the Dutch were." Thus, the English agreed to enter into the covenant that the Dutch had originally made with the Iroquois "and to become one People" with the Indians.

Canasatego then told the story of how New York's governor strengthened the multicultural alliance between the colony and the Iroquois by linking the two peoples by a "Silver Chain":

> And by his further Care in looking into what had passed between us, he found that the Rope which tied the Ship to the great Mountain was only fastened with Wampum, which was liable to break and rot, and to perish in a Course of Years; he therefore told us, he would give us a Silver Chain, which would be much stronger, and would last for ever. This we accepted, and fastened the Ship with it, and it has lasted ever since.[85]

For the Iroquois, the story of the Covenant Chain extended back in time to the period of their first encounters and ensuing treaty relationships with the strange and alien European newcomers to their lands. As a matter of constitutional principle, both the Iroquois and the English were obligated to sustain this story of multicultural unity that had proven to be of such great value to both parties in their struggles for survival in North America. This, of course, accorded precisely with Iroquois constitutional tradition, for as the story of the founding of their own ancient confederacy had told, human solidarity can only be achieved if different peoples imagine the possibilities of linking arms together.

A Tradition of Tellings

The idea that stories are essential to sustaining a tradition is central to American Indian tribal life. Leslie Marmon Silko, the contemporary Laguna Pueblo writer, dedicates her appropriately titled autobiography, *Storyteller*, "to the storytellers as far back as memory goes and to the telling which continues and through which they all live and we with them."[86] The storyteller, Silko's work tells us, is situated in a tradition of tellings. Our very act of speech is the product of these many tellings. We are literally constituted as individuals and as groups by our stories and the traditions these stories sustain. By them, we are made whole.[87]

The power of stories to sustain the traditions that bind a society together was widely recognized in Encounter era Indian diplomacy.[88] For the Iroquois, the Covenant Chain was simply the telling of one story in the perpetuation of an ancient tradition of multicultural unity achieved by the Iroquois at the founding of their league. In their American Indian vision of law and peace, the Iroquois saw themselves as constitutionally obligated by Deganawidah's divine command to bring all nations under the spreading branches of the Great Tree of Peace and to establish the law of the Great Peace.[89]

Throughout the Covenant Chain treaty literature, Iroquois diplomats draw on the constitutional tradition inaugurated by Deganawidah's founding of their league for the basic vocabulary of their treaty relationship with the English. "[T]he Covenant that is betwixt the Governor General and us is inviolable," a group of Iroquois declared a few months after the Albany agreement establishing the Chain. Then, invoking the imagery of Deganawidah's founding act, the Iroquois described their treaty relationship with New York as being "so strong that if the very thunder should break upon the Covenant Chain, it would not break it asunder."[90]

Two years later, at Albany, a group of Mohawk chiefs told New York's governor Edmond Andros that "they belong to his government and desire the Covenant chain may be strong and binding."[91] The Iroquois then reenacted Deganawidah's command at the founding of their own confederacy by taking hold of the governor's arm and declaring their desire that "their arms may remain fast together and that there may be no misunderstanding."[92]

In 1775, an Oneida speaker explained the bonds created by the chain of friendship between the Iroquois and the English by reference to the founding epic of the confederacy: "[W]hen our ancestors first met, they agreed that they should take each other by the hand, and that no storms, not even thunder, should be able to break their union."[93]

The Deganawidah epic provided more than just a well-rehearsed vocabulary of metaphors, rhetorical devices, and symbolic gestures for the Iroquois' treaty relationship with the English. The constitutional tradition of multicultural treaty making established by the Deganawidah story generated the structuring principles of the Covenant Chain alliance as well. Jennings describes the original 1677 treaty in Albany between the Iroquois and New York as establishing "a constitutional basis (in the English sense)" for the Covenant Chain.[94] That basis derived directly from the principles of multicultural unity accepted by the Iroquois at the founding of their own league. At a 1691 meeting in Albany, an Iroquois speaker reprised Deganawidah's message of unity to the league to define the reciprocal treaty obligations comprehended by the Covenant Chain with the English as follows:

> We have been informed by our Forefathers that in former times a Ship arrived here in this Country which was matter of great admiration to us, especially our desire was to know what was within her Belly. In that Ship were Christians . . . with whom we made a Covenant of Friendship, which covenant has since been tied together with a chain and always ever since kept inviolable by the Brethren and us, in which Covenant it was agreed that whoever should hurt or prejudice the one should be guilty of injuring all, all of us being comprehended in one common league.[95]

The ancient constitutional tradition of a treaty as linking two peoples together was drawn on by another Iroquois speaker, Sadeganaktie, at Albany in 1694 to describe the unifying principles governing the Covenant Chain. He emphasized the importance of "keeping the Chain firm and inviolable and all that are linked therein." According to his ancient Iroquois vision of the constitutional principles governing a treaty relationship, "The least Member cannot be touched, but the whole Body must feel and be sensible; if therefore an Enemy hurt the least part of the Covenant Chain, we will join to destroy that Enemy, for we are one Head, one Flesh, and one Blood."[96]

One of the most memorable retellings of the sodalital obligations derived from Iroquois constitutional tradition occurs relatively late during the Encounter era, at a 1796 treaty council in New York. At this council, the Iroquois sought to renew the chain of friendship that had been sustained since ancient times with the New Yorkers.[97] Now, however, the New Yorkers were a part of the United States, not England. The "brothers" of the United States seemed ignorant of the principles that had traditionally governed the Iroquois Covenant Chain alliances with the New Yorkers. These principles derived directly from the Deganawidah epic. "Brothers," a Mohawk speaker lamented, "[i]t seems that, before a nation can get justice of another, they must first go to war, and spill one another's blood; but brothers, we do not like this mode of settling differences; we wish justice to be done without."[98] Declaring his peoples' "earnest wish to live in friendship and unity" with the United States—"a just people" who would never wrong the Indians of lands that "justly" belonged to them—the Mohawk speaker patiently elaborated his American Indian vision of human solidarity achieved between the different peoples of North America:

> [L]et justice take place betwixt you and us, and in place of arbitrary power: for that brothers, you very well know, is a thing that never gave contentment to any people or nation whatsoever.
>
> Brothers: Formerly we enjoyed the privilege we expect now is called freedom and liberty; but since our acquaintance with our brother white people, that which we call freedom and liberty, becomes an entire stranger to us. . . .
>
> Brothers: We pray you to take this matter into good consideration, and do by us as you would wish to be done by Brothers, this is what we wish for; that every brother might have their rights throughout the continent, and all to be of one mind, and to live together in peace and love, as becometh brothers; and to have a chain of friendship made between you and us, too strong ever to be broke, and polished and brightened so pure as never to rust. This is our sincere wishes.[99]

For the Iroquois, the story of the Covenant Chain sustained a constitutional tradition of human solidarity between different peoples inaugurated by Deganawidah's founding of the league in ancient time. Important structuring principles were generated by this tradition. The strong sense of solidarity and connection achieved over time by a successful treaty enabled the two sides to rely on their friendship as a source of "security, peace, and happiness" in a hostile and dangerous world. According to ancient Iroquois constitutional tradition, by linking arms together, different peoples can imagine a world of human solidarity in which "no storms, not even thunder, should be able to break their union."[100]

The Covenant Chain as Multicultural Constitution

Numerous factors explain the Iroquois' dominant influence on the intercultural diplomacy of the Encounter era. Certainly not least among them, however, is the Iroquois' unique vision of a treaty as a way of sustaining their own ancient constitutional tradition of different peoples achieving solidarity by linking arms together.

The Covenant Chain functioned as a multicultural constitution in North America from 1677 until the middle of the eighteenth century. The scope of the Chain's influence within British America during this time was extensive. No tribe or tribal group appears more frequently or with such prominence as the Iroquois in the treaty literature of the colonial period. The multiracial and multicultural relationships established under the Iroquois Covenant Chain influenced events throughout most of the territory of England's mid-Atlantic colonies. The Chain also protruded into the relations between tribes and colonies in New England. Virginia's dealings with the southern tribes frequently were complicated by the Covenant Chain and Iroquois power maintained under it. Throughout the Encounter era, other colonies, particularly Pennsylvania, connived to supplant New York as the leading colony on the English side of the Chain. Iroquois influence through the Chain, either direct or indirect, was palpable throughout virtually the entire eastern North American diplomatic system.

From both the English and the Iroquois perspective, the Covenant Chain adequately fulfilled its intended function of perpetuating a highly valued treaty relationship of trade and collective security.[101] Because of its function in reconciling the interests of so many different groups of peoples for such a relatively long period of time on the colonial frontier, the Covenant Chain represents a unique story of accommodation and cooperation between peoples "of different ethnicity, different cultures, and different social and political structures."[102] The Chain operated as a multicultural constitution on the Encounter era frontier through principles that transcended notions of tribe, state, and empire. According to this American Indian treaty vision of law and peace, human solidarity is achieved by a constitutional tradition of imagining the possibilities of different peoples linking arms together.

American Indian Multicultural Constitutionalism

We can briefly summarize some of the important lessons we have come to better understand by looking at several of the different ways Indians of the Encounter era envisioned treaties as constitutions. According to American Indian multicultural constitutionalism, different peoples in a relationship of close connection were expected to embrace the sacredly revealed truth of their shared humanity as a basis of normative action toward each other. As a matter of constitutional principle, they could rely on the customary bonds of multicultural unity created by their treaty relationship in times of crisis or need. They imagined themselves as obligated to sustain a constitutional tradition of human solidarity with each other. These values, customs, and traditions reflected a basic paradigm of American Indian visions of law and peace: as human beings in a world of diversity and conflict, we are under an obligation to link arms together.

Conclusion

Understanding American Indian Treaty Visions of Law and Peace

Treaties as Relationships of Trust

This book has explored a few of the ways Indians of the Encounter era spoke about treaty relationships. Only the broadest of themes—those easiest to identify and pursue at the outset of such an immense interpretive project—have been developed here. Many other pathways are to be discovered for understanding the complex language of Indian forest diplomacy. Variations and the distinctive vocabularies of large numbers of tribes remain to be examined in all of their rich, diverse particularity. Discontinuities and adaptations over time to the absorptive dynamics of the West's "will to empire" need to be explained in serious and detailed scholarly analyses. What has been essentialized must now be dissolved by scrutinizing the singular responses of different tribes to the centrifugal forces of colonizing power. Innumerable counterstories and countermythologies can be brought into existence through retellings of the history of American Indian visions of law and peace.[1]

Yet even the cursory readings of a few themes from the Encounter era treaty literature set out in this book can teach us several important lessons about American Indian visions for achieving law and peace in a multicultural world. As we now have come to better understand, the language of Encounter era Indian diplomacy sought to make it possible for different peoples to embrace the good news of peace that all of us are connected as one. It did this through a variety of stories, metaphors, and other narrative devices that sought to imagine a world of human solidarity. By using this language, Indians believed it possible to perpetuate a tradition of law and peace between the different peoples of North America. For Indians, this language defined the paradigms for behavior in a multicultural world.

Indians of the seventeenth and eighteenth centuries, it should be noted, were not primitive idealists, at least when it came to understanding human nature. They did not presume that potential treaty partners were ordinarily predisposed to embrace their vision of a treaty relationship and act as relatives toward stranger groups. They recognized that the paradigms defined by their language of diplomacy could only be accepted by treaty partners who had learned to rely on each other in a chaotic and hostile world.[2] One of the most important things to understand about the language of Encounter era forest diplomacy, therefore, is that it reflected the deeply held Indian belief that a successful treaty relationship, first and foremost, is built on a foundation of trust.

This is one reason why, throughout the treaty literature, Indians insist on acts of commitment from their treaty partners—signs that human beings, in a world of diversity and conflict, can learn to trust each other. Smoking the pipe of peace, taking hold of a treaty partner by the hand, exchanging hostages, and presenting valuable gifts were just some of the ways human beings could demonstrate their steadfast commitment to upholding their treaty relationships. Indians believed strongly that through such "confident example-setting" (to borrow from the contemporary philosopher Annette C. Baier) justice is initiated between groups and "made settled by the fact that the first or early performers' example is followed, their confidence confirmed, general expectation of further conformity strengthened and so a general custom launched."[3] In the language of Indian diplomacy, by linking arms together in the circle of "security, peace, and happiness,"[4] different peoples embrace each other in a relationship of trust.

I conclude this book with the theme of trust in American Indian forest diplomacy, not only because of its centrality in the Encounter era treaty literature but also because creating relationships of trust and reliance has been a central story line in the work of a number of contemporary North American theorists on justice in our society. Feminist philosophers and theorists like Annette Baier[5] and Martha Minow,[6] liberal philosophers like Richard Rorty,[7] critical legal studies theorists like Roberto Unger[8] and Joseph Singer,[9] and other progressive thinkers and writers of our century[10] have increasingly called our attention to the importance of trust in creating healthy social relationships. Thus, understanding some of the ways that Indians of the Encounter, through their "confident example-setting," sought to create relationships of trust with their treaty partners can teach us important lessons about how we might achieve law and peace between different groups of peoples in a multicultural world.

The Common Bowl

"Confident example-setting" by Indians is one of the thematic constants of the Encounter era treaty literature. Numerous devices were available to treaty partners to demonstrate their commitment to the treaty as a relationship of trust and reliance. Take, for example, the metaphor of treaty partners eating out of a "common bowl." In the language of Indian forest diplomacy, this compelling image was used to signify an agreement between different groups in a treaty relationship to share their hunting lands. Each could hunt for game in the other's territories. Each had a coequal and reciprocal right to freely trade and share in the resources of the great commons formed by their treaty agreement.

By conjoining their lands into a common bowl, treaty partners eliminated one of the most frequent causes of conflict and distrust between the tribal peoples of indigenous North America: competition for hunting grounds and resources.[11] But in agreeing to this act of commitment, they did much more: They obligated themselves to act as relatives toward each other in times of crisis or need. Each could be trusted and relied on steadfastly by the other.[12] The metaphor of the common bowl helped to launch, in Baier's phrasing, "a general custom"[13] of different peoples acting to mutualize and converge their interests, thereby creating a set of conditions that Indian forest diplomacy regarded as essential to a successful multicultural treaty relationship.

"The Interest of Any One Nation Should Be Interests of Us All"

The centrality of trust as an organizing theme in the language of Indian diplomacy is demonstrated by the wide diffusion of the common bowl metaphor across the Encounter era frontier. The Algonquian alliance in Canada used the metaphor as part of its language of intertribal diplomacy to represent peace, solidarity, and friendship.[14] The Iroquois located the metaphor as a central part of the Deganawidah epic, the founding narrative of their ancient tribal confederacy.[15] After agreeing to join hands together in the circle of "security, peace and happiness" according to the command of Deganawidah,[16] the Iroquois decided to embrace the lawgiver's instruction that the separate tribes of the confederacy share their resources together as one people. "We have still one matter left to be considered," said Deganawidah, "and that is with reference to the hunting grounds of our people from which they derive their living." The fifty sachems of the league resolved to open their individual tribes' hunting grounds as a commons benefiting all the different nations of the confederacy.[17] In agreeing to perform this act of commitment, they declared:

> We shall now do this: We shall only have one dish (or bowl) in which will be placed one beaver's tail and we shall all have coequal right to it, and there shall be no knife in it, for if there be a knife in it, there would be danger that it might cut someone and blood would thereby be shed.[18]

For the Iroquois, the metaphor of the common bowl stood for the constitutional principle that different peoples in a treaty relationship mutualize and converge their interests, thereby eliminating the sources of distrust between them.[19] Joseph Brant, the famous Mohawk Iroquois diplomat of the Revolutionary period, drew on this fundamental principle of Iroquois multicultural constitutionalism in his efforts to construct a pan-Indian alliance between the Iroquois and Algonquian peoples. Following the Revolutionary War, these ancient tribal enemies came to recognize the need for intertribal unity in dealing with the United States, the formidable new nation of white men claiming a superior sovereignty over the Indians' lands. Brant urged a treaty relationship between all of the surviving Indian tribes of eastern North America who would join their lands together into a great commons. Brant narrated that a century ago, "a Moon of Wampum was placed in this country with four roads leading to the center for the convenience of the Indians from different quarters to come and settle or hunt here. A dish with one spoon was likewise put here with the Moon of Wampum."[20]

In 1786, at the Huron village of Brownstown, Iroquois diplomats explained what was expected of the tribes that had entered into this relationship of trust represented by the "dish with one spoon":

> If we make a war with any Nation, let it result from the Great Council fire, if we make peace, let it also proceed from our unanimous Councils. But whilst we remain disunited, every inconvenience attends us. The Interest of any one Nation should be Interests of us all, the welfare of one should be the welfare of all others.[21]

The far-ranging power of the common bowl metaphor in Indian forest diplomacy is illustrated by the fact that the Sioux, on the westernmost fringes of the Encounter era frontier, used it as part of their treaty language. In 1805, a Sauk chief visited British army headquarters at Amherstberg, Canada, to report that the Sioux had presented them with a war pipe, along with a talk about a common dish and spoon. Through these signs, the Sioux were proposing to the Sauks that the two groups hold their territories in common and fight against the United States, the "White Devil with his mouth wide open ready to take possession of our lands by any means."[22]

Even as the Encounter era was drawing to a close in eastern North America, the principle represented by the common bowl metaphor continued to play an energizing role in sustaining major tribal alliances in the region. The great Shawnee patriot chief Tecumseh organized his early nineteenth-century challenge to European-American colonial hegemony on the continent around the theme of common Indian ownership of land.[23] "The white usurpation in our common country must be stopped, or we, its rightful owners, be forever destroyed and wiped out as a race of people," he pleaded to a gathering of southern tribes in 1811. "Let us form one body, one heart, and defend to the last warrior our country, our homes, our liberty, and the graves of our fathers."[24]

Significantly, Indians of the Encounter era did not restrict application of the principle represented by the metaphor of the common bowl solely to treaty relationships with other Indian tribes. The Indian vision of the different peoples of North America learning to trust each other by agreeing to mutualize and converge their interests is a compelling force at a number of important points in the history of Indian-white treaty relations during the Encounter era. The principle was propounded, for instance, by the great diplomat/storyteller Kiotseaeton at the Three Rivers Treaty Council in 1645.[25] At that meeting, the French and their allied Canadian tribes were invited by Kiotseaeton to link arms together with the Iroquois in a great multicultural treaty alliance.[26] As part of the agreement creating this proposed union, the Iroquois would open their hunting grounds to their new treaty partners; the two sides would eat out of a common bowl. "Our country is well stocked with fish, with venison, and with game, it is everywhere full of deer, of elk, and beaver," Kiotseaeton declared: "come and get good meat with us." There was no longer any reason for distrust between the two sides: "The road is cleared; there is no longer any danger."[27]

More than a century later, in 1763, the metaphor appears as part of the treaty language of the Georgia Creeks in negotiations with John Stuart, the English colonial Indian superintendent. With the French and Indian War recently concluded in favor of the victorious English, Stuart hoped to ensure future good relations with all of the southern tribes. He must have been pleased, therefore, to hear a group of Lower Creek headmen announce their intent "to keep peace with the white people their Friends as long as the Water Runs, that their Children may come to Perfection. . . . [W]e still eat with one spoon, and feed upon one victuals as Friends. I still hold you by the hand as friends not intending to let it slip."[28]

The metaphor of the common bowl was used even by the Indians of the upper Ohio Valley to envision a relationship of trust with the United States in the tumultuous decade following the end of the Revolutionary War. The Western Indians' crushing 1791 defeat of Arthur St. Clair, governor of the Northwest Territory, had required the United States to reassess its aggressive land policies against the tribes of the region. In 1792 and 1793, President George Washington and Secretary of War Henry Knox sent a series of peace missions to the Western Indians, seeking to avoid further warfare and protect white frontier settlements from attack.[29] On several of these missions, emissaries from the Iroquois confederacy in New York were asked to speak on behalf of the United States. The Iroquois had come to terms of peace with the United States and had received guarantees that they could retain the territory in which they lived. Their task was to convince the Western Indians to pursue the same peaceful course with the white man. At a council at Buffalo Creek in 1792, a speaker from the Shawnee Nation responded to the message of peace from the United States delivered by the Iroquois by invoking the common bowl metaphor: "You have given us a dish and one spoon, desiring the whole combination [of peoples] to eat with them; we accept of them, and shall do accordingly."[30]

In envisioning the possibility of European-Americans sharing from a common bowl with Indian peoples, these Indian diplomats were drawing from a rich narrative tradition in indigenous North America. In American Indian visions of law and peace, the different peoples who embraced the metaphor of the common bowl as a structuring principle of their treaty relationship agreed to mutualize and converge their interests. They were united by the strength of their commitment to sustaining a strong relationship of trust and reliance between the different peoples of North America. In the language of Indian diplomacy, by agreeing to eat out of a common bowl, "the interest of One Nation should be interests of us all, the welfare of one should be the welfare of all others."

"We Shall Treat One Another as Brethren to the Latest Generation"

The metaphor of the common bowl was one of many devices Indians used to express their vision of a treaty as a relationship of trust. By harmonizing their interests with European-Americans, Indians believed it was possible to sustain a new kind of society on the emerging multicultural frontiers of Encounter era North America, a society in which "confident example-setting" created conditions of trust and reliance, making possible the achievement of justice between different groups of peoples.

We have already seen, for instance, that the Conestoga Indians granted some of their lands as a means of cementing a treaty relationship of trust and reliance with William Penn and the Pennsylvania colony.[31] As Conestoga chief Civility explained to Pennsylvania's colonial officials in 1735, when his people gave their lands to Governor Penn long ago, they told him that "he and they should live on those lands like Brethren, in Love and Friendship together . . . whereby they became all as one People and one Nation, joined together so strongly that nothing should ever disunite them, but that they should continue one People for ever."[32]

Throughout the treaty literature, Indians attempt to converge their interests with European-Americans through this "confident example-setting" device of granting land settlement rights to the strange newcomers to their world. Hendrick, the Iroquois diplomat, for example, expected unqualified acceptance of the principle that a treaty created a relationship of trust in offering a large grant of land to the English at the Albany Congress of 1754:

> What We are now going to say is a Matter of great moment, which we desire you to remember as long as the Sun and Moon lasts. We are willing to sell you this large tract of land for your people to live upon, but We desire this may be considered as Part of our Agreement, that when we are all dead and gone, your Grandchildren may not say to our Children, that your Forefathers sold the land to our Forefathers, and therefore be gone off them. This is wrong. Let us all be Brethren as well after as before of giving you deeds for land. After we have sold our land, we in a little time have nothing to shew from it, but it is not so with you, your Grandchildren will get something from it as long as the world stands, our Grandchildren will have no advantage from it. They will say we were fools for selling so much land for so small matter, and curse us; therefore let it be a part of the present agreement that we shall treat one another as Brethren to the latest generation, even after we shall not have left a foot of land.[33]

This distinctive vision of a treaty granting land settlement rights as a way for American Indians to harmonize their interests and create a relationship of trust with a stranger group was rejected as alien by European-Americans of the Encounter era. As the distinguished historian Reginald Horseman has explained, European-Americans saw these treaties with Indian tribes as an expedient means of securing something white Americans desperately needed and desired—Indian lands—"with the least conflict and expense."[34]

For most white Americans, treaties with Indians were not valued for the enduring connections of trust they established and maintained between communities at a distance on a multicultural frontier. Most whites had no steadfast desire to link arms together or eat out of the same bowl with the indigenous tribal peoples of North America. Indians were simply seen as obstacles to the survival and ultimate flourishing of the superior society white Americans assumed they were destined to create in America. Indians, in the national mythology of white conquest, became groups of *other*, different, and inferior types of human beings competing for the vast lands and rich resources of the continent.[35]

This very different way European-Americans had of envisioning their treaty relationships with tribes, as our American history books tell us, gained precedence in North America during the century-long period of frontier Indian wars and conquests following the Encounter era. In the language of conquest used by European-Americans, Indian grants of land settlement rights to whites represented a way to divide these two very different peoples seen as having radically divergent interests in the resources of the continent. Treaties were a means to acquire by cheaper, peaceful methods what European-Americans thought they had a natural right to acquire from "savage" Indian tribes, even by force if ultimately necessary—Indian-held lands. As summarized by Horseman, because of these attitudes of cultural superiority, the treaties European-Americans made with Indian tribes, quite simply, "were made to be broken."[36]

Thus, the white man failed to learn one of the essential lessons taught by American Indian visions of law and peace. A vital term of many of the very treaties that made it possible for Europeans to settle the land in North America, this lesson teaches us that different peoples achieve justice between each other by agreeing to build relationships of trust and reliance. In the language of Indian diplomacy, they imagine the possibility of sharing from a common bowl.

Reasons for Developing a Better Understanding of American Indian Visions of Law and Peace

The theme of trust in the language of Encounter era Indian diplomacy teaches us many important lessons about American Indian visions of law and peace. For Indians of the Encounter era, relationships of trust with different peoples were essential to survival and flourishing in a multicultural world. The language of Indian forest diplomacy reflected this basic understanding in a richly evocative vocabulary describing the paradigms for behavior that Indians believed nurtured trust and reliance in a treaty relationship. In Indian diplomacy, such acts of "confident example-setting" as granting land settlement rights to stranger groups, agreeing to eat out of a common bowl, linking arms together, clearing the path of peace, and sharing each other's sacred stories and rituals signified the commitment of treaty partners to behave as relatives toward each other. These acts, according to American Indian treaty visions of law and peace, initiated the process by which different groups learned to build justice in a multicultural world.

We thus come full circle. In the Introduction to this book, I claimed that our understandings of the role of American Indian visions of law and peace in the Encounter era treaty literature are incomplete and inaccurate and that by reviving and reconstructing these visions we begin the process of elaborating a new theoretical framework for interpreting Indian rights. More important, I claimed that these ancient Indian visions can speak to difficult challenges we confront in achieving justice in our own multicultural world.[37] In concluding this book, I would like to show how the theme of trust in the language of Encounter era Indian diplomacy can be used to support these ambitious claims for American Indian visions of law and peace.

The White Man's Indian Law

As I wrote in the Introduction, the white man's Indian law has dominated our past historical understandings of Indian tribalism's rights to survival in our society.[38] The story of the white man's Indian law teaches us that the legal rules and principles that have sustained the degree of "measured separatism"[39] belonging to Indian peoples as a right under U.S. law are the exclusive by-products of the Western legal tradition brought to North America from the Old World. The Indian vision of a treaty as a relationship of trust, however, can be used to show that Indian legal ideas and values also have been instrumental in protecting and promoting indigenous American tribalism's cultural survival over time in our history.

The Indian vision of a treaty as a relationship of trust is reflected, for example, in the landmark Indian rights decisions of the early nineteenth-century U.S. Supreme Court. In the *Cherokee Cases,*[40] Chief Justice John Marshall set out what modern federal Indian law recognizes as a central pillar of Indian tribalism's core right to a degree of "measured separatism" in U.S. society, the trust doctrine.[41]

In the first of these seminal cases, *Cherokee Nation v. Georgia,*[42] Marshall wrote that "the relation of the Indians to the United States is marked by peculiar and cardinal distinctions which exist nowhere else."[43] The guiding principles of our Indian law, the chief justice explained, derived from the fact that the Indians recognize a relationship of trust arising out of their treaties with the United States: "[T]hey [the Indians] look to our government for protection; rely upon its kindness and its power; appeal to it for relief to their wants; and address the president as their great father."[44]

The next year in the second of the *Cherokee Cases, Worcester v. Georgia,*[45] Marshall elaborated further on the United States' unique trust responsibilities arising out of its treaties with the Indian tribes of America. Specifically analyzing the late Encounter era treaties between the United States and the Cherokee Nation (Treaty of Hopewell, 1785; Treaty of Holston, 1791), Marshall held that the status of the Indians under these agreements "was that of a nation claiming and receiving the protection of one more powerful; not that of individuals abandoning their national character and submitting as subjects to the laws of a master."[46]

The United States, therefore, under Marshall's legal analysis, had a duty to protect Cherokee rights. This duty arose under the express and implied terms of the treaty relationship between the tribes and the United States. These terms, of course, were terms of trust. As we have come to understand, these terms were derived from Indian understandings of their treaty rights with the United States.[47]

The *Cherokee Cases* represent the first formal recognition by the U.S.

Supreme Court of the trust doctrine as a source of protection for Indian rights under our law.[48] Under this doctrine, the United States "has charged itself with moral obligations of the highest responsibility and trust. Its conduct, as disclosed in the acts of those who represent it in dealings with the Indians, should be judged by the most exacting fiduciary standards."[49] Confirmed by numerous subsequent court decisions, congressional statutes, and executive action, the trust doctrine has served, at important times in our history, as a positive, purposive force in protecting and promoting Indian tribalism's rights to cultural survival in U.S. society.

The theme of trust in the language of Indian diplomacy shows us that the white man's Indian law was not the sole source of legal principles that spoke to the importance of protecting Indian tribalism's right to a "measured separatism" under U.S. law. By recognizing the central principle of Encounter era Indian diplomacy that a treaty is a relationship of trust, we begin the complex process of rendering a more complete accounting of the importance of Indian ideas and values in protecting Indian rights under U.S. law. The trust doctrine was not the exclusive by-product of the Western legal tradition brought to North America from the Old World. This central protective principle of Indian tribal rights under our law has deep roots in Encounter era Indian visions of law and peace.

Federal Indian Law Today: Dilemmas and Challenges

This, of course, is not the Encounter era. The ability of Indians to ask that their visions of their rights be respected and accommodated by the dominant society has been overcome by two centuries of white conquest and colonization in North America. The major challenges confronting American Indian tribalism's struggles for cultural survival today arise from a different calculus of racial power on the continent—tribal Indians are a small minority demanding rights from a far larger white majority. As Robert Clinton, an authority in the field of federal Indian law, has written, the task of ridding modern U.S. law of its "colonial roots" and of creating a "decolonized federal Indian law" more protective of tribal rights confronts a formidable reality: the lack of what he calls "[w]idespread non-Indian political leadership or support for restoring Indian tribes to their rightful measure of sovereignty and resources."[50]

Charles Wilkinson, another noted contemporary authority in federal Indian law, makes a similar point. The most cherished rights of Indian peoples, Wilkinson writes, "are not based on equality of treatment under the Constitution and general civil rights laws." Rather, Indians make claims to "special rights," based on centuries-old and seemingly anachronistic treaties and laws. Because these special rights are not enjoyed by other groups in our society, they are invariably looked upon with suspicion and skepticism by most Americans. Thus, goes Wilkinson's analysis:

> One barrier that American Indians have faced, then, is that public understanding of their distinctive issues comes slowly. Their special rights are complex and history-based, emerging from the deep past rather than being ignited by the fire of moment. . . . In every instance, the Indian position is fragile because it ultimately depends on the capacity and willingness of the majority society to explore unfamiliar intellectual terrain.[51]

The understandings of tribal rights offered by such contemporary federal Indian law scholars as Clinton and Wilkinson alert us to the difficult nature of the contemporary challenges confronting Indian tribalism's struggles for cultural survival in America. Like other minority groups in our society, tribal Indians must demonstrate a convergence of their interests with dominant group interests in promoting their rights. For Indians, however, this "interest convergence dilemma" (to borrow Derrick Bell's term)[52] is made all the more intense and difficult to resolve by the fact that the rights they claim seem so alien and opposed to the dominant white society's legal, political, and cultural traditions. To protect tribal rights, the white majority must surrender its privileges of racial power acquired by a centuries-old tradition of conquest and colonization of Indian tribes.

Will Kymlicka, the noted international human rights law scholar, in fact, has written directly on the intense, racialized nature of the challenges confronting indigenous rights advocates in Western settler-state societies. These societies steadfastly abide by what Kymlicka describes as "the traditional liberal concerns for civil and political liberties."[53] As he notes, Supreme Court justices in countries such as Canada and the United States can only understand "aboriginal [i.e., indigenous] rights by relating them to their own experiences and traditions." Since these judges are likely in most cases to be members of the dominant Westernized culture, they can be expected to adopt what Kymlicka calls "the standard interpretation of liberalism." According to that interpretation,

> aboriginal rights are viewed as matters of discrimination and/or privilege, not of equality. They will always, therefore, be viewed with the kind of suspicion that [leads] liberals . . . to advocate their abolition. Aboriginal rights, at least in their robust form, will only be secure when they are viewed, not as competing with liberalism, but as an essential component of liberal political practice.[54]

The works of such scholars as Clinton, Wilkinson, Bell, and Kymlicka show us the need for overcoming the suspicions of the dominant white society about the claims of tribal Indians to special rights. The theme of trust in Encounter era Indian diplomacy can help us begin the process of developing a new, decolonized, theoretical framework for Indian rights addressing that need.

The vision of a treaty as a relationship of trust was the organizing principle of the diplomatic agreements of the Encounter era negotiated between American Indians and European-Americans. The metaphor of the common bowl was one of many ways in which Indians used the language of forest diplomacy in seeking to overcome the concerns of white Americans about recognizing tribal rights. By converging their interests with those of European-Americans, Indians believed it possible to nurture the trust necessary to imagine a sharing of power between different peoples over the lands and resources of America.

The treaties of the Encounter era reflect the enormous decolonizing potential of American Indian visions of law and peace. In these treaties, Indians secured "special rights" to engage in bilateral governmental relations with white Americans. These treaties recognized, as well, important rights of Indian tribes to exercise power over their lands and resources and to maintain their internal forms of self-government free of the white man's control.[55] We need to develop a much fuller understanding of how Indians used the language of forest diplomacy to convince white Americans to agree to respect and protect these and other "robust" forms of important tribal rights to cultural survival. We need to revive the visions that once made it possible for white Americans to imagine tribal rights as harmonizing with their interests. We need to test the potential of these reconstructed visions for transforming the present calculus of racial power in America. Most important, we need to begin the process of learning how to nurture the trust that is necessary for Indian tribalism and the dominant white society to survive and flourish together in North America, according to American Indian visions of law and peace.

Placing Our Lives in Each Other's Hands

How do different groups of peoples survive and flourish together in a multicultural world? This most difficult question has figured prominently in the works of a number of contemporary North American political and legal theorists.[56] Analyzing the intense challenges to the achievement of justice in a world of human diversity and conflict, these thinkers, like Indians of the Encounter era, tell us that trust is an essential condition for creating healthy social relationships.

Baier, for example, whose insights on "confident example-setting" have helped frame much of the discussion in this concluding chapter, utilizes the theme of trust as a central organizing principle in her work on justice in society. The "justice-inventors" of a society, she writes, know that "cooperation and mutual trust are both possible and advantageous . . . between non-friends, non-lovers (and those who are not intended lovers) and non-kin (or those not recognized as kin)."[57]

Similar to Baier, the feminist legal theorist Martha Minow has also stressed the importance of building conditions of trust in our social relationships. Arguing for a jurisprudential approach that "assumes that there is a basic connectedness between people,"[58] Minow's work seeks to change our understanding of the source of legal obligations by focusing on the need to protect the ability of individuals to rely on the continuation of vital relationships of interdependence. According to the vision of social life Minow elaborates, our law needs to allow different people to develop relationships that promote conditions of trust.[59]

Other contemporary North American theorists on justice in our society similarly have called our attention to the importance of trust and reliance in creating healthy social relationships. The liberal philosopher Richard Rorty, whose ideas have been discussed previously in this book,[60] has written insightfully about the difficult challenges of nurturing trust in a multicultural world. In Rorty's view, we need to develop an ever-increasing ability "to see the similarities between ourselves and people very unlike us as outweighing the differences. . . . The relevant similarities are not a matter of sharing a deep true self which instantiates true humanity, but are such little, superficial, similarities as cherishing our parents and our children."[61]

Critical legal studies scholars have also drawn our attention to the theme of trust in many of their works. Roberto Unger, for example, has written that focusing on trust and cooperation, rather than on the language of rights, is a better way of understanding the source and nature of many of the obligations that arise under our law.[62] Joseph Singer, another major voice in the critical legal studies movement, has declared that in a complex, rapidly changing, and diverse society such as ours, "we in fact have an obligation to learn what it would take for us to create the kind of society in which we could trust each other enough to place our lives in each other's hands."[63]

We can now better understand how these contemporary writers and theorists are continuing an important indigenous North American narrative tradition. With their emphases on the connections that relate us to each other, on the need to treat each other as relatives, and on nurturing trust, reliance, and cooperation in our social relationships, these thinkers, like Indians of the Encounter era, speak to the difficult challenges we confront in achieving justice on the frontiers of our emerging multicultural world.

Indians of the Encounter era developed a number of innovative and fruitful approaches for meeting the difficult challenges of building relationships of trust between communities at a distance. Different peoples, according to American Indian visions of law and peace, nurtured trust between each other by sharing sufferings, clearing all barriers to communication, exchanging stories, forgiveness, and goodwill, and mutualizing their interests; they agreed to treat each other as relatives, "to the latest generation."[64] These are just a few of the many acts of commitment we read about in the Encounter era treaty literature that show us how American Indians went about the difficult process of society building on a rapidly changing multicultural frontier. Such acts speak with insight and imagination to the challenges of creating a society in which different, conflicting groups of peoples learn to trust each other enough to place their lives in each other's hands. According to American Indian visions of law and peace, they must first agree to link arms together.

Notes

Introduction

1. Robert A. Williams, Jr., *The American Indian in Western Legal Thought: The Discourses of Conquest* (1990).

2. Edward W. Said, *Culture and Imperialism* xii (1993). "Never was it the case that the imperial encounter pitted an active intruder against a supine or inert non-Western native; there was *always* some form of active resistance." *Id.*

3. For the purposes of this book, the North American Encounter era is understood as running from roughly the early sixteenth through the late eighteenth century, the period during which, as Stephen Cornell describes,

> Europe spun a web about the world, and in the process the world was remade. During those and subsequent years, various peoples, nations, and ideas would struggle within the grasp of that web. Some would flourish, some would disappear; but few would entirely escape the ever-expanding network of connections that made this world so very new.

Stephen Cornell, *The Return of the Native: American Indian Political Resurgence* 11 (1988).

Professor Cornell divided this "incorporative process" of the Encounter era into six major periods, "distinguished by the prevalence in each of more or less distinct sets of economic and political relationships" between North American tribes and European-American society. *Id.* at 12.

In this book, I focus primarily on North American Indian visions of law and peace between different peoples that emerge in the treaty literature of the first of these periods, identified by Cornell as the "market period." *Id.* As demarcated by

Cornell, this early period of multicultural encounter in North America "lasted from shortly after Indian-White contact into the last half of the eighteenth century. Its centerpiece was the fur trade of the eastern woodlands, which incorporated Indians, as producers of peltry, into a European market and, as potential allies, into the system of competitive trans-Atlantic European politics." *Id.*

Of all the major periods of Indian-white contact in North America, this period is unique in that European-Americans sought reciprocal trade with Indian tribes rather than direct control of Indian tribal natural resources, especially land. As Wesley Craven explains, European colonizers in this early Encounter period relied heavily on the profits of trade, primarily in beaver and other furs, to underwrite their North American ventures. Wesley F. Craven, *The Colonies in Transition, 1660–1713* 112 (1968). Success and profit in early North American mercantile ventures depended largely on forging alliances with tribal trading partners. *See* Cornell, *supra,* at 17.

Thus, during the early Encounter era, tribes were often treated in fact, if not wholly regarded in theory, as rough political, economic, and military equals by their European trading partners. In this unique period of increasing interdependence between the different cultural and racial groups engaged in trade, and in the politics of accommodation and conflict surrounding trade, North American indigenous peoples proclaimed their visions of law and peace. Significantly, for the purposes of this study, these visions were expressed in a language and metaphors still largely uncorrupted, though not wholly uninfluenced, by the subsequent corrosive and pervasive effects of incorporation, increased Indian dependence, and European-American hegemony.

4. G. Edward White, "Reflections on the 'Republican Revival': Interdisciplinary Scholarship in the Legal Academy," 6 *Yale J. L. & Human.* 1, 23 (1994).

5. *See* Robert A. Williams, Jr., "The Algebra of Federal Indian Law: The Hard Trail of Decolonizing and Americanizing the White Man's Indian Jurisprudence," 1986 *Wis. L. Rev.* 219, 293–299 [hereinafter "The Algebra"]; Robert A. Williams, Jr., "Encounters on the Frontiers of International Human Rights Law: Refedining the Terms of Indigenous Peoples' Survival in the World," 1990 *Duke L. J.* 660; Robert A. Williams, Jr., "Sovereignty, Racism, Human Rights: Indian Self-Determination and the Post-Modern World Legal System," 2 *Rev. Const. Stud.* 146 (1995).

6. *See* "Report of the Working Group on Indigenous Populations on Its Sixth Session," *U.N. ESCOR* CN. 4, U.N. Doc. E/CN. 4/Sub. 2/1988/24, at 7 (1988). On the oral tradition of the *Gus-Wen-Tah, see generally* Oren Lyons, "The American Indian in the Past," in *Exiled in the Land of the Free* 41–42 (1992).

7. *See* Williams, *supra* note 1, at 325–328.

8. *See Indian Self-Government in Canada, Report of the Special Committee* (back cover) (1983).

9. *See* Robert A. Williams, Jr., "Encounters on the Frontiers of International Human Rights Law: Redefining the Terms of Indigenous Peoples' Survival in the World," 1990 *Duke L. J.* 660, 676–685, for a discussion of the Working Group and the Draft Declaration of the Rights of Indigenous Peoples.

S. James Anaya has analyzed the indigenous human rights movement and those groups understood as included within this movement in "Indigenous Rights Norms in Contemporary International Law," 8 *Ariz. J. Int'l & Comp. L.* 1 (1991).

> The conceptual category of indigenous peoples or populations has emerged within the human rights organs of international organizations and other venues of international discourse. The category is generally understood to include not only the native tribes of the American continents, but also other culturally distinctive, non-state groupings such as the Australian aboriginal communities and tribal peoples of southern Asia, that similarly are threatened by the legacies of colonialism.
>
> The subject groups are themselves largely responsible for the mobilization of the international human rights program in their favor. During the 1970's, indigenous peoples organized and extended their efforts internationally to secure legal protection for their continued survival as distinct communities with historically based cultures, political institutions, and entitlement to land.

Id. at 1.

10. As Robert Cover writes:

> A legal tradition . . . includes not only a corpus juris [body of law] but also a language and mythos—narratives in which the corpus juris is located by those whose wills act upon it. These myths establish the *paradigms for behavior.* They build relations between the normative and the material universe, between the constraints of reality and the demands of an ethic. These myths establish a repertoire of moves—a lexicon of normative action—that may be combined into meaningful patterns culled from the meaningful patterns of the past.

Robert M. Cover, "*Nomos* and Narrative," 97 *Harv. L. Rev.* 4, 9 (1983) (emphasis added).

11. *See generally* "The Algebra," *supra* note 5, at 252–289 (discussing European-American jurisprudence on American Indian rights).

12. Audre Lord, "The Master's Tools Will Never Dismantle the Master's House," in *Sister Outsider: Essays and Speeches* 110 (1984).

13. Contemporary scholars of federal Indian law are becoming more acutely aware of the fundamental defects in our contemporary legal framework for understanding and protecting tribal rights. The idea that Indian tribalism's "right" to survival should be subjected to the political and legal processes of the majority society has been increasingly questioned by a growing number of federal Indian law scholars. *See, e.g.,* Nell Jessup Newton, "Federal Power over Indians: Its Sources, Scope, and Limitations," 132 *U. Pa. L. Rev.* 195 (1984); Rennard Strickland, "Genocide-at-Law: A Historical and Contemporary View of the Native American Experience," 24 *U. Kan. L. Rev.* 713 (1986); Robert N. Clinton, "Isolated in Their Own Country: A Defense of Federal Protection of Indian Autonomy and Self Government," 33 *Stan. L. Rev.* 979 (1981); David Williams, "The Borders of the Equal Protection Clause: Indians as Peoples," 38 *UCLA L. Rev.* 759 (1991); Russell L. Barsh & James Y. Henderson, *The Road: Indian Tribes and Political Liberty* (1980); Milner S. Ball, "Constitution, Court, Indian Tribes," 1987 *Am. B. Found. Res. J.* 1.

14. Richard White, *The Middle Ground: Indians, Empires, and Republics in the Great Lakes Region, 1650–1815* (1991).

15. *Id.* at xiv.

16. *Id.*

17. *See* Williams, *supra* note 1.

18. Lawrence C. Wroth, "The Indian Treaty as Literature," 17 *Yale Rev.* 749, 766 (1928).

19. *Id.* at 766.

20. One of the underlying bedrock principles of U.S. law on American Indian rights is that treaties between Indian tribes and the federal government are the supreme law of the land and must be interpreted as the Indians themselves would have understood them. This view of treaties can be traced to Chief Justice Marshall's early nineteenth-century seminal decision on Indian rights, *Worcester v. Georgia,* 31 U.S. (6 Pet.) 515, 582 (1832). *See also Choctaw Nation v. Oklahoma,* 397 U.S. 620, 631 (1970); *United States v. Shoshone Tribe,* 304 U.S. 111, 116 (1938); *Starr v. Long Jim,* 227 U.S. 613, 622–623 (1913).

An excellent discussion and analysis of the canons of construction for interpreting Indian treaties under U.S. law can be found in Charles F. Wilkinson & John M. Volkman, "Judicial Review of Indian Treaty Abrogation: 'As Long as Water Flows or Grass Grows upon the Earth'—How Long a Time Is That?," 63 *Cal. L. Rev.* 601, 608–619 (1975).

21. *See* Charles F. Wilkinson, *American Indians, Time, and the Law* (1987). Wilkinson's elaboration of "a measured separatism" for tribes in the U.S. polity is discussed *id.* at 53–54, 121–122.

22. *See supra* text accompanying notes 6–7.

23. *See* Williams, *supra* note 7.

24. *See supra* sources cited in note 5.

25. J. G. A. Pocock, *Politics, Language, and Time* 25 (1971).

26. *See generally* Mary A. Druke, "Iroquois Treaties: Common Forms, Varying Interpretations," in *The History and Culture of Iroquois Diplomacy* 85–92 (Francis Jennings et al. eds., 1985) (discussing types of treaty documents that produce evidence of treaty negotiations during the seventeenth, eighteenth, and early nineteenth centuries).

27. *See* Frantz Fanon, *The Wretched of the Earth* 51 (1968).

> The settler makes history and is conscious of making it. And because he constantly refers to the history of his mother country, he clearly indicates that he himself is the extension of that mother country. Thus the history which he writes is not the history of the country which he plunders but the history of his own nation in regard to all that she skims off, all that she violates and starves.

Id.

28. According to Walter Benjamin:

> All rulers are the heirs of those who conquered before them. Hence, empathy with the victor invariably benefits the rulers. Historical materialists know what that means. Whoever has emerged victorious participates to this day in the triumphal procession in which the present rulers step over those who are lying prostrate. They are called cultural treasures, and a historical materialist views them with cautious detachment. For without exception the cultural treasures he surveys have an origin which he cannot contemplate without honor. They owe their existence not only to the efforts of the

> great minds and talents who have created them, but also to the anonymous folk of their contemporaries. There is no document of civilization which is not at the same time a document of barbarism and just as such a document is not free of barbarism, barbarism taints also the manner in which it was transmitted from one owner to another. A historical materialist therefore dissociates himself from it as far as possible. He regards it as his task to brush history against the grain.

Walter Benjamin, *Illuminations* 256–257 (Hannah Arendt ed., 1969).

29. On the Indian vision of a treaty relationship as a linking of arms together, *see infra* Chapter 5.

Chapter 1

1. "We have had many myths about the West, but the principal one was a story about a simple, rural people moving into an extraordinary land . . . and creating there a peaceful, productive life." Donald Worster, "Beyond the Agrarian Myth," in *Trails: Toward a New Western History* 7 (Patricia Nelson Limerick, Clyde A. Milner II, & Charles E. Rankin eds., 1991).

Assaults on the national mythology of western frontier conquest have been taken up in earnest by scholars of the New Western History. As Patricia Nelson Limerick writes, in "this enriched and deepened perspective" on the West,

> that unitary term "the white man" dissolves, revealing a wide range of people with various ethnic origins, occupations, values and characters. Rather than seeing a single Anglo waive moving West across a continent, we see one set of waves, predominantly but not wholly Anglo, encountering other waves: one Hispanic from the south, another Asian from the Far West, and amid it all, we find enduring yet dynamic Native American cultures.

Patricia Nelson Limerick, "Preface," in *id.* at xi.

The "fierce race of savages" phraseology in the text is borrowed from Frederick Jackson Turner, creator of the frontier thesis in American historiography. *See* Frederick Jackson Turner, *The Frontier in American History* 269 (1947).

Limerick summarizes Turner's paradigm-defining historical thesis of the American frontier experience in her landmark book, *The Legacy of Conquest: The Unbroken Past of the American West* (1987), as follows:

> The center of American history, Turner had argued, was actually to be found at its edges. As the American people proceeded westward, "the frontier [was] the outer edge of the wave—the meeting point between savagery and civilization and the line of most effective and rapid Americanization." The struggle with the wilderness turned Europeans into Americans, a process Turner made the central story of American history: "The existence of an area of free land, its continuous recession, and the advance of American settlement westward, explain American development."

Id. at 20–21.

2. Bronislaw Malinowski, *Magic, Science and Religion* 108–109 (1954). "[F]or myth is not only looked upon as a commentary of additional information, but it is a warrant, a charter, and often even a practical guide to the activities with which it is connected."

3. Roy Harvey Pearce, *The Savages of America: A Study of the Indian and the Idea of Civilization* 1–49 (rev. ed. 1965).

4. My use of the term "narrative tradition" to describe the corpus of texts and familiar arguments in American public rhetoric on Indian tribalism's cultural inferiority combines a number of sources on traditions and narratives, J. G. A. Pocock writes: "An essential feature of society is tradition—the handing on of formed ways of acting, a formed way of living, to those beginning or developing their social membership." J. G. A. Pocock, *Politics, Language, and Time* 233–234 (1971). Mark Tushnet, in a discussion of "traditions" and their role in political and legal discourse, has said: "Traditions are not systematic, well-organized bodies of thought; rather, they help people to understand the world by providing some familiar categories to use." *Red, White and Blue: A Critical Analysis of Constitutional Law* 6 (1988). *See also* Robert Cover, "Forward: *Nomos* and Narrative," 97 *Harv. L. Rev.* 4, 5–7 (1983).

> No set of legal institutions or prescriptions exist apart from the narratives that locate it and give it meaning. For every constitution there is an epic, for each decalogue a scripture. Once understood in the context of the narratives that give it meaning, law becomes not merely a system of rules to be observed, but a world in which we live.

Id. at 4–5.

I use "narrative tradition" to refer to those related sets of stories, myths, and other narrative forms handed down from generation to generation by a given society that help the members of that society understand the world, particularly the normative world, in which they live.

5. Pearce, *supra* note 3, at 41.

6. Cotton Mather, "The Wonders of the Invisible World" (1693), *quoted in Puritans, Indians and Manifest Destiny* 49 (C. Segal & D. Stineback eds., 1977) (emphasis in original).

Massachusetts's first colonial governor, the Puritan John Winthrop, writing in the early seventeenth century, could cite scripture in support of his legal proposition that the New World's Indian tribes' failure to cultivate the land divested them of any rights to the countries they claimed:

> The whole earth is the Lord's Garden and he hath given it to the sons of men, with a general condition, Gen[esis] 1.28. Increase and multiply, replenish the earth and subdue it. . . . And for the Natives of New England they enclose no land neither have any settled habitation nor any tame cattle to improve the land by and so have no other but a natural right to those countries so as if we leave them sufficient for their use we may lawfully take the rest, there being more than enough for them and us.

Quoted in Francis Paul Prucha, *American Indian Policy in the Formative Years: The Indian Trade and Intercourse Acts, 1790–1834* 240 (1962).

Throughout this book I have made changes in seventeenth- and eighteenth-century orthography as a convenience to the reader. Letters or words in colonial documents have been changed to conform to modern usage; abbreviations have been expanded, italics removed, and capital letters replaced when their use reflected idiosyncrasies of period and style rather than substantive emphasis. *See, e.g.*, Alden T. Vaughan, *New England Frontier: Puritans and Indians, 1620–1675* lxxi–lxxii (3d ed. 1995).

7. Samuel Purchas, "Virginia's Verger: Or a Discourse Showing the Benefits Which May Grow to This Kingdom from American English Plantations," 19 *Hakluytus Posthumus or Purchas His Pilgrims* 231 (1905–1907).

8. Thomas Hobbes, *Leviathan, or the Matter, Forme & Power of a Commonwealth Ecclesiastical and Civil* (Crawford B. Macpherson ed., 1968).

9. *Id.* at 186–187.

10. *Id.*

11. John Locke, *Two Treatises of Government* (1963).

12. *Id.* at 343. On the relation between Locke, Hobbes, and American Indians, *see* Robert F. Berkhofer Jr., *The White Man's Indian* 21–22 (1979).

13. Locke, *supra* note 11, at 338–339.

14. Emmerich Vattel, *The Law of Nations or the Principles of Natural Law* (Classics of International Law ed., 1964).

15. *Id.* at 37. "Of all the arts," Vattel wrote, "agriculture is without doubt the most useful and most necessary. It is the chief source from which the state is nourished." *Id.* at 37. The sovereign of a nation was instructed by Vattel to "do all in his power" to have the lands under his control as well cultivated as possible. *Id.*

16. *Id.* at 38.

17. *Id.* Commenting further on the right of a civilized agrarian state to dispossess a savage nation that did not properly utilize the soil, Vattel explored the reasons justifying the displacement of American Indians in the New World:

> There is another celebrated question which has arisen principally in connection with the discovery of the New World. It is asked whether a Nation may lawfully occupy any part of a vast territory in which are to be found only wandering tribes whose small numbers cannot populate the whole country. We have already pointed out, in speaking of the obligation of cultivating the earth, that these tribes cannot take to themselves more land than they have need of or can inhabit and cultivate. Their uncertain occupancy of these vast regions cannot be held as a real and lawful taking of possession; and when the nations of Europe, which are too confined at home, come upon lands which the savages have no special need of and are making no present and continuous use of, they may lawfully take possession of them and establish colonies in them. We have already said that the earth belongs to all mankind as a means of sustaining life. But if each Nation had desired from the beginning to appropriate to itself an extent of territory great enough for it to live merely by hunting, fishing, and gathering wild fruits, the earth would not suffice for a tenth part of the people who now inhabit it. Hence, we are not departing from the intentions of nature when we restrict the savages within narrower bounds.

Id. at 85–86.

He did view favorably, nonetheless, the moderation shown by the New England Puritans who "bought from the savages the lands they wished to occupy." This "praiseworthy example," according to Vattel's *Law of Nations,* was followed by William Penn and the colony of Quakers he established in Pennsylvania. *Id.* at 85–86. He did not conclude, however, that such a practice was or should be part of the European Law of Nations.

18. Another critical source of ideas about the American Indian that both benefited from and contributed to the narrative traditions concerning tribalism's deficiency can be found in the works of eighteenth-century Scottish Enlightenment writers on society. Several of these writers drew on the narrative tradition of American Indian tribalism's cultural inferiority in developing a broad range of sociological speculations on the progress of history, "from barbarism to civilization, from a warrior society marked by primitive virtue toward a state of commerce, refinement, and humanity." J. G. A. Pocock, *The Machiavellian Moment: Florentine Political Thought and the Atlantic Republican Tradition* 499 (1975).

The broad intention of the Scottish school, which included Francis Hutcheson, Thomas Reid, Adam Ferguson, Lord Kames, and William Robertson, was to construct a historical analysis of social progress. These writers, as Roy Harvey Pearce has explained, believed man's "original nature" to be unchanging yet reducible to discernible laws of development. Pearce, *supra* note 3, at 82–83. The development of human institutions and customs "was judged to be progressive, of the nature of a continuous movement with no breaks, as growth has no breaks, a movement directed by Nature." Gladys Bryson, *Man and Society: The Scottish Inquiry of the Eighteenth Century* 242–243 (1945), *quoted in* Pearce, *supra* note 3. The study of "primitive peoples," particularly the American Indian, provided grist for the mill for this particular school of Western social thought that sought to understand the processes by which human beings, their institutions, and their customs developed and evolved.

Adam Ferguson's *Essay on the History of Civil Society,* first published in 1767, is regarded as one of the classic sociological texts of the eighteenth-century Scottish school. A self-described "natural history" of man from his "rude" to "polished" state, it frequently cites the "savage nations" of America as examples of "rude nations prior to the establishment of property." *Id.* at 81–82.

Property, in particular landed property, assumes a defining role in Ferguson's sociological history of humankind's progress, from its "rudest state" to its most civilized achievements:

> It must appear very evident, that property is a matter of progress. It requires among other particulars which are the effects of time, some method of defining possession. The very desire of it proceeds from experience; and the industry by which it is gained, or improved, requires such a habit of acting with a view to distant objects, as may overcome the present disposition to sloth or to enjoyment. This habit is slowly acquired, and is in reality a principal distinction of nations in the advanced state of mechanic and commercial arts.

Id. at 82.

According to Ferguson, property was "the principal distinction" between "rude" nations, such as those "in most parts of America," and "advanced" or "polished" nations. The savage nations, while mixing "with the practice of hunting some species of rude agriculture," did not recognize individual property rights in the crops their labor had created but rather, according to Ferguson, "enjoy the fruits of the harvest in common." *Id.*

Ferguson's *Essay* sought to demonstrate that savage nations, lacking in the advantages bestowed upon society by the institution of property, inevitably yielded to more advanced nations:

> For want of these advantages, rude nations in general, though they are patient of hardship and fatigue, though they are addicted to war, and are qualified by their stratagem and valor to throw terror into the armies of a more regular enemy; yet, in the course of a continued struggle, always yield to the superior arts, and the discipline of more civilized nations. Hence the Romans were able to over-run the provinces of Gaul, Germany, and Britain: and hence the Europeans have a growing ascendancy over the nations of Africa and America.

Id. at 95.

Ferguson's focus on individual property as a distinguishing norm between superior "civilized" and inferior "savage" peoples was a prominent feature in the works of other Scottish school writers. Adam Smith's *Wealth of Nations* (1776) asserted that private property and the division of labor generally accounted for the superiority of "civilized" societies compared to "savage" ones.

19. "George Washington to James Duane, September 7, 1783," in *Documents of United States Indian Policy* 1–2 (Francis Paul Prucha ed., 2d ed. 1990).

20. In his 1802 oration before the Sons of the Pilgrims, Adams drew liberally from the narrative tradition of tribalism's cultural inferiority to provide a homiletic apologia for the sins of the Pilgrim forefathers committed against the Indian:

> There are moralists who have questioned the right of Europeans to intrude upon the possessions of the aborigines in any case and under any limitations whatsoever. But have they maturely considered the whole subject? The Indian right of possession itself stands, with regard to the greatest part of the country, upon a questionable foundation.

Quoted in C. Royce, *Indian Land Cessions in the United States, 18th Annual Report of the Bureau of American Ethnology, 1896–1897,* pt. 2, at 536 (1899).

Adams's oration went on to ground Indian property rights in the narrative tradition's central legitimizing normative text: the "law of nature." Europeans had recognized the Indians' right to "[t]heir cultivated fields, their constructed habitations, a space of ample sufficiency for their substance, and whatever they had annexed to themselves by personal labor." But Adams asked rhetorically: "What is the right of a huntsman to the forest of a thousand miles which he has accidentally ranged in quest of prey? Shall the liberal bounties of Providence to the race of man be monopolized by one of the thousand for whom they were created?" *Id.*

Adams's speech continued with a rhetorical cavalcade of questions designed to illustrate the unassimilable nature of the Indian's claims over the lands of America with the expansionary needs of U.S. society: "Shall the lordly savage not only disdain the virtues and enjoyments of civilization himself, but shall he control the civilization of a world?" *Id.*

Adams argued in his oration that it was Indian tribalism's divergence from the norms governing a civilized society's use of land that provided the source of white society's privileges to the New World. The Indian was a "tenant of the woods," whose claims to territorial sovereignty violated natural law—a law followed by the white man in cultivating the Indian's wastelands. *Id.* at 537.

Adams's final and definitive answer to the series of rhetorical questions he posited as to whether America's Indians possessed rights to the lands they claimed was, of course, "no." "Heaven has not been this inconsistent in the works of its hands. Heaven has not thus placed at irreconcilable strife its moral laws with its physical creation." *Id.*

21. "John Quincy Adams' Message to Congress" (Dec. 2, 1828), in 2 *A Compilation of Messages and Papers of the Presidents* 415–416 (J. Richardson ed., 1907).

22. Act of May 28, 1830, ch. 148, 4 Stat. 411.

23. *See* Turner, *supra* note 1, at 269.

24. *See, e.g.,* International Convention on the Elimination of All Forms of Racial Discrimination, 5 *International Legal Materials* 352 (1966), in which the states' parties to the convention "condemn all propaganda and all organizations which are based on ideas or theories of superiority of one race or group of persons of one colour or ethnic origin." *Id.,* Art. 4. The United States signed the convention in 1966, the year in which it was promulgated, but has not yet ratified its text. Eighty other countries have ratified the convention, which entered into force in 1969.

25. 348 U.S. 272 (1955).

26. *Id.* at 288–290.

27. *See, e.g., United States v. Sioux Nation of Indians,* 448 U.S. 371 (1980), a case involving the illegal taking (as found by an eight-justice majority) of the Black Hills from the Sioux. Associate Justice Rehnquist wrote in lone dissent: "There were undoubtedly greed, cupidity, and other less-than-admirable tactics employed by the Government during the Black Hills episode in the settlement of the West, but the Indians did not lack their share of villainy either." *Id.* at 435.

28. 435 U.S. 191 (1978).

29. *Id.* at 202.

30. Speaking to a group of students at Moscow University in the Soviet Union in 1988, President Ronald Reagan, the Great Communicator himself, demonstrated the sustaining force of the myth in his paradigmatic effort to explain the Indian as marginal on the present-day American cultural landscape:

> Let me tell you just a little something about the American Indian in our land. We have provided millions of acres of land for what are called—preservations—or the reservations, I should say.
>
> They, from the beginning, announced that they wanted to maintain their way of life, as they always had lived there in the desert and plains and so forth. And we set up their reservations so they could, and have a Bureau of Indian Affairs to help take care of them.
>
> At the same time, we provide education for them—schools on the reservations. And they're free also to leave the reservations and be American citizens among the rest of us, and many do.
>
> Some still prefer, however, that way of—that early way of life. And we've done everything we can to meet their demands as to what they—how they want to live.
>
> Maybe we made a mistake. Maybe we should not have humored them in that, wanting to stay in that primitive kind of lifestyle. Maybe we should have said, "No, come join us. Be citizens with the rest of us."

"Comments on American Indians," Associated Press Wire Service, June 1, 1988, *reprinted in* David H. Getches, Charles F. Wilkinson, & Robert A. Williams, Jr., *Federal Indian Law: Cases and Materials* 277–278 (3d ed. 1993).

31. Francis Jennings, *The Ambiguous Iroquois Empire* 367 (1984).

32. As Richard White has explained, "[F]or long periods of time in large parts of the colonial world whites could neither dictate to Indians nor ignore them. Whites needed Indians as allies, as partners in exchange, as sexual partners, as friendly neighbors." Richard White, *The Middle Ground: Indians, Empires, and Republics in the Great Lakes Region, 1690–1815* x (1991).

33. Immanuel Wallerstein, *The Modern World-System I: Capitalist Agriculture and the Origins of the European World-Economy in the Sixteenth Century* 347 (1974).

34. *See infra* note 45. *See also* Eric P. Wolf, *Europe and the People without History* 158–194 (1982).

35. *See, e.g.*, Wilbur R. Jacobs, "Unsavory Sidelights on the Colonial Trade," in *Dispossessing the American Indian: Indians and Whites on the Colonial Frontier* 31–40 (1972) (discussing white attitudes toward Indians involved in the colonial trade).

36. *See* Francis Paul Prucha, *American Indian Treaties: The History of a Political Anomaly* (1994).

37. *See supra* text accompanying notes 9–11.

38. *See* Robert A. Williams, Jr., *The American Indian in Western Legal Thought: The Discourses of Conquest* 216–219 (1990).

39. *See* 15 *Handbook of North American Indians: Northeast* 92–94 (Bruce G. Trigger vol. ed., 1978) [hereinafter 15 *Handbook*].

40. *Quoted in* John Phillip Reid, *A Better Kind of Hatchet: Law, Trade, and Diplomacy in the Cherokee Nation during the Early Years of European Contact* 72 (1976).

41. *See* Hobbes, *supra* note 8; *supra* text accompanying note 10.

42. Stephen Cornell, *The Return of the Native* 17 (1988).

43. Even Frederick Jackson Turner himself conceded the significance of the Indian trade in his thesis on the "Americanization" of the frontier: "[T]he Indian trade pioneered the way for civilization. . . . The trails widened into roads and the roads into turnpikes, and these in turn transformed into railroads." Turner, *supra* note 1, at 14–15.

44. The links of interdependence, of course, extended beyond Indian-European cooperative ventures in the multicultural world of the North American Encounter era. Europeans from different cultural backgrounds and with initial conflicts of interest quickly discovered the benefits of multicultural cooperation in the New World. The "French" in Canada were an unruly mix of Normans, Flemings, Jesuits, and French nobility; they were as culturally diverse as the "Algonquian" Indians to whom they were allied. In English America, the Dutch merchants of Albany contributed significantly to the New York colony's commercial development. William Penn promoted the settlement of his proprietary colony by encouraging German and other continental Europeans to immigrate to the New World. The Irish and Scotch helped develop the southern colonies' fur trade.

45. The idea of different cultural groups in an "original position" of rough equality on a multicultural frontier is adapted from the philosopher John Rawls's

famous text, *A Theory of Justice* (1971). In describing his notion of the "original position," Rawls explains:

> This original position is not, of course, thought of as an actual historical state of affairs, much less as a primitive condition of culture. It is understood as a purely hypothetical situation characterized so as to lead to a certain conception of justice. Among the essential features of this situation is that no one knows his place in society, his class position or social status, nor does any one know his fortune in the distribution of natural assets and abilities, his intelligence, strength, and the like. I shall even assume that the parties do not know their conceptions of the good or their special psychological propensities.

Id. at 12.

Rawls concedes that his original position of equality is a philosophical construct. It corresponds, he says, "to the state of nature in the traditional theory of the social contract." *Id.* Rawls also states that the principles of justice selected by the parties in this original position are chosen behind a veil of ignorance. "This ensures that no one is advantaged or disadvantaged in the choice of principles by the outcome of natural chance or the contingency of social circumstances. Since all are similarly situated and no one is able to design principles to favor his particular condition, the principles of justice are the result of a fair agreement or bargain." *Id.*

As has already been noted, the American Indian played an important role in developing many of the central principles of the Enlightenment era's natural law tradition within which Rawls writes. *See supra* text accompanying notes 9–19. Rawls himself explicitly states that his aim "is to present a conception of justice which generalizes and carries to a higher level of abstraction the familiar theory of the social contract as found say, in Locke, Rousseau [who helped invent the 'noble savage' theme], and Kant." *Id.* at 11.

My idiosyncratic adaptation of Rawls's "original position" in the historical context of cultural-group relations in the North American Encounter era scripts, in effect, a potential counterrole for the American Indian in the Western philosophical tradition. I am suggesting that American Indian visions of law and peace reflected in the treaties negotiated with whites in the seventeenth and eighteenth centuries can be used as alternative starting points to develop principles of justice for the basic structure of a multicultural society.

46. *See* Frantz Fannon, *The Wretched of the Earth* 51 (1968).
47. *Quoted in* Leo Marx, *The Machine in the Garden* 41 (1964).
48. *Id.*
49. *See* 15 *Handbook, supra* note 39, at 89.
50. Cover, *supra* note 4, at 1–11.
51. Jennings, *supra* note 31, at 375.
52. *See supra* note 45.
53. Clifford Geertz, *The Interpretation of Cultures* 49 (1973).
54. *Id.* at 48.
55. *See* Dorothy V. Jones, "British Colonial Indian Treaties," in 4 *Handbook of North American Indians* 185 (Wilcomb E. Washburn vol. ed., 1988).
56. *Id.*
57. I use the term "law and peace" throughout the book as a generalized

description of two core ideals reflected in the language of Indian diplomacy during the Encounter era. As captured most effectively in the Iroquois "Great Law of Peace" (*see infra* Chapter 2), the language of Indian diplomacy spoke of a treaty as establishing a law, through its shared rituals, assumed duties, and acknowledged traditions, that when faithfully followed secured a long-standing and highly beneficial peace between different peoples. Law *and* peace were therefore virtually synonymous words in this language. There could be no peace between people without law, and no law without peace. The myriad ways in which Eastern Woodlands Indians sought to achieve law and peace with their treaty partners are discussed *infra* Chapters 2–5.

58. *See* Williams, *supra* note 38, at 206–207.

59. Wesley F. Craven, *The Southern Colonies in the Seventeenth Century, 1607–1689* 80 (1949).

60. "Captain John Smith's Summary: A Map of Virginia," in *The Jamestown Voyages under the First Charter, 1606–1609* 413 (D. C. Barbour ed., 1969) [hereinafter *Jamestown Voyages*].

61. *Id.* at 414.

62. Jones, *supra* note 55, at 185.

63. T. J. Brasser, "Early Indian-European Contacts," in 15 *Handbook, supra* note 39, at 83–85.

64. *See id.*

65. *See id.*

66. *See* Williams, *supra* note 38, at 206–207.

67. *Jamestown Voyages, supra* note 60, at 369.

68. *See, e.g.,* Brasser, *supra* note 63, at 85.

69. James Tuck, "Northern Iroquoian Prehistory," in 15 *Handbook, supra* note 39, at 330–331.

70. *Selected Writings of Edward Sapir* 162 (David Mandelbaum ed., 1949).

71. *See* Harold Driver, *Indians of North America* 25 (2d ed. 1969); Alice B. Kehoe, *North American Indians* 160–286 (2d ed. 1992). We do know that there was remarkable linguistic diversity among Eastern Woodlands Indians in North America. Consider the major tribal groupings on the eastern half of the continent: the Creeks in Georgia and Alabama and the Choctaws and Chickasaws in Mississippi spoke differing Muskogean languages. A large number of different Algonquian languages were spoken throughout the middle and northern parts of eastern North America—by Powhatan's confederacy in Virginia, by the Shawnee in Kentucky, and by the Delaware, Munsee, Piscataway, and Nanticoke of the mid-Atlantic region. The Montauk on Long Island, the Mohicans in the Hudson Valley, the Pequot and Mohegan in Connecticut, the Narragansett and Wampanoag in Massachusetts, and the Passamaquody, Penobscot, and Abenaki in Maine spoke differing Algonquian languages, as did the Ottawa, Algonquin, and Ojibwa in Canada. Iroquoian languages were spoken by the Five Nations group of Senecas, Cayugas, Onondagas, Oneidas, and Mohawks, but a Seneca Iroquoian speaker might not always have been easily understood in a Mohawk village. The Hurons, Wyandots, Petuns, Neutrals, Eries, and Susquehonock Conestoga Indians spoke different branches of Iroquoian. The Cherokees of the Carolinas, Georgia, and Tennessee and the Tuscaroras of North Carolina spoke related branches of Iroquoian, but the difference between Cherokee and the other languages of the Iroquoian family "are of a magnitude that is appreciably

greater than that of the differences among the various languages of the Germanic family or among the languages of the Romance family." Floyd G. Lounsbury, "Iroquoian Languages," in 15 *Handbook, supra* note 39, at 334. *See generally* Alice B. Kehoe, *North American Indians* 160–286 (2d ed. 1992).

72. *See supra* sources cited in note 71.

73. Pocock, *supra* note 4, at 22.

74. Daniel K. Richter, "Rediscovered Links in the Covenant Chain: Previously Unpublished Transcripts of New York Indian Treaty Minutes, 1677–1691," 92 *Proc. Am. Antiquarian Soc'y* 45, 47–48 (1982).

75. Clifford Geertz, *Local Knowledge* 151 (1983). According to this type of multicultural interpretive perspective:

> The problem of how a Copernican understands a Ptolemaian, a fifth republic Frenchman an *ancien régime* one, or a poet a painter is seen to be on all fours with the problem of how a Christian understands a Muslim, a European an Asian, an anthropologist an aborigine, or vice versa. We are all natives now, and everybody else not immediately one of us is an exotic. What looked once to be a matter of finding out whether savages could distinguish fact from fancy now looks to be a matter of finding out how others, across the sea or down the corridor, organize their significative world.

76. *See infra* Chapter 2.

77. Pocock, *supra* note 4, at 22–26.

> If at this stage we are asked how we know the languages adumbrated really existed, or how we recognize them when we see them, we should be able to reply empirically: that the languages in question are simply there, that they form individually recognizable patterns and styles, and that we get to know them by learning to speak them, to think in their patterns and styles until we know that we are speaking them and can predict in what directions speaking them is carrying us.

Id. at 26.

78. *See infra* Chapter 3.

79. *See infra* Chapter 4.

80. *See infra* Chapter 5.

81. *See infra* Conclusion.

82. *See* Lawrence Wroth, "The Indian Treaty as Literature," 17 *Yale Rev.* 749 (1928).

83. One could no more "essentialize" the language of Encounter era Eastern Woodlands Indian diplomacy by partially listing its paradigms than one could essentialize the language of seventeenth-century English Enlightenment thought by neatly summarizing the major ideas of Hobbes and Locke. *See, e.g., supra* text accompanying notes 11–14. Nor should one assume that the language of diplomacy used by one group of Indians in an anthropologically defined "culture area" called the Eastern Woodlands is somehow related to the idioms, symbols, and metaphors used by other distinct groups of indigenous tribal peoples in their diplomatic relations with Europeans during the period of their colonization without further multicultural investigation of the historical record. (On the concept of culture areas, *see* Kehoe, *supra* note 71, at 11–13.)

Chapter 2

1. William N. Fenton, writing on Iroquois traditions of diplomacy as recorded in the treaty literature, said:

> The ethnohistorian in examining this [treaty] literature is confronted by the paradox of change and stability. Iroquois culture was indeed radically affected by its growing dependency on the European trade. The most obvious changes occurred in material culture; while social organization and political institutions remained relatively unaffected. Learning a few Dutch, French or English words did not alter their grammar; and as in language, the underlying patterns of their rituals remained stable over long periods of time. Content changed but structure persisted.

William N. Fenton, "Structure, Continuity and Change in the Process of Iroquois Treaty Making," in *The History and Culture of Iroquois Diplomacy* 5 (Francis Jennings, William N. Fenton, Mary A. Druke, & David R. Miller eds., 1985) [hereinafter *Iroquois Diplomacy*].

Fenton labels the ethnohistorian's method of utilizing the living tradition "for interpreting the past" as "upstreaming." *Id.* at 4. The method, as Fenton himself concedes, has its limitations and should be used with caution. The structure of a tradition itself evolves, some elements drop out, others are inserted, so that "the two patterns of sequence are not identical at both ends of the time span." *Id.* at 5. *See also* Richard White, *The Middle Ground: Indians, Empires and Republics in the Great Lakes Region, 1650–1815* (1991). "If assimilationist studies have a built-in bias toward the disappearance of earlier culture, then upstreaming has a bias toward continuity." *Id.* at xiv.

2. This is roughly the ceremony as I have seen it customarily practiced on important occasions in Indian country. The ritual varies in its details from tribe to tribe, of course, but the pipe is smoked in the solemn manner described generally in the text to honor a visiting leader from another tribe, to commence a meeting at which an important court case is to be discussed, or as a purely religious observance, for example.

3. *The Sacred Pipe: Black Elk's Account of the Seven Rites of the Oglala Sioux* xiv–xv (Joseph Epes Brown ed., 1953).

4. *Id.* at 3–4.

5. *Id.* at 5.

6. *Id.* at 5–6.

7. *Id.* at 7.

8. *Id.* at 8.

9. *Id.*at 8 n. 14.

10. *Id.* at 13.

11. *Id.* at 10.

12. So serious, in fact, that in 1890, the U.S. government prohibited the Sioux from performing the rite of the "keeping of the soul," requiring that on a certain day established by law, all souls kept by the Sioux must be released. *Id.* at 10 n. 1.

13. *Id.* at 7.

14. *Id.* at 101.

15. *Id.* at 101–102.

16. *Id.* at 102. Those who have seen the movie *Dances with Wolves* will recall that the Sioux are depicted as being at war with the Pawnees.

17. *Id.*

18. *Id.* at 102–103.

19. *Id.* at 110.

20. *Id.* at 112.

21. *Id.* at 113.

22. *Id.* at 113–114.

23. *Id.* at 115.

24. *Quoted in Native America in the Twentieth Century: An Encyclopedia* 73 (Mary B. Davis ed., 1994).

25. *See* Alice B. Kehoe, *North American Indians: A Comprehensive Account* 302–305 (2d ed. 1992).

26. Black Elk's rendition of Sioux tradition traces the introduction of the calumet pipe to Matohoshila's vision and subsequent diplomatic relations with the Caddoan Rees. Other evidence suggests, however, that the peace pipe tradition may have actually spread to the Sioux by way of the Pawnees, a Caddoan language–speaking group located on the western frontiers of Sioux territory who were closely related to the Rees. By the mid-seventeenth century, many of the Great Lakes region tribes had adopted the pipe as part of their diplomacy, and soon after, the pipe appears as part of the rituals practiced by the Iroquois and other Eastern Woodlands tribes. *See* White, *supra* note 1, at 29.

27. The early relations between the Yamacraws and Georgia are concisely reported in *Early American Indian Documents: Treaties and Laws, 1607–1789,* vol. 11, *Georgia Treaties, 1733–1763* 1–6 (John T. Juricek ed., 1989).

28. The council is reprinted in *id.* at 7–9, from which all quotes are taken.

29. The council is reprinted in *Early American Indian Documents: Treaties and Laws, 1607–1789,* vol. 4, *Virginia Treaties, 1607–1722* 266–267, from which all quotes are taken.

30. *See* White, *supra* note 1, at 6–7.

31. John Richard Alden, *John Stewart and the Southern Colonial Frontier: A Study of Indian Relations, War, Trade and Land Problems in the Southern Wilderness, 1754–1775* 218 (1944).

32. The Jesuit missionary's *Customs of the American Indians Compared with the Customs of Primitive Time* (1724) (William N. Fenton & Elizabeth Moore eds. and trans., 2 vols., 1974–1977) has been called an "ethnological classic" by the editors of *Iroquois Diplomacy, supra* note 1, at 266.

33. Dorothy V. Jones, "British Colonial Indian Treaties," in 4 *Handbook of North American Indians: History of Indian-White Relations* 186 (Wilcomb E. Washburn vol. ed., 1988).

34. *Quoted in id.*

35. *Quoted in* White, *supra* note 1, at 21.

36. *See generally id.* at 20–21 (describing the use of the pipe by the tribes of the Great Lakes region).

37. *See* Wilbur R. Jacobs, *Dispossessing the American Indian: Indians and Whites on the Colonial Frontier* 51 (1972).

38. Richard White, speaking to the importance of the pipe in Encounter era diplomacy on the North American colonial frontier, has written:

> The importance of the calumet ceremony can hardly be overstated. It formed a part of a conscious framework for peace, alliance, exchange, and full movement among peoples in a region. By arresting warriors, the calumet produced a truce during which negotiations took place; when negotiations were successful, the full calumet ceremony ratified the peace and created a fictive kinship relation between the person offering the pipe and the person specifically honored by the calumet. These people became responsible for maintaining that peace.

White, *supra* note 1, at 21–22. On the pipe, *see also* Donald Blakeslee, "The Calumet Ceremony and the Original Fur Trade Rituals," *W. Canadian J. Anthropology* 81–82 (1977); William N. Fenton, "The Iroquois Eagle Dance: An Offshoot of the Calumet Dance," *Bureau Am. Ethnology Bull.* 156 (1953).

39. Robert Cover, "*Nomos* and Narrative," 97 *Harv. L. Rev.* 4, 9 (1983).

40. Jones, *supra* note 33, at 186.

41. The council is reprinted in *Early American Indian Documents: Treaties and Laws, 1607–1789,* vol. 1, *Pennsylvania and Delaware Treaties, 1629–1737* 105–106 (Donald H. Kent ed., 1979), from which all quotes are taken.

42. The July 7, 1793, meeting is reprinted in 18 *National State Papers* 24 (1985).

43. The meeting is reprinted in *Early American Indian Documents: Treaties and Laws, 1607–1789,* vol. 5, *Virginia Treaties, 1723–1775* 272 (W. Stitt Robinson ed., 1983).

44. *Quoted in* Jacobs, *supra* note 37, at 113.

45. Marshall D. Sahlins, *Tribesmen* 98 (1968).

46. Bronislaw Malinowski, "Magic, Science and Religion," in *Magic, Science and Religion and Other Essays,* 28–29 (Robert Redfield ed., 1954). Malinowski was speaking specifically of the reliance on magic, which he distinguished from religious rites, to control forces beyond the native's control, but his influential thesis, as Sahlins notes, can be generalized to include "a variety of religious beliefs and practices." Sahlins, *supra* note 45, at 98.

47. Sahlins, *supra* note 45, at 97–99.

> Since it is in spiritual ways that social pressure exercises itself, it could not fail to give men the idea that outside themselves there exist one or several powers, both moral and, at the same time, efficacious, upon which they depend. They must think of these powers, at least in part, as outside themselves, for these address them in a tone of command. . . . As long as scientific analysis does not come to teach it to them, men know well that they are acted upon, but they do not know by whom. So they must invent by themselves the idea of these powers which they feel themselves in connection.

Id. at 97.

48. *See supra* text accompanying notes 33–34.

49. *See supra* text accompanying notes 12–24.

50. Sahlins, *supra* note 45, at 97.

51. Cover, *supra* note 39, at 7.

52. *See supra* Introduction, text accompanying note 6.

53. *See* Bert Salwen, "Indians of Southern New England and Long Island:

Early Period," in 15 *Handbook of North American Indians: Northeast* 166 (Bruce G. Trigger vol. ed., 1978) [hereinafter 15 *Handbook*]. "The wampum trade appears to have existed in pre-contact times, and both the manufacture and distribution of the beads are well-described by Lescarbot as observed in about 1606." *Id.*

54. On the uses of wampum in Indian-white trade and diplomacy, *see generally* 1 Lewis H. Morgan, *League of the Ho-De-No Sau-Nee or Iroquois* (Human Relations Area Files 1954) 114–115 (1901) (discussing the use of wampum in mourning councils); W. M. Beauchamp, "Wampum Used in Council and as Currency," 20 *Am. Antiquarian* 1 (1898); William N. Fenton, "The Hiawatha Wampum Belt of the Iroquois League for Peace: A Symbol for the International Congress of Anthropology," in *Men and Cultures* 3 (Anthony F. C. Wallace ed., 1960) (analyzing the Hiawatha wampum belt as a device for remembering the founding of the original League for Peace); William N. Fenton, "The New York State Wampum Collection: The Case for the Integrity of Cultural Treasures," 115 *Proc. Am. Phil. Soc'y* 437 (1971) (discussing wampum in the context of claims for the restoration of cultural objects to Indian heirs); Michael K. Foster, "Another Look at the Function of Wampum in Iroquois-White Councils," in *Iroquois Diplomacy, supra* note 1, at 99 (focusing on the Indian's own understanding of the function of wampum in the councils); J. S. Slotkin & Karl Schmitt, "Studies of Wampum," 51 *Am. Anthropologist* 223 (1949) (discussing the use of wampum before and after white contact); George S. Snyderman, "The Functions of Wampum," 98 *Proc. Am. Phil. Soc'y* 469 (1954) (discussing wampum from the Indian's own point of view to eradicate misconceptions perpetuated by the failure of whites to understand Indian culture); Elisabeth Tooker, "The League of the Iroquois: Its History, Politics, and Ritual," in 15 *Handbook, supra* note 53, at 418, 422–424 (discussing the uses of wampum in a variety of different contexts); Mary Druke, "Iroquois Treaties: Common Forms, Varying Interpretations," in *Iroquois Diplomacy, supra* note 1, at 88–90 (discussing the wampum belt as a treaty document).

55. *Reprinted in Iroquois Diplomacy, supra* note 1, at 127–153, from which all quotes are taken.

56. *See infra* Chapter 4.

57. *See* Francis Jennings, *The Ambiguous Iroquois Empire* 84–112 (1984).

58. Anthony F. C. Wallace, *The Death and Rebirth of the Seneca* 43 (1972).

59. *See* Eric Wolf, *Europe and the People without History* 170 (1982); White, *supra* note 1, at 102–104.

60. *See supra* text accompanying notes 13–24.

61. Eric Wolf, *Europe and the People without History* 164 (1982).

62. Anthony F. C. Wallace, "The Career of William N. Fenton and the Development of Iroquoian Studies," in *Extending the Rafters: Interdisciplinary Approaches to Iroquois Studies* 1 (Michael K. Foster et al. eds., 1984) (providing a comprehensive bibliographical essay on the career and influence of the man "[u]niversally recognized as the dean of Iroquoian studies"). *See also id.* at 401–417 (giving a complete bibliography of Fenton's works to 1982).

63. *Iroquois Diplomacy, supra* note 1, at 4.

64. Fenton, in describing the program of the Condolence Council, identifies sixteen discrete events "arranged in a pattern of sequence that has governed its performance since early times." *Id.* at 18–19.

65. Michael K. Foster, "Another Look at the Function of Wampum in Iroquois-White Councils," in *id.* at 105.

66. *Id.* at 106.
67. *Id.*
68. *See supra* text accompanying notes 56–57.
69. *See Iroquois Diplomacy, supra* note 1, at 17–19 (describing the use of wampum in the Condolence Council).
70. *See id.* at 20.
71. *See id.* at 19–20.
72. *See id. See generally* Robert A. Williams, Jr., "Gendered Checks and Balances: Understanding the Legacy of White Patriarchy in an American Indian Cultural Context," 24 *Ga. L. Rev.* 1019, 1036–1043 (1990) (discussing the Iroquois system of using gender-specific roles as cultural checks and balances).
73. *Iroquois Diplomacy, supra* note 1, at 18.
74. *Id.* at 28.
75. *See, e.g., Iroquois Diplomacy, supra* note 1, at 20–21.
76. Cadwallader Colden, *The History of the Five Indian Nations* 104–105 (1958) (1727, 1747).
77. *Id.* The Iroquois diplomat continued his lengthy presentation of belts as follows:

> We are now come to the House where we usually renew the Chain; but alas! we find the House polluted, polluted with Blood. All the Five Nations have heard of this, and we are come to wipe away the Blood, and clean the House. We come to invite Corlear [New York's governor], and every one of you . . . *to be revenged of the Enemy,* by this fifth Belt.
>
> We will never desist. . . . We are of the Race of the Bear, and a Bear you know never yields, while one Drop of Blood is left. *We must all be Bears;* giving a sixth Belt.
>
> Brethren be patient, this Disaster is an Affliction which has fallen from Heaven upon us. The Sun, which hath been cloudy, and sent this Disaster, will shine again with its pleasant Beams. Take Courage, said he, Courage, repeating the Word several times as they gave a seventh Belt.

Id.
78. *Id. See Iroquois Diplomacy, supra* note 1, at 20.
79. *See id.* at 20, 44–46.
80. Although there is no written record of the founding of the League of the Haudenosaunee (the Iroquois' own name for their multitribal confederacy), anthropologists and ethnohistorians generally concede its existence prior to European contact. It may have been in existence by the fifteenth century, if not earlier. *See* Wallace, *supra* note 58, at 41 (dating the league's emergence at "about 1450"); *Iroquois Diplomacy, supra* note 1, at 16 ("It is certain . . . that the League was founded before European settlement, probably about A.D. 1500, give or take twenty-five years"); Daniel Richter, "Ordeals of the Longhouse: The Five Nations in Early American History," in *Beyond the Covenant Chain: The Iroquois and Their Neighbors in Indian North America, 1600–1800* 16 (Daniel K. Richter & James H. Merrell eds., 1987) [hereinafter *Beyond the Covenant Chain*] ("native traditions and scholarly interpretations point to various eras between A.D. 1400 and A.D. 1600 as the date of the League's founding").
81. *Iroquois Diplomacy, supra* note 1, at 14.

> The Deganawidah Epic in all of its versions comprises one genre, which in the words of Levi-Strauss "can be thought of as belonging together," and in this sense have a single identity over time. But even in societies like the Iroquois who aspire to verbatim recall, each narrator has his own version of the myth: he never tells it twice in precisely the same way, and there is bound to be substitution of content over time. Listeners, nevertheless, recognize the several versions as belonging to the one myth, even though the narrators are unable to agree on details or the precise order of incidents. One need not pursue the search for one true version; it never existed. One can, however, reconstruct its main outlines and plot.

Id. (footnotes omitted).

The descriptions of the league's founding and the Deganawidah epic summarized in this chapter are based on the following sources: Arthur C. Parker, "The Constitution of the Five Nations, or The Iroquois Book of the Great Law" [hereinafter Parker, "Constitution of the Five Nations"], in *Parker on the Iroquois* (William N. Fenton ed., 1968); Paul Wallace, *The White Roots of Peace* (1946); *Iroquois Diplomacy, supra* note 1, at 14–18; William N. Fenton, "The Lore of the Longhouse: Myth, Ritual and Red Power," 48 *Anthropological Q.* 131 (1975); *Beyond the Covenant Chain, supra* note 80, at 16–19; Anthony F. C. Wallace, "The Dekanawideh Myth Analyzed as the Record of a Revitalization Movement," 5 *Ethnohistory* 118 (1958); Paul A. W. Wallace, "The Iroquois: A Brief Outline of Their History" [hereinafter P. Wallace, "The Iroquois"], in *The Livingston Indian Records, 1666–1723,* 15, 15–18 (Lawrence H. Leder ed., 1956).

My retelling and interpretation of the Iroquois Deganawidah charter epic and its integral relation to an understanding of Iroquois political and legal traditions during the Encounter era borrow heavily from Bronislaw Malinowski's essay, "Myth in Primitive Psychology," in *Magic, Science and Religion and Other Essays* 74, 94 (Robert Redfield ed., 1954). Malinowski sets out to demonstrate that "an intimate connection exists between the word, the mythos, the sacred tales of a tribe, on the one hand, and their ritual acts, their moral deeds, their social organization, and even their practical activities, on the other." *Id.* at 74. A myth thus serves as "a warrant, a charter, and often even a practical guide to the activities with which it is connected." *Id.* at 85. "[O]nce we begin to study the social function of myth, and so to reconstruct its full meaning, we are gradually led to build up the full theory of native social organization." *Id.* at 94.

As Clifford Geertz notes, there has been "little conceptual advance" in the field over Malinowski's theory-building efforts. Clifford Geertz, *The Interpretation of Cultures* 103 (1973). Geertz's work itself reflects the influence of Malinowski's "sociological" approach on the field of anthropology. Geertz has paraphrased the broad goal of this approach in one characteristically brilliant and pithy sentence (contained in an essay discussing Malinowski's traits as an anthropologist): "The trick is to figure out what the devil they [the 'natives'] think they are up to." Clifford Geertz, *Local Knowledge* 58 (1983). The approach outlined in Geertz's essay, "The Way We Think Now: Toward an Ethnography of Modern Thought," in *id.* at 147, illuminates somewhat the limited goals I have set out for my own research in the field of multicultural legal studies:

> The primitive form of the "primitive thought" formulation—that is, that while we, the civilized, sort matters out analytically, relate them logically,

> and test them systematically, as can be seen by our mathematics, physics, medicine, or law, they, the savage, wander about in a hodgepodge of concrete images, mystical participations, and immediate passions, as can be seen by their myth, ritual, magic, or art—has, of course, been progressively undermined as more about how the other half thinks has become known (and more, too, about just how unvirginal reason is); though it persists in certain sorts of developmental psychology, certain styles of comparative history, and certain circles of the diplomatic service. The error, as in rather different ways both Boas and Malinowski gave much of their careers to demonstrating, lay in attempting to interpret cultural materials as though they were individual expressions rather than social institutions. Whatever the connection between thought as process and thought as product might be, the Rodin model—the solitary thinker mulling facts or spinning fantasies—is inadequate to clarify it. Myths are not dreams, and the rational beauties of mathematical proof are guarantees of no mathematician's sanity.

Id. at 49.

82. Bronislaw Malinowski, "Myth in Primitive Psychology," in *Magic, Science and Religion and Other Essays* 116 (Robert Redfield ed., 1954).

83. *See, e.g., Beyond the Covenant Chain, supra* note 80, at 19.

84. *See, e.g.*, Parker, "Constitution of the Five Nations," *supra* note 81, at 14–15.

85. *See, e.g., Beyond the Covenant Chain, supra* note 80, at 16.

86. *Id.* at 16.

87. *Id.*

88. A. Wallace, *supra* note 58, at 101. *See also* Daniel Richter, "War and Culture: The Iroquois Experience," 40 *Wm. & Mary Q.* 528 (1983). In his article, Richter asserts that the psychology of the mourning war was "deeply rooted in Iroquois demography and social structure" and emphasizes its function in "the maintenance of stable population levels." *Id.* at 529 n. 4, 530. *Cf.* Marian W. Smith, "American Indian Warfare," 13 *Transactions N.Y. Acad. Sci.* 348, 352–355 (1951) (stressing the psychological and emotional functions of the mourning war).

89. According to Anthony Wallace:

> Generally speaking, whatever economic or political considerations might be involved in the tensions that led to war, the actual formation of war parties was either inspired or rationalized by the obligation to avenge dead relatives. . . . [U]ntil there had been retaliatory killings and tortures, it was as if the blood of the murdered one had not been wiped away and his corpse not covered. War-caused bereavement was a state of unavenged insult and shame.

A. Wallace, *supra* note 58, at 101.

90. *Id.* at 101.

91. *See id.*

92. *Beyond the Covenant Chain, supra* note 80, at 16.

93. *Id.*

94. P. Wallace, "The Iroquois," *supra* note 81, at 17.

95. *Iroquois Diplomacy, supra* note 1, at 14.
96. *Beyond the Covenant Chain, supra* note 80, at 16–17.
97. *Id.* at 17.
98. *Iroquois Diplomacy, supra* note 1, at 15.
99. *See* P. Wallace, "The Iroquois," *supra* note 81 at 17. *See also* Parker, "Constitution of the Five Nations," *supra* note 81, at 8–9.

> I am Dekanawideh and with the Five Nations' confederate lords I plant the Tree of the Great Peace. I plant it in your territory Adodarhoh and the Onondaga Nation, in the territory of you who are fire keepers.
>
> I name the tree the Tree of the Great Long Leaves. Under the shade of this Tree of the Great Peace we spread the soft, white, feathery down of the globe thistle as seats for you, Adodarhoh and your cousin lords. . . .
>
> There shall you sit and watch the council fire of the Confederacy of the Five Nations.
>
> Roots have spread out from the Tree of the Great Peace . . . and the name of these roots is the Great White Roots of Peace.
>
> If any man of any nation outside of the Five Nations shall show a desire to obey the laws of the Great Peace . . . they may trace the roots to their source . . . and they shall be welcomed to take shelter beneath the Tree of the Long Leaves.
>
> The smoke of the confederate council fire shall ever ascend and shall pierce the sky so that all nations may discover the central council fire of the Great Peace.

Id.

100. Parker, "Constitution of the Five Nations," *supra* note 81, at 8–9.
101. *Beyond the Covenant Chain, supra* note 80, at 17. Besides arranging the council in two moieties for purposes of condoling and mourning, Deganawidah also arranged "a tripartite seating" for purposes of business at the Great Council Fire. The Mohawks and Senecas sat to the East, the Oneidas and Cayugas to the West, and the "firekeepers," the Onondagas, to the north, acting as arbiters of the two opinions. *Iroquois Diplomacy, supra* note 1, at 15. *See generally* Parker, "Constitution of the Five Nations," *supra* note 81, at 30–33 (describing the structure of the Great Council in terms of the league's principles).

The Deganawidah epic was not recorded in writing until late in the nineteenth century. *See Iroquois Diplomacy, supra* note 1, at 15. In describing the council seating arrangements, Fenton cites the version of the epic recorded and edited by Arthur C. Parker, an Iroquois anthropologist, published in Parker's 1916 work, "Constitution of the Five Nations," *supra* note 81. According to Fenton, the efforts by "native annalists" to codify the charter for the League of Five Nations pointed to "a process of projection and feedback of content, structure and ritual process that is yet evolving." *Iroquois Diplomacy, supra* note 1, at 15 (footnote omitted). Not surprisingly, then, several of Parker's renditions of the "bylaws" governing the league's internal structure and rituals contain "a distinct nineteenth century tone," though others "hark back to aboriginal times." *Id.*

In relating the epic of Deganawidah's founding of the league, I have sought to convey the basic outlines of the story as generally agreed on by most of the major sources consulted in my research. These include primarily Parker, "Constitution of the Five Nations," *supra* note 81; J. N. B. Hewitt, "Legend of the Founding of the Iroquois League," 5 *Am. Anthropologist* 131 (1892). For critical commentary on the various versions of the Iroquois "Constitution," see William N. Fenton, "Introduction to Arthur C. Parker," in *Parker on the Iroquois, supra* note 81, at 38–46; *Iroquois Diplomacy, supra* note 1.

102. *Beyond the Covenant Chain, supra* note 80, at 18.

103. *Id.* at 17.

104. John P. Reid, *A Better Kind of Hatchet: Law, Trade, and Diplomacy in the Cherokee Nation during the Early Years of European Contact* 16 (1976). Reid is referring to the Cherokees' concept of peace, but the notion applies equally to the Iroquois. *See* Richter, *supra* note 80, at 18.

105. *See* Fenton, *Iroquois Diplomacy, supra* note 1, at 13 (discussing the importance of attaining "one mind" in the Iroquois system of government).

106. *Beyond the Covenant Chain, supra* note 80, at 18.

107. Parker, "The Constitution of the Five Nations," *supra* note 81, at 15.

108. P. Wallace, *The Iroquois, supra* note 81, at 17. The Deganawidah epic provided what Wallace calls a "patriotic incentive" that bound the Iroquois together as a confederated people. He argues that the league's frequent wars throughout the Encounter era assumed "something of the complexion of religious crusades." *Id.*

109. A. Wallace, *supra* note 58, at 43.

110. Parker, "Constitution of the Five Nations," *supra* note 81, at 9.

111. J. G. A. Pocock, *Politics, Language, and Time* 237 (1971).

112. Malinowski, *supra* note 46, at 100.

> And this brings us once more to our original contention that the really important thing about the myth is its character of a retrospective, ever-present, live actuality. . . . It is clear that myth functions especially where there is a sociological strain, such as in matters of great difference in rank and power, matters of precedence and subordination, and unquestionably where profound historical changes have taken place. So much can be asserted as a fact, though it must always remain doubtful how far we can carry out historical reconstruction from the myth.

Chapter 3

1. "On a most basic level, humans who did not establish and maintain relationships—persons who had no friends, kin, or alliances—faced grim prospects. (Indeed, they were at times found destitute in or near Indian villages)." Mary A. Druke, "Linking Arms: The Structure of Iroquois Intertribal Diplomacy," in *Beyond the Covenant Chain: The Iroquois and Their Neighbors in Indian North America, 1600–1800* 32–33 (Daniel K. Richter & James H. Merrell eds., 1987) [hereinafter *Beyond the Covenant Chain*].

2. "Gain at the cost of other communities," Thornstein Veblen once wrote in an oft-cited passage, "particularly *communities at a distance,* and more especially such as are felt to be aliens, is not obnoxious to the standards of homebred use and wont." *Quoted in* Marshall Sahlins, *Tribesmen* 82 (1968) (emphasis added).

3. Eric R. Wolf, *Europe and the People without History* 89 (1982).

4. *Id.* at 91.

5. As Wolf writes, kinship involves

> (a) symbolic constructs ("filiation/marriage; consanguinity/affinity") that (b) continually place actors; born and recruited, (c) into social relations with one another. These social relations (d) permit people in variable ways to call on the share of labor carried by each, in order to (e) effect the necessary transformations of nature.

Id.

6. A sixth nation, the Tuscaroras of North Carolina, came north as refugees and joined the confederacy during the early eighteenth century. *See* William N. Fenton, "Structure, Continuity, and Change in the Process of Iroquois Treaty Making" [hereinafter Fenton, "Iroquois Treaty Making"], in *The History and Culture of Iroquois Diplomacy* 7–9 (Francis Jennings et al. eds., 1985) [hereinafter *Iroquois Diplomacy*].

7. Villages, at least during the early Encounter era, were typically composed of a cluster of 30 to 150 longhouses, surrounded by a palisade, outlying agricultural fields, and then the forest, usually a range of territory encompassing the village's hunting and gathering grounds. Ideally, a village would be situated on a height of land accessible to drinking water and not too far removed from a waterway. *See* William N. Fenton, "Northern Iroquoian Cultural Patterns," in 15 *Handbook of North American Indians: Northeast* 306 (Bruce G. Trigger vol. ed., 1978) [hereinafter 15 *Handbook*]. Within the villages, the chief's home typically served as a council house, where ambassadors to the village would call and where the village would assemble to hear an ambassador's message. Fenton, "Iroquois Treaty Making," *supra* note 6, at 9.

8. Anthony Wallace has described an Iroquois longhouse as "a dark, noisy, smoke-filled family barracks; a rectangular, gable-roofed structure anywhere from fifty to seventy-five feet in length, constructed of sheets of elm bark lashed on stout poles." Anthony F. C. Wallace, *The Death and Rebirth of the Seneca* 22 (1972).

9. Fenton, "Iroquois Treaty Making," *supra* note 6, at 9–10. Fenton has described the matrilineal clan organization of the Iroquois in the following terms:

> Stemming from the fireside family and including any living siblings of the wife's mother, both male and female, the wife's brothers and sisters, the wife's children, and her daughter's children, and the descendants of any of the preceding women in the female line, is the household of fact and legal fiction, or the continuing maternal family. Ascending the matrilineal scale, the senior living woman is the matriarch and she presides over the household and makes ultimate decisions on social and political matters. This lineage of persons tracing descent from a common mother forms an isogamic incest group, members of which must take their spouses from other similar matrilineages. In time such a lineage might occupy several longhouse in several villages, giving rise to segments of a clan.

Id. at 10.

10. *Id.*

11. *See* Wallace, *supra* note 8, at 14–15.

12. *Id.* at 34. Cultivation of this ideal of autonomous responsibility explains the Iroquois' strong belief that no one could tell another person in the tribe what

to do. As Wallace explains, Europeans found such tribal methods of socialization difficult to accept:

> The Europeans who observed this pattern of child experience were by no means unfavorably impressed although they were sometimes amazed. They commented, however, almost to a man, from early Jesuit to latter-day Quaker, on a consequence that stood out dramatically as they compared this "savage" maturation with "civilized." "There is nothing," wrote the Jesuit chronicler of the Iroquois mission in 1657, "for which these peoples have a greater horror than restraint. The very children cannot endure it, and live as they please in the houses of their parents, without fear of reprimand or chastisement." One hundred and fifty years later, the Quaker Halliday Jackson observed that "being indulged in most of their wishes, as they grow up, liberty, in its fullest extent, becomes their ruling passion." The Iroquois themselves recognized the intensity of their children's resentment at parental interference.

Id. at 38 (footnotes omitted).

13. *See generally* Wallace, *supra* note 8, at 14–15 ("clan members are expected to maintain a generally friendly attitude toward one another, as if they were all members of one big and more or less happy family").

14. *See generally id.* at 14–15.

15. *Id.* at 23.

16. On the role of women in Iroquois culture, *see* Arthur C. Parker, "Iroquois Uses of Maize and Other Food Plants," in *Parker on the Iroquois* 5, 21–24 (William N. Fenton ed., 1968) (discussing the division of labor by gender); Judith K. Brown, "Economic Organization and the Position of Women among the Iroquois," 17 *Ethnohistory* 151 (1970); Martha C. Randle, "Iroquois Women, Then and Now," 149 *Bureau Am. Ethnology Bull.* 167 (1951); Elisabeth Tooker, "Women in Iroquois Society," in *Extending the Rafters: Interdisciplinary Approaches to Iroquoian Studies* 109 (Michael K. Foster et al. eds., 1984); Robert A. Williams, Jr., "Gendered Checks and Balances: Understanding the Legacy of White Patriarchy in an American Indian Cultural Context," 24 *Ga. L. Rev.* 1019 (1990).

17. The Seneca, for example, divide themselves into Wolf, Bear, Beaver, and Turtle clans on one moiety or side and Deer, Hawk, Snipe, and Heron on the other. *See* Wallace, *supra* note 8, at 14–15.

18. *Id.* at 15.

19. Fenton, "Iroquois Treaty Making," *supra* note 6, at 10–12.

20. *Id.* at 12.

21. *See id.* at 10–11.

22. Harold E. Driver, *Indians of North America* 221 (2d ed. 1969). By contrast, as Driver notes, "European marriage and family practices were almost uniform." *Id.*

23. John Phillip Reid, *A Law of Blood: The Primitive Law of the Cherokee Nation* 37 (1970).

24. *Id.* at 10.

25. *Id.*

26. *See id.* at 38–39.

27. Rennard Strickland, *Fire and the Spirits: Cherokee Law from Clan to Court* 27 (1975).

28. *Quoted in* Reid, *supra* note 23, at 39.

29. *Id.* at 48. "We should stress not the familial divisions of clanship, but the legal cohesiveness provided by the mutual rights and duties existing between clan members—for it was this which united the Cherokee into a 'nation' in the fullest sense of the term." *Id.*

30. Strickland, *supra* note 27, at 27.

31. Reid, *supra* note 23, at 78–79; Strickland, *supra* note 27, at 27–28.

32. "There are two fundamental principles at the basis of primitive law: first, controversy should be prevented; second, controversy should be terminated." J. W. Powell, "Tribal Marriage Law," in *Primitive and Ancient Legal Institutions* 277, 278 (Albert Kocourek & John H. Wigmore eds., 1915).

33. The discussion in this section relies on the following sources: Ives Goddard, "Delaware," 15 *Handbook, supra* note 7, at 225–239; Charles Callender, "Shawnee," in *id.* at 622–639; Charles Callender, "Fox," in *id.* at 636–667.

34. Callender, "Fox," in 15 *Handbook, supra* note 7, at 640.

35. Robert Cover, "Foreword: *Nomos* and Narrative," 97 *Harv. L. Rev.* 4, 4–11 (1983).

36. Francis Jennings defines a tribe as "a coherent and self-conscious political entity integrated by kinship rather than bureaucracy and coercion; it functions as a nation in external affairs and as a family internally." Francis Jennings, "Pennsylvania Indians and the Iroquois," in *Beyond the Covenant Chain, supra* note 1, at 187 n. 4. A useful and concise account of tribal cultures can be found in Sahlins, *supra* note 2. Sahlins's account stresses the vital importance of kinship connections in tribal life: "The tribe is a constellation of communities and relations between communities. The main elements of this structure are in substance major groupings of kinsmen. Descent groups in particular often comprise the nuclei of tribal sections; certain types of descent groups can provide a framework for the entire tribal organization." *Id.* at 49.

37. *See* Sahlins, *supra* note 2.

38. *Id.* at 82.

39. Marcel Mauss, *The Gift* 79 (1954).

40. 27 *National State Papers of the United States 1789–1817,* pt. 2, *Texts of Documents, Administration of George Washington, 1789–1797, December 7, 1795–December 31, 1795* 22 (Eileen Daney Carzo ed., 1985) [hereinafter *National State Papers*].

41. The meeting is related in Francis Jennings, *The Ambiguous Iroquois Empire* 193 (1984).

42. On the symbolic usage of kinship terms in Iroquois treaty diplomacy, *see* Fenton, "Iroquois Treaty Making," *supra* note 6, at 11, 21–22. Andros, the experienced colonial official, clearly appreciated that the terms held distinct meanings for the Iroquois. He told the Indians, "[Y]ou take notice of the word[s] Brothers and Children." The governor, however, chose to ignore the Iroquois preferences in his discourse. "[L]eave it to me," he said; "they are both words of relation and friendship, but Children the nearer." *Quoted in id.*

43. One year before Andros's meeting with the Mohawks, a group of Seneca chiefs tried to explain their understnding of their treaty status as "brethren" with the New York colony as follows. Although the English enjoyed the privilege of

calling the Indians the "subjects" of their king, the Seneca nonetheless regarded themselves "no ways obliged to hanker to him." *Id.* at 194.

44. *See* Jennings, *supra* note 41, at 193.

45. *See* Fenton, "Iroquois Treaty Making," *supra* note 6, at 11, 22.

46. *See* Reid, *supra* note 7, at 40–41.

47. *Early American Indian Documents: Treaties and Laws, 1607–1789* (Alden T. Vaughan gen. ed.), vol. 6, *Maryland Treaties, 1632–1775* 285 (W. Stitt Robinson ed., 1987).

48. *See* Mary A. Druke, "Linking Arms: The Structure of Iroquois Intertribal Diplomacy," in *Beyond the Covenant Chain, supra* note 1, at 31.

49. Witham Marshe, "Journal of the Treaty Held with the Six Nations by the Commissioners of Maryland, and Other Provinces, at Lancaster, in Pennsylvania, June, 1744," *reprinted in* 7 *Collections of the Massachusetts Historical Society, for the Year 1800* 171, 193 (1801).

50. *See Iroquois Diplomacy, supra* note 6, at 240; Richard White, *The Middle Ground: Indians, Empire and Republics in the Great Lakes Region, 1650–1815* 84, 112–113 (1991).

51. *See Iroquois Diplomacy, supra* note 6, at 246.

52. *See id.* at 235.

53. *See supra* text accompanying note 49.

54. *See* Wolf, *supra* note 3, at 88–96; Sahlins, *supra* note 2, at 12–13. Sahlins quotes the Chinese philosopher-sage Confucius: "Ceremonies are the bond that holds the multitudes together, and if the bond be removed, the multitude fall into confusion." *Quoted in id.* at 12.

55. *See supra* Chapter 2, text accompanying notes 1–11.

56. *See Early American Indian Documents: Treaties and Laws, 1607–1789* (Alden T. Vaughan gen. ed.), vol. 5, *Virginia Treaties, 1723–1775* 361 (W. Stitt Robinson ed., 1983) [hereinafter *Virginia Treaties, 1723–1775*].

57. *Id.* at 363.

58. *See id.* at 23.

59. 18 *National State Papers, supra* note 40, at 25.

60. 27 *National State Papers, supra* note 40, at 23.

61. *See supra* Chapter 2, text accompanying notes 53–58.

62. *See Early American Indian Documents: Treaties and Laws, 1607–1789* (Alden T. Vaughan gen. ed.), vol. 8, *New York and New Jersey Treaties, 1609–1682* 39 (Barbara Graymont ed., 1985) [hereinafter *New York Treaties*].

63. *Quoted in* 9 *The Papers of Sir William Johnson,* 14 vols., 604 (James Sullivan, Alexander C. Flick, et al. eds., 1921–1965).

64. Fenton, "Iroquois Treaty Making," *supra* note 6, at 17.

65. *See id.* at 12, 24–25.

66. *See New York Treaties, supra* note 62, at 40–41.

67. *See Early American Indian Documents: Treaties and Laws, 1607–1789* (Alden T. Vaughan gen. ed.), vol. 1, *Pennsylvania and Delaware Treaties, 1629–1737* 52 (Donald H. Kent ed., 1979).

68. *Virginia Treaties, 1723–1775, supra* note 56, at 287.

69. *See Early American Indian Documents: Treaties and Laws, 1607–1789* (Alden T. Vaughan gen. ed.), vol. 4, *Virginia Treaties, 1607–1722* 265–266 (W. Stitt Robinson ed., 1983).

70. *See* Sahlins, *supra* note 2, at 9 ("exchange in tribal societies generally

proceeds under certain constraints. Competition and gain are often excluded, either in the attempt to make friendly relations or at least to avoid unfriendly ones").

71. *See id.* at 10. Professor Sahlins explains the purpose served by these "instrumental exchanges" in tribal diplomacy: "Reciprocity in exchange is economic diplomacy: the mutuality of the material flow symbolizes willingness to consider the other party's welfare, a disinclination to selfishly prosecute one's own." *Id.* This insight into tribal economics can be traced in Thomas Hobbes's work. As Sahlins notes, Hobbes declared that the first law of nature enjoins humans to seek peace. This, in turn, means that reciprocity is a law of nature. As Hobbes put it:

> [N]o man giveth, but with intention of Good to himself; because Gift is Voluntary; and of all Voluntary Acts, the Object is to every man his own Good; of which if men see they shall be frustrated, there will be no beginning of benevolence, or trust; nor consequently of mutual help; nor of reconciliation of one man to another; and therefore they are to remain still in the condition of *War;* which is contrary to the first and fundamental Law of Nature, which commands men to *Seek Peace.*

Quoted in id. at 9.

72. *See, e.g.*, the account of treaty councils held with Georgia's colonial officials reprinted in *Early American Indian Documents: Treaties and Laws, 1607–1789* (Alden T. Vaughan gen. ed.), vol. 11, *Georgia Treaties, 1733–1763* 10–11, 12–13, 94, 188–191 (John T. Juricek ed., 1989).

73. *Id.* at 5.

74. *See* "Alured Clarke's Account of the Royal Audience," *reprinted in id.* at 22–23 [hereinafter "Clarke"]; "The Earl of Egmont's Report of the Royal Audiences," *reprinted in id.* at 23–24 [hereinafter "Egmont"]; "Tomochici's Audience with King Geroge II and Queen Carolina [*Gentlemen's Magazine*]," *reprinted in id.* at 21–22 [hereinafter *Gentlemen's Magazine*].

75. *See* "Egmont," *supra* note 74, at 23.

76. *See* "Clarke," *supra* note 74, at 22.

77. *See Gentlemen's Magazine, supra* note 74, at 21.

78. "Clarke," *supra* note 74, at 22.

79. *Gentlemen's Magazine, supra* note 74, at 21.

80. "Clarke," *supra* note 74, at 23.

81. "Egmont," *supra* note 74, at 23.

82. *See Georgia Treaties, supra* note 72, at xxi–xxiii.

83. *Id.* at 54.

84. *See supra* text accompanying note 83.

85. *See* Richard White, *The Middle Ground: Indians, Empires and Republics in the Great Lakes Region, 1650–1815* 93 (1991).

Chapter 4

1. On stories and storytelling as techniques in critical race and feminist theories of law and jurisprudence, *see generally* Derrick Bell, *And We Are Not Saved* (1987) (elaborating on ten different forms of antiblack discrimination by telling ten separate stories); Patricia A. Cain, "Feminist Jurisprudence: Grounding the

Theories," 4 *Berkeley Women's L.J.* 191 (1990) (retelling stories of lesbian individuals to ground feminist legal theory in the experiences of women); Richard Delgado, "Storytelling for Oppositionists and Others: A Plea for Narrative," 87 *Mich. L. Rev.* 2411 (1989) [hereinafter, Delgado, "A Plea for Narrative"] (discussing storytelling as a modern academic tool); Richard Delgado, "When a Story Is Just a Story: Does Voice Really Matter?," 76 *Va. L. Rev.* 95 (1990); Toni M. Massaro, "Empathy, Legal Storytelling, and the Rule of Law: New Words, Old Wounds?," 87 *Mich. L. Rev.* 2099 (1989) (elevating storytelling as an academic method of inductive education); Mari J. Matsuda, "Looking to the Bottom: Critical Legal Studies and Reparations," 22 *Harv. C.R.-C.L. L. Rev.* 323 (1987) (encouraging scholars to listen to the stories of people experiencing discrimination before developing grand normative theories of justice); Mari J. Matsuda, "Public Response to Racist Speech: Considering the Victim's Story," 87 *Mich. L. Rev.* 2320 (1989) [hereinafter, Matsuda, "Racist Speech"] (retelling the stories of victims of racial harassment); Carrie Menkel-Meadow, "Portia in a Different Voice: Speculations on a Women's Lawyering Process," 1 *Berkeley Women's L.J.* 39 (1985) (discussing how the entry of women into the legal academy has led to an increase in the use of storytelling as an academic methodology); Martha Minow, "Feminist Reason: Getting It and Losing It," 38 *J. Legal Educ.* 47 (1988) (pursuing the perpetual critique initiated by feminist research while searching for practical justice rather than theory); Patricia Williams, "The Obliging Shell: An Informal Essay on Formal Equal Opportunity," 87 *Mich. L. Rev.* 2128 (1989) (retelling the story of minority set-asides in the case of *City of Richmond v. J. A. Croson Co.*, 488 U.S. 469 (1989), as part of a broader essay on formal equal opportunity); Patricia J. Williams, "Alchemical Notes: Reconstructing Ideals from Deconstructed Rights," 22 *Harv. C.R.-C.L. L. Rev.* 401 (1987) (relating parables to a critique of the critical legal studies movement).

2. *See* Symposium, "Legal Storytelling," 87 *Mich. L. Rev.* 2073 (1989).

3. Delgado, "A Plea for Narrative," *supra* note 1.

4. *Id.* at 2438.

5. Matsuda, "Racist Speech," *supra* note 1, at 2325 n. 32.

6. *Id.* at 2325 (footnote omitted).

7. Arnold Krupat, "The Dialogic of Silko's Storyteller," in *Narrative Chance: Postmodern Discourse of Native American Indian Literatures* 59 (Gerald Vizenor ed., 1993) [hereinafter *Narrative Chance*].

8. *Id.* at 63 ("[S]tories—both the mythic-traditional tales passed down among the people and the day-to-day narratives of events—do make things happen").

9. On jurisgenesis, the creation of legal meaning as a collective and social process, *see* Robert M. Cover, "Foreword: *Nomos* and Narrative," 97 *Harv. L. Rev.* 4, 11–19 (1983).

10. 8 *Documents Relative to the Colonial History of the State of New York* 43 (E. B. O'Callaghan ed., 1857) [hereinafter *D.R.C.H.S.N.Y.*]. Johnson is quoted in Theda Perdue's "Cherokee Relations with the Iroquois in the Eighteenth Century," in *Beyond the Covenant Chain: The Iroquois and Their Neighbors in Indian North America, 1600–1800* 137 (Daniel K. Richter & James H. Merrell eds., 1987). Perdue provides a concise historical account of the background of Cherokee-Iroquois conflict during the Encounter era. On Ouconastota, "[t]he

distinguished Chief who visisted England in the days of George II," *see* 8 *D.R.C.H.S.N.Y., supra,* at 41 n. 2.

11. On the reasons for Chota's ascendancy during the mid-eighteenth century in Cherokee political affairs, *see* John Phillip Reid's careful analysis in *A Law of Blood* 17–27 (1970).

12. *See D.R.C.H.S.N.Y., supra* note 10, at 43.

13. The 1763 treaty council at Augusta, Georgia, was one of the most significant multicultural encounters of the eighteenth century. The council was called by Lord Egremont, secretary of state for the Southern Department in the Crown's Ministry with responsibility for colonial affairs. Along with James Stuart, the royal government's superintendent of Indian affairs in the South, the conference was attended by the colonial governors of Virginia, North and South Carolina, and Georgia. Indian embassies to the council included delegations from the Creeks, Catawbas, Cherokees, Chickasaws, and Choctaws. The purpose of the conference was to explain the territorial changes resulting from the Peace of Paris, which ended the French and Indian War. British victory in the war meant the surrender of France's major territorial claims in eastern North America. Spanish influence in the southern part of North America ended as well when east and west Florida came under British control after the war. *See Early American Indian Documents: Treaties and Laws, 1607–1789* (Alden T. Vaughan gen. ed.), vol. 5, *Virginia Treaties, 1723–1775,* 250–252 (W. Stitt Robinson ed., 1983) [hereinafter *Virginia Treaties*].

14. *Id.* at 288.

15. The Treaty of Greenville, June 1795, was a crucial event in the early history of U.S.-Indian relations. Since the end of the Revolutionary War, the Indians of the Old Northwest had staunchly resisted white settlement on Indian lands beyond the Ohio River. In 1794, General Anthony Wayne, instructed to advance with his army into the Ohio country, met and defeated the Western tribes in the decisive battle of Fallen Timbers near the rapids of the Maumee River. In the treaty offered by Wayne to the Indians and signed at Greenville in 1795, the United States drew a boundary line that separated the races but required the Western Indians to cede the eastern and southern sections of what is now Ohio and a small portion of present-day Indiana. Reginald Horsman assesses the significance of the Treaty of Greenville as follows:

> The Treaty of Greenville, by bringing peace to the frontier and asserting the dominance of the United States in the [Old] Northwest, made possible the future American settlement of the area. . . .
>
> But while the Indians were comparatively calm and boundaries relatively stable, American settlers pounced across the Ohio into the land ceded by the Indians at Greenville. They were soon pushing up to and across the Greenville line, and all the promises of the early 1790's meant nothing.

Reginald Horsman, *Expansion and American Indian Policy, 1783–1812* 103 (1992).

16. 27 *National State Papers of the United States, 1789–1817,* pt. 2, *Texts of Documents, Administration of George Washington, 1789–1797, December 7, 1795–December 31, 1795* 17 (Eileen Daney Carzo ed., 1985) [hereinafter 27 *National State Papers*].

17. *See supra* Chapter 2, text accompanying notes 55–57.

18. *The History and Culture of Iroquois Diplomacy* 140 (Francis Jennings et al. eds., 1985) [hereinafter *Iroquois Diplomacy*].
19. *Id.*
20. *Id.*
21. *Id.*
22. *Id.* at 140–141.
23. *Id.* at 141.
24. N. Scott Momaday, "The Man Made of Words," *Indian Voices: The First Convocation of American Indian Scholars* 55 (1970).
25. *Virginia Treaties, supra* note 13, at 272.
26. *See Early American Indian Documents: Treaties & Laws, 1607–1789* (Alden T. Vaughan gen. ed.), vol. 3, *New York and New Jersey Treaties, 1609–1682* 86 (Barbara Graymont ed., 1985).
27. *Id.*
28. *Id.*
29. *Id.* at 86–87.
30. Robert M. Cover, "Foreword: *Nomos* and Narrative," 97 *Harv. L. Rev.* 4, 4–5 (1983).
31. *See supra* text accompanying notes 3–4.
32. *Iroquois Diplomacy, supra* note 18, at 139.
33. *Id.*
34. Michael Foster, "Another Look at the Function of Wampum in Iroquois-White Councils," in *Iroquois Diplomacy, supra* note 18, at 104.
35. *Id.* at 106–107.
36. *Iroquois Diplomacy, supra* note 18, at 139.
37. *Id.*
38. *Id.* at 139–140.
39. *Id.* at 140.
40. *Id.* at 144.
41. Richard Rorty, *Contingency, Irony, and Solidarity* (1989).
42. *Id.* at xvi, 192.
43. *Id.* at xvi.
44. *Id.*
45. *See supra* Chapter 1, text accompanying notes 8–10.
46. Rorty, *supra* note 41, at xvi.
47. *See supra* text accompanying note 42.
48. Cover, *supra* note 30, at 40.
49. *Id.* at 4–5.
50. *See* Matsuda, "Racist Speech," *supra* note 1, at 2325 n. 25.
51. 15 *National State Papers of the United States, 1789–1817*, pt. 2, *Texts of Documents, Administration of Geroge Washington, 1789–1797, 2nd Congress, 2nd Session, December 3, 1792–February 8, 1793* (Eileen Daney Carzo ed., 1985).
52. *Id.*
53. *Id.*
54. *Id.*
55. *Id.*
56. *See supra* Chapter 2, text accompanying notes 38–40.
57. *See* Cover, *supra* note 30, at 11–19.
58. *Id.* at 45.

59. *See supra* Chapter 2, text accompanying notes 57–61.
60. 27 *National State Papers, supra* note 16, at 21.
61. *Id.*
62. *Id.*
63. *Id.*
64. *See supra* text accompanying notes 16–23.
65. *Iroquois Diplomacy, supra* note 18, at 141.
66. *See* Arthur C. Parker, "The Constitution of the Five Nations, or the Iroquois Book of the Great Law," in *Parker on the Iroquois* 31 (William N. Fenton ed., 1968).
67. *Id.* at 112.
68. We know little of Kiotseaeton, who conducted the remarkable treaty negotiations at Three Rivers, other than that he was called Le Crochet (The Hook) by the French and was from the Mohawk tribe, the "eastern door" of the League of the Iroquois. We do know, however, that he was well versed in the narrative traditions of the league and translated these traditions into a remarkably effective language for diplomacy.

Kiotseaeton staged the entire negotiations at Three Rivers as an elaborate play, with positions and dialogue scripted according to the ritualized patterns of the Iroquois Condolence Council. From the banks of the river, he addressed the French and their allied tribes as his "brothers," the traditional form of address used between the two sides in council ritual. His opening words of peace, "I come therefore to enter into the designs of the French. . . . I come to make known to you the thoughts of all my country," represented, in essence, a scaled-down version of the inaugural "wood's edge" ceremony of the Condolence Council.

His actual presentation of treaty terms at Three Rivers further relied on ritual council patterns. In the courtyard of the French fort, "over which large sails had been spread to keep off the heat of the Sun," Kiotseaeton stepped onto center stage. Two poles had been planted with a rope stretched between them at the center of the stage. As explained by Father Vimont, the purpose of the device was to "hang and tie the words that they were to bring us—that is to say, the presents they wished to make us, which consisted of seventeen collars of porcelain beads, a portion of which were on their bodies." *Iroquois Diplomacy, supra* note 18, at 137–139.

As prescribed by council ritual, Kiotseaeton raised his eyes up to the sun, then cast them over the whole company assembled in the courtyard. Slowly, he moved to the line of wampum gifts strung between the two poles in the center of the stage and took a collar of wampum in hand. Looking directly at the French governor, Huault de Montmagny, whom he called *Onontio* (or Great Mountain), he "commenced," in Father Vimont's words, "to harangue in a loud voice."

> Onontio, lend me ear. I am the mouth for the whole of my country; thou listenest to all the Iroquois in hearing my words. There is no evil in my heart; I have only good songs in my mouth. We have a multitude of war songs in our country; we have cast them all on the ground; we have no longer anything but songs of rejoicing.

Id. at 139.

With this dramatic pronouncement of his country's desire to end all hostilities with the French and their allied tribes of Canada, Kiotseaeton next burst into the Condolence Council song of peace: "[H]e began to sing; his countrymen responded; he walked about the great space as if on the stage of theater; he made a thousand gestures; he looked up to Heaven; he gazed at the Sun; he rubbed his arms as if he wished to draw from them the strength that moved them in war." *Id.* at 137–139.

69. Delgado, "A Plea for Narrative," *supra* note 1, at 2438.

Chapter 5

1. *See supra* Chapter 2.
2. *See supra* Chapter 3.
3. *See supra* Chapter 4.
4. *See supra* Chapter 1.
5. U.S. Constitution, Preamble. Orlando Patterson, in his essay, "Freedom, Slavery, and the Modern Construction of Rights," in *Historical Change and Human Rights: The Oxford Amnesty Lectures, 1994* (1995), states that the idea, reflected in the written charters of the English North American colonies, "that a political community should be established on the basis of certain clearly defined legal principles" was "unprecedented." *Id.* at 149. The colonial charter of Massachusetts, the Fundamental Order of Connecticut, and Roger Williams's "remarkable" charter for Rhode Island, *id.*, not to mention the Articles of Confederation adopted during the Revolutionary period, were all important precedents for the Founders' Constitution. On the Anglo-European and Anglo-American constitutional tradition, *see* J. G. A. Pocock, *The Machiavellian Moment* (1975) (describing "constitutional thought" in that tradition as "thought about the forms and institutions of joint action between citizens," *id.* at 99).

I have assiduously tried to avoid in this chapter overt engagement in the academic debate about the degree of influence of American Indian political ideas on the Founders of the United States and their drafting of the Constitution of 1787. *See, e.g.*, Donald A. Grinde Jr., *The Iroquois and the Founding of the American Nation* (1977); Jack M. Weatherford, *Indian Givers: How the Indians of the Americas Transformed the World* (1988); Gregory Schaaf, "From the Great Law of Peace to the Constitution of the United States: A Revision of America's Democratic Roots," 14 *Am. Indian L. Rev.* 323, 324–331 (1989); *Indian Roots of American Democracy* (José Barreiro ed., 1992); Bruce E. Johansen, *Forgotten Founders* (1982) (exploring evidence of Iroquoian influence on the U.S. Constitution). *But see* Erik M. Jensen, "The Imaginary Connection between the Great Law of Peace and the United States Constitution: A Reply to Professor Schaaf," 15 *Am. Indian L. Rev.* 295, 295–298 (1990); Michael Newman, "Founding Feathers: The Iroquois and the Constitution," *New Republic*, Nov. 7, 1988, at 17–18; Elisabeth Tooker, "The United States Constitution and the Iroquois League," 35 *Ethnohistory* 305 (1988).

Even the Congress of the United States has weighed in on the historical controversy with a formal resolution acknowledging "the contribution of the Iroquois Confederacy of Nations to the development of the Constitution." H. Con. Res. 331, 100th Cong., 2d sess. (1988). *See also Iroquois Confederacy of Nations: Hearing before the Select Comm. on Indian Affairs*, 100th Cong., 1st sess. (1987).

As I hope this chapter shows, American Indian visions of law and peace as proclaimed in the Encounter era treaty literature are worthy of serious study precisely because the language of American Indian multicultural constitutionalism employed a vocabulary so unlike anything brought by Europeans to America or implemented by them once they got here and acquired power over the continent. *See generally* Rennard Strickland, "Genocide-at-Law: A Historic and Contemporary View of the Native American Experience," 34 *U. Kan. L. Rev.* 713 (1986) (looking at the role of law in the historical and contemporary genocidal experience of North American natives); Robert A. Williams, Jr., "Document of Barbarism: The Contemporary Legacy of European Racism and Colonialism in the Narrative Tradition of Federal Indian Law," 31 *Ariz. L. Rev.* 237 (1989) (comparing the early nineteenth-century Cherokee discourse of tribal sovereignty with the opposing legal discourse deployed by Removal era whites in response to Indian resistance to white hegemony).

6. The text expands on an important point made by Francis Jennings. Analyzing the Covenant Chain, the Encounter era multicultural constitution between the Iroquois and the British colonies (*see infra,* text accompanying notes 77–102), Jennings writes: "There was enough identifiable structure in the Chain to warrant being called a constitution—not in the American sense of one basic law, but rather as the British use that word to embrace a whole body of traditions, customs, and practices basic to the polity." Francis Jennings, *The Ambiguous Iroquois Empire* 368 (1984).

7. *See supra* Chapter 2.

8. 27 *National State Papers of the United States, 1789–1817,* pt. 2, *Texts of Documents, Administration of George Washington, 1789–1797* 23 (Eileen Daney Carzo ed., 1985) [hereinafter 27 *National State Papers*].

9. *Early American Indian Documents: Treaties and Laws, 1607–1789,* vol. 11, *Georgia Treaties, 1733–1763* 55 (John T. Juricek vol. ed., 1989) [hereinafter *Georgia Treaties*].

10. 19 *National State Papers of the United States, 1789–1817,* pt. 2, *Texts of Documents, Administration of George Washington, 1789–1797* 207 (Eileen Daney Carzo ed., 1985).

11. 14 *National State Papers of the United States, 1789–1817,* pt. 2, *Texts of Documents, Administration of George Washington, 1789–1797* 159 (Eileen Daney Carzo ed., 1985).

12. *See supra* Chapter 2, text accompanying note 105.

13. *See supra* text accompanying note 8.

14. *See supra* Chapter 2, text accompanying notes 111–112.

15. *Early American Indian Documents: Treaties and Laws, 1607–1789,* vol. 2, *Pennsylvania Treaties, 1737–1756* 269–272 (Donald H. Kent vol. ed., 1984) [hereinafter *Pennsylvania Treaties, 1737–1756*].

16. *Id.* at 282–283.

17. *Id.* at 283.

18. *Id.*

19. *Id.*

20. *Id.* at 289.

21. *See supra* Chapter 2, text accompanying notes 101–110.

22. *See supra* Chapter 3, text accompanying notes 35–36.

23. 27 *National State Papers, supra* note 8, at 14.

24. *Georgia Treaties, supra* note 9, at 36.

25. *Early American Indian Documents: Treaties and Laws, 1607–1789* (Alden T. Vaughan gen. ed.), vol. 5, *Virginia Treaties, 1723–1775* 216 (W. Stitt Robinson vol. ed., 1983 [hereinafter *Virginia Treaties, 1723–1775*].

26. *See supra* Chapter 3, text accompanying notes 30–32.

27. *Virginia Treaties, 1723–1775, supra* note 25, at 216.

28. *Id.*

29. *Id.* at 217.

30. *Early American Indian Documents: Treaties and Laws, 1607–1789,* vol. 6, *Maryland Treaties, 1632–1775* 231–232 (W. Stitt Robinson vol. ed., 1987).

31. Richard White, *The Middle Ground: Indians, Empires, and Republics in the Great Lakes Region, 1650–1815* (1991). This section on the French-Algonquian treaty alliance relies primarily on White's superb book.

32. *Id.* at x.

33. On the Beaver Wars, *see generally* Francis Jennings, *The Ambiguous Iroquois Empire, supra* note 6; Robert A. Goldstein, *French-Iroquois Diplomatic and Military Relations, 1609–1701* (1969); George T. Hunt, *The Wars of the Iroquois: A Study in Intertribal Trade Relations* (1940).

34. *Quoted in* White, *supra* note 31, at 24.

35. *See id.* at 30.

36. Algonquian unity, sufficient to repulse and, in time, perhaps even to defeat the Iroquois, was central to French strategy on the continent. Only France had the power to create such unity by bringing together all of these tribes under the protective power of *Onontio,* the governor of New France. As Intendant Duchesneau recognized in 1681, it was in the French "interest to keep these people united and to take cognizance of all their differences, however trifling these may be, to watch carefully that not one of them terminate without our mediation and to constitute ourselves in all things their arbiters and protectors." *Quoted in id.* at 31.

37. *Quoted in id.* at 36.

38. *See id.* at 83–94.

39. *Id.* at 93.

40. *Id.* at 129.

41. *Id.* at 112.

42. Wilbur R. Jacobs, *Dispossessing the American Indian: Indians and Whites on the Colonial Frontier* 56 (1985).

43. *Quoted in* White, *supra* note 31, at 141.

44. *Id.* at 130.

45. These principles permitted the alliance to achieve a remarkable degree of success in the half century leading up to the culminating contest between France and England for European imperial hegemony in North America—the French and Indian War. During this period, the alliance of the *pays d'en haut* enabled the Algonquians to reoccupy the territories seized from them by the Iroquois. The French based their security and ultimately their imperial strategy for control of the North American continent on the strength of this unique multicultural treaty relationship. *See generally* White, *supra* note 31.

46. *Early American Indian Documents: Treaties and Laws, 1607–1789,* vol. 1, *Pennsylvania and Delaware Treaties, 1629–1737* 26 (Donald H. Kent vol. ed., 1979) [hereinafter *Pennsylvania and Delaware Treaties*].

47. *Id.*

48. *Pennsylvania Treaties, 1737–1756, supra* note 15, at 8.
49. *Georgia Treaties, supra* note 9, at 36.
50. *Id.* at 267.
51. *Quoted in* Dorothy V. Jones, "British Colonial Treaties," in 4 *Handbook of North American Indians: History of Indian-White Relations* 187 (Wilcomb Washburn vol. ed., 1988).
52. The Conestogas were a remnant group of Susquehannock Indians who settled near the confluence of Conestoga Creek and the Susquehanna River in Pennsylvania during the late seventeenth century. They entered into a treaty with William Penn in 1701. *See* Francis Jennings, "Susquehannocks," in 15 *Handbook of North American Indians: Northeast* 362–367 (Bruce G. Trigger vol. ed., 1978).
53. *Pennsylvania and Delaware Treaties, 1629–1737, supra* note 46, at 147.
54. *Id.* The day after the Conestoga speech, Pennsylvania's council instructed that the Indians be informed

> [t]hat the bond of friendship and Brotherhood made by the Proprietor, Willm. Penn, with their nation, was so strong, that we Doubted not that it would ever be broken; that both we and they had hitherto Inviolably kept it, and we were Glad to see them on their parts Desirous to strengthen it, and therefore took their presents very kindly.

Id. at 149.
55. *Id.* at 400.
56. *Id.*
57. *Id.*
58. *Quoted in* Peter Wraxall, *An Abridgement of the Indian Affairs* 217 (Charles H. McIlwain ed., 1915).
59. *Georgia Treaties, supra* note 9, at 267–268.
60. "Sir William Johnson to the Lords of Trade, July 17, 1756," in 8 *Documents Relative to the Colonial History of the State of New York* 119 (John R. Brodhead ed., 1853).
61. *Pennsylvania Treaties, 1737–1756, supra* note 15, at 182.
62. *See supra* Chapter 4.
63. *See* Robert A. Williams, Jr., "Linking Arms Together: Multicultural Constitutionalism in a North American Indigenous Vision of Law and Peace," 82 *Cal. L. Rev.* 981, 1005 (1994). Portions of this section on the Iroquois multicultural constitutional tradition are adapted from the above article.
64. The narrative tradition of the Iroquois as "Romans of the New World" can be traced back to the influential colonial period writer Cadwallader Colden. His two-part study, *The History of the Five Nations Depending on the Province of New York in America* (pt. 1, 1727; pt. 2, 1747) (1922), drew frequent comparisons to the Romans and Greeks in speaking of the Iroquois. Other writers followed in the tradition. DeWitt Clinton, a member of the New York Tammany Society, in an 1812 address before the Historical Society of New York, stated that the Iroquois, in "eloquence, in dignity, and in all characteristics of profound policy, surpassed an assembly of feudal barons, and were perhaps not inferior to the great . . . Council of Greece." *Quoted in* Donald A. Grinde Jr., "Iroquois Political Theory and the Roots of American Democracy," in *Exiled in the Land of the Free* 277 (Oren Lyons et al. eds., 1992). It was Clinton who called the Iroquois

"the Romans of the Western World." *Quoted in id.* at 272. Lewis Henry Morgan, in his classic *League of the Ho-De-No Sau-nee* (1851), continued the narrative tradition with comparisons of the Iroquois to the classic Romans and Greeks throughout his text. *See generally* Jennings, *supra* note 6, at 10–24 (discussing the "mythology" of the Iroquois in American historical writing).

65. Jones, *supra* note 51, at 186.

66. Elisabeth Tooker, "The League of the Iroquois: Its History, Politics, and Ritual," in 15 *Handbook of North American Indians: Northeast* 418 (Bruce G. Trigger vol. ed., 1978).

67. *Id.* at 421, table 1.

68. *See, e.g.,* Jennings, *supra* note 6, at 14, 141–142.

69. *See supra* Chapter 2.

70. Arthur C. Parker, "The Constitution of the Five Nations or the Iroquois Book of the Great Law," in *Parker on the Iroquois* 102 (William N. Fenton ed., 1968).

71. *See* Richard Haan, "Covenant and Consensus: Iroquois and English, 1676–1760," in *Beyond the Covenant Chain: The Iroquois and Their Neighbors in Indian North America, 1600–1800* 41–57 (Daniel K. Richter & James H. Merrell eds., 1987) [hereinafter *Beyond the Covenant Chain*].

72. *Quoted in* Michael K. Foster, "Another Look at the Function of Wampum in Iroquois-White Councils," in *The History and Culture of Iroquois Diplomacy* 110 (Francis Jennings et al. eds., 1985).

73. *See, e.g., supra* Chapter 2, text accompanying notes 55–56, and Chapter 4, text accompanying notes 32–40.

74. *The History and Culture of Iroquois Diplomacy* 141 (Francis Jennings et al. eds., 1985).

75. *Id.*

76. *Id.*

77. The seminal work on the Covenant Chain is Jennings, *supra* note 6. Other works on the Covenant Chain include Richard Aquila, *The Iroquois Restoration: Iroquois Diplomacy on the Colonial Frontier, 1701–1754* (1983); Stephen Saunders Webb, *1676: The End of American Independence* (1985); Francis Jennings, "Iroquois Alliances in American History," in *The History and Culture of Iroquois Diplomacy* 37–65 (Francis Jennings, William N. Fenton, Mary Druke, & David R. Miller eds., 1985 [hereinafter *Iroquois Diplomacy*]. *See also* Morgan, *supra* note 64.

The treaty literature of the Encounter era indicates that the Iroquois sought to apply the constitutional principles embodied in the Covenant Chain to their other multicultural relationships as well. Ethnohistorian Richard Haan states that there were many "chains" linking the Iroquois with the different English colonies. The term "Covenant Chain," Haan states, was generally used by English colonists to describe these types of multicultural alliances. The evidence indicates, for example, that Pennsylvania likely maintained what it regarded as a separate chain with the Iroquois with a "fire" that burned at Philadelphia rather than at Albany. *See* Richard L. Haan, "Covenant and Consensus: Iroquois and English, 1676–1760," in *Beyond the Covenant Chain, supra* note 71, at 41–57.

78. *Quoted in* Jennings, *supra* note 6, at 370.

79. *Id.* at 148.

80. *Id.*

81. *Id.*

82. *See id.* at 148–149, 167; *Beyond the Covenant Chain, supra* note 71, at 43–49.

83. *Quoted in* Jennings, *supra* note 6, at 145.

84. *Pennsylvania Treaties, 1737–1756, supra* note 15, at 84–85.

85. *Id.*

86. *Quoted in* Arnold Krupat, "The Dialogic of Silko's *Storyteller,*" in *Narrative Chance: Postmodern Discourse on Native American Literatures* 60 (Gerald Vizenor ed., 1993).

87. *Id.*

88. *See supra* Chapter 4.

89. *See supra* Chapter 2. The responsibility of the league for perpetuating the Great Peace was tied closely to the Iroquois conception of political time. As J. G. A. Pocock has explained:

> Societies exist in time, and conserve images of themselves as continuously so existing. It follows that the consciousness of time acquired by the individual as a social animal is in large measure consciousness of his society's continuity and of the image of its continuity which that society possesses; and the understanding of time, and of human life as experienced in time, disseminated in a society, is an important part of that society's understanding of itself—of its structure and what legitimates it, of the modes of action which are possible to it and in it. There is a point at which historical and political theory meet, and it can be said without distortion that every society possesses a philosophy of history—a set of ideas about what happens, what can be known and what done, in time considered as a dimension of society—and its functioning.

J. G. A. Pocock, *Politics, Language, and Time* 233 (1974).

For the Iroquois, their images and ideas about political time arose out of the Deganawidah epic, which taught that the organization of their confederated league had brought order and stability out of a time of intense chaos, crises, and suffering. Maintaining the league as an institution devoted to sustaining and renewing the Great Peace was the Iroquois' best assurance for preventing the degeneration of the Iroquois back into that time of constant pain, sorrow, and mourning wars.

Deganawidah had therefore imposed a most weighty responsibility on the Iroquois: they were obligated to perpetuate the continuity in time of the league of the Iroquois as one united people. This vitally regarded duty was visualized as extending to future generations of Iroquois. The chiefs of the council were charged by Deganawidah as follows: "Be of strong mind, O chiefs! Carry no anger and hold no grudges. Think not forever of yourselves, O chiefs, nor of your own generation. Think of continuing generations of our families, think of our grandchildren and of those yet unborn, whose faces are coming from beneath the ground." Anthony F. C. Wallace, *The Death and Rebirth of the Seneca* 42 (1972). Wallace explains the league's primary focus in assuring the continuity and unity of the Iroquois confederacy of tribes through time and extending the long branches of the Tree of Peace to other nations as follows:

> The minimum purpose of the League was to maintain unity, strength, and good will among the Five Nations, so as to make them invulnerable to

> attack from without and to division from within. The native philosophers who rationalized the League in later years conceived also a maximum purpose: the conversion of all mankind, so that peace and happiness should be the lot of the peoples of the whole earth, and all nations should abide by the same law and be members of the same confederacy.

Id.

Peace, not war, according to the Deganawidah epic, was supposed to be the predisposition of the Iroquois toward other nations not confederated to the League. "The white roots of the Great Tree of Peace will continue to grow," Deganawidah had prophesied,

> advancing the Good Mind and Righteousness and Peace, moving into territories of peoples scattered through the forest. And when a nation, guided by the Great White Roots, shall approach the Tree, you shall welcome her here and take her by the arm and seat her in the place of council. She will add a brace or leaning pole to the longhouse and will thus strengthen the edifice of Reason and Peace.

Id. at 42–43.

As the Iroquois said: "[T]he land shall be beautiful, the river shall have no waves, one may go everywhere without fear." *Id.* at 43.

90. Jennings, *supra* note 6, at 166.

91. Daniel K. Richter, "Rediscovered Links in the Covenant Chain: Previously Unpublished Transcripts of New York: Indian Treaty Minutes, 1677–1691," 92 *Proc. Am. Antiquarian Soc'y* 45, 56 (1982).

92. *Id.*

93. *Quoted in* Mary A. Druke, "Linking Arms: The Structure of Iroquois Intertribal Diplomacy," in *Beyond the Covenant Chain, supra* note 71, at 33.

94. Jennings, *supra* note 6, at 165–166.

95. Richter, *supra* note 91, at 74–75.

96. *Quoted in Iroquois Diplomacy, supra* note 68, at 22.

97. 33 *National State Papers of the United States, 1789–1817,* pt. 2, *Texts of Documents, Administration of George Washington, 1789–1797,* 261 (Eileen Daney Carzo ed., 1985).

98. *Id.* at 261.

99. *Id.*

100. *See supra* text accompanying note 93. The principle that those linked by a treaty relationship were under an obligation to protect each other's interests helps us understand one of the most important events related in the Covenant Chain treaty literature—the Iroquois grant of lands in the Susquehanna Valley to the New York colony in 1681. From the English perspective, New York gained a valuable piece of real estate when the Iroquois assigned to the governor of New York the vast territories the confederacy claimed in the Susquehanna Valley by right of supposed prior conquests over the tribes of the region. The transaction was accompanied, however, by an Iroquois declaration of the principles informing the grant—principles that were determined by reliance on the ancient constitutional tradition that sustained the Covenant Chain treaty relationship:

> When the English came to the Manhattans, i.e. New York; Aragiske, i.e. Virginia & to Jaquokranagare, i.e. Mayland; they were but a small people and we a great people, and finding they were a good people, we gave them

> Lands, & Treated them civilly. And now since you are a Great People & we but small, *your will protect us from the French,* which if you do not, we shall loose all our Hunting & Beavers, & the French will have all our Beavers, who are angry with us for bringing them to the Brethren. We have put *all our lands & ourselves* under the Protection of the Great Duke of York, & Give him the *Susquehanna River* which we *Won with the Sword,* and desire it may be a Branch of the Great Tree that grows here, under which we shall shelter ourselves from the French or any other peoples.

Quoted in Richter, *supra* note 91, at 66.

The grant in trust of the Susquehanna Valley was not intended by the league as an acknowledgment of New York's suzerainty over the Iroquois under the chain. The legal meanings of the grant derived from the principles of Iroquois constitutional tradition. According to those traditional principles, the Iroquois and English had agreed to link arms together by their alliance. The English therefore owed the Iroquois a duty of protection "from the French and any other peoples." This meant that the English had a constitutional duty to protect the lands assigned in the grant for the benefit of their chain treaty partners, the Iroquois, in perpetuity. This Iroquois understanding of the grant as controlled by the constitutional principles of the chain is indicated quite clearly by a statement made by the league's spokesman at the end of the above speech: "[A]s we are free People United to the English we give our Land to what Sachem [chief] we please." No Englishman present at the speech sought to contradict this statement. The principle perpetuated by the constitutional tradition embodied in the Covenant Chain required the English to acknowledge the Iroquois' independence, at least as far as the Iroquois understood that term. *Id.*

101. Jennings stresses that the English regarded the chain "as an instrument" to serve their own purposes, as did the Iroquois. For the Iroquois, however, "their economic dependence on the inter-societal trade controlled by Europeans" placed real limits on their power, limits "largely determined by what services they could perform for the English." Nonetheless, the two sides of the chain needed each other for their own "expedient" purposes. The chain served as a constitutional device for organizing the interests of the various parties allied through it, and as Jennings notes, "the interests of all the parties coincided often enough, and mutual concessions were made frequently enough, to hold the rickety edifice more or less together for a century." Jennings, *supra* note 6, at 373–374. *See also Beyond the Covenant Chain, supra* note 71, at 48.

102. Jennings, *supra* note 6, at 374–375.

Conclusion

1. *See* Frantz Fanon, *The Wretched of the Earth* 51 (1978): "The immobility to which the native is condemned can only be called in question if the native decides to put an end to the history of colonization—the history of pillage—and to bring into existence the history of the nation—the history of decolonization."

2. *See supra* Chapter 5, text accompanying notes 22–30.

3. Annette C. Baier, *A Progress of Sentiments: Reflections on Hume's Treatise* 232 (1991).

4. *See supra* Chapter 5, text accompanying note 70.

5. *See* Baier, *supra* note 3. *See also* Annette C. Baier, "Hume, the Women's Moral Theorist?," in *Women and Moral Theory* 40 (Eva Kitay & Diana Meyers eds., 1987).

6. Martha Minow, "Beyond State Intervention in the Family: For Baby Jane Doe," 18 *U. Mich. J. L. Reform* 933 (1995), urges the position that decisions about family relations should be based on the extent to which they build conditions for trust. *See id.* at 989–1009. *See also* Martha Minow, "Many Silent Worlds," 9 *W. New Eng. L. Rev.* 197 (1987) (describing the legal obligations of persons seen situated in a complex network of relationships built on trust).

7. Following up on Baier, *supra* note 5, Richard Rorty, "Human Rights, Rationality, and Sentimentality," in *On Human Rights: The Oxford Amnesty Lectures, 1993* (Stephen Shute & Susan Hurley eds., 1993) [hereinafter *The Oxford Amnesty Lectures*], states that the substitution of "trust" for "obligation" as the fundamental moral notion requires the progressive development of the ability "to see the similarities between ourselves and people very unlike us as outweighing the differences." *Id.* at 129. *See also* Richard Rorty, *Contingency, Irony, and Solidarity* 192 (1989) (arguing that moral progress in the direction of greater human solidarity [i.e., trust] requires developing "the ability to think of people wildly different from ourselves as included in the range of 'us'").

8. Roberto Unger, a leading critical legal studies theorist, has pointed to the fact that focusing on trust and cooperation rather than on the language of rights is a better way of understanding the source and nature of many of the obligations that arise from contractual relationships of interdependence. In mapping the premises of this "countervision" to the dominant approach to contract problems in American law, Unger states:

> [O]bligations do arise primarily from relationships of mutual dependence that have been only incompletely shaped by government-imposed duties or explicit and perfected bargains. The situations in which either of these shaping factors operates alone to generate obligations are, on this alternative view, merely the extremes of a spectrum. Toward the center of this spectrum, deliberate agreement and state-made or state-recognized duties become less important, though they never disappear entirely. The closer a situation to the center, the more clearly do rights acquire a two-staged definition: the initial, tentative definition of any entitlement must now be completed. Here the boundaries are drawn and redrawn in context according to judgments of both the expectations generated by interdependence and the impact that a particular exercise of a right might have upon other parties to the relation or upon the relation itself.

Roberto M. Unger, *The Critical Legal Studies Movement* 80–81 (1986). *See also* Roberto Unger, *Passion* 72–74 (1984) (arguing that rights can be justified within a common enterprise to the extent that they promote trust between persons).

9. Writing on the rights and obligations of workers and plant owners in the context of a "company town" plant closing, Joseph Singer, another leading critical legal theorist, demonstrates that American property law, like American contract law, already recognizes numerous relationships of trust, mutuality, and interdependence as property rights. Other relationships, however, such as those between plant owners and plant workers, plant and plant suppliers, and plant and town as interdependent entities supporting and sustaining each other over

decades, stand for very little in our property law. *See* Joseph William Singer, "The Reliance Interest in Property," 40 *Stanford L. Rev.* 611, 621–623.

Singer's relational vision of property rights encourages us to ask a set of questions about the plant closing situation not usually considered in the language of rights in our contemporary American vision of property law:

> Rather than asking "who owns the factory?" we should ask "what relationships should we nurture?" We should encourage people to rely on relationships of mutual dependence by making it possible for everyone to form such relationships and by protecting those who are most vulnerable when those relationships end. Property rights can be justified morally within a common enterprise to the extent they allow people to develop relationships that promote conditions of trust. . . . [W]e have an obligation to learn what it would take for us to create the kind of society in which we could trust each other enough to place our lives in each other's hands.

Id. at 751

10. The theme of trust, particularly with respect to obligations arising out of reliance on long-term relationships, has been prominent in the works of a number of twentieth-century progressive political and legal thinkers. Leon Green, for example, writing in 1937 at the height of the legal realist movement, carefully outlined the realist position that the modern market system should protect relational interests. *See* Leon Green, "The Case for the Sit-Down Strike," 90 *New Republic,* Mar. 24, 1937, at 199. Green, focusing on the specific context of sit-down strikes, acknowledged that the industrial relation between employer and employee initially is the result of a "contractual nexus." But, he wrote,

> as in the case of family, corporate, partnership, carrier, and all other important relations, the slender tie of the initial contract is overgrown by a network of tissue, nerves and tendons, as it were, which gives the relation its significance. . . .
>
> Both groups are joint adventurers, as it were, in industrial enterprise. Both have and necessarily must have a voice in the matters of common concern. Both must have protection adequate to their interests as against the world at large as well as against the undue demands of each other.

Id. at 199.

Extending his analysis beyond the confines of the industrial relation between employer and employee, Green declared a fundamental principle that emerges in the works of a number of major legal realists of the 1930s, as well as in the works of subsequent generations of legal scholars who were heavily influenced by their contributions: "All institutions built upon relational interests of the groups concerned must submit to the obligations which have grown up around the particular relation, and if it is to be destroyed it must be done subject to such obligations." *Id.* at 200.

In the 1960s and 1970s, law and society scholars such as Ian Macneil and Stewart Macaulay sought to extend these realist insights on relational interests in contract law using the empirical research tools of the modern social sciences. Their interdisciplinary work on long-term supplier contracts and other commercial contexts focused scholarly attention on the reciprocal legal rights, expectations, and obligations arising from various types of contractual relationships of mutuality and interdependence. *See* Ian R. Macneil, *The New Social Contract: An Inquiry into Modern Contractual Relations* (1980) (arguing that modern contractual relations collectively are analogous to Rousseau's concept of the social contract); Ian R. Macneil, "Contracts: Adjustment of Long-Term Economic Relations under Classical, Neoclassical and Relational Contract Law," 72 *Nw. U. L. Rev.* 854 (1978); Ian R. Macneil, "Economic Analysis of Contractual Relations: Its Shortfalls and the Need for a Rich Classification Apparatus," 75 *Nw. U. L. Rev.* 1018 (1981); Ian R. Macneil, "Relational Contract: What We Do and Do Not Know," 1985 *Wis. L. Rev.* 483.

See also Stewart Macaulay, "Elegant Models, Empirical Pictures, and the Complexities of Contract," 11 *Law & Soc'y Rev.* 507 (1977) (arguing that the empirical picture of the contract process in capitalist societies differs sharply from the classical model). *See also* Robert W. Gordon, "Macaulay, Macneil and the Discovery of Solidarity and Power in Contract Law," 1985 *Wis. L. Rev.* 565 (focusing on the substantial departures of Macaulay and Macneil from the conventional contracts scholarship); Gidon Gottlieb, "Relationism: Legal Theory for a Relational Society," 50 *U. Chi. L. Rev.* 567 (1983) (arguing that the function of law is dependent on social context).

11. *See, e.g.,* Francis Jennings, *The Ambiguous Iroquois Empire* 84–112 (1984) (describing the Iroquois Beaver Wars of the seventeenth century); 15 *Handbook of North American Indians: Northeast* 384–386 (Bruce G. Trigger vol. ed., 1978) (describing Woodlands Indian warfare).

12. *See generally* Richard White, *The Middle Ground: Indians, Empires, and Republics in the Great Lakes Region, 1650–1815* 441–515 (1991) (describing and referencing uses of the common bowl metaphor among Indian tribes of eastern North America).

13. Baier, *supra* note 3, at 232.

14. White, *supra* note 12, at 441.

15. *See supra* Chapter 5, text accompanying notes 69–72.

16. *See supra* Chapter 5, text accompanying note 70.

17. *See* Arthur C. Parker, "Constitution of the Five Nations," in *Parker on the Iroquois* 103 (William N. Fenton ed., 1968).

18. *Id.*

19. *Id.* As Parker's relation of the epic explains of this act:

> This one dish or bowl signifies that they will make their hunting grounds one common tract and all have a coequal right to hunt within it. The knife being prohibited from being placed in the dish or bowl, signifies that all danger would be removed from shedding blood by the people of these different nations of the confederacy caused by differences of the right of the hunting grounds.

Id. at 103.

20. *Quoted in* White, *supra* note 12, at 441. *See also* Isabel Thompson Kelsay, *Joseph Brant, 1743–1806: Man between Two Worlds* 410 (1984).

21. *Quoted in* White, *supra* note 12, at 441. As White aptly notes, "Brant's symbol of the common dish paralleled an American republican vision of a common land of plenty, open to all migrants who would live together in harmony and peace. But for the American vision to reach fruition, the Americans would have to destroy the Indian's competing vision." *Id.* at 442.

22. *Id.* at 512.

23. *See* 15 *Handbook of North American Indians: Northeast* 631–632 (Bruce G. Trigger vol. ed., 1978). In the early nineteenth century, Tecumseh, with English encouragement, tried to form the Indian tribes of the Old Northwest into an alliance that would agree to sell no more land to the United States. His brother, Tenskwatawa (the Prophet), preached a nativistic movement supporting this goal. The Kickapoo, Potawatomi, Delaware, Sauk, and Winnebago were among the tribes most strongly attached to Tecumseh's resistance movement.

> Recognizing the threat as serious, William Henry Harrison, the governor of the Indiana Territory, led an army to Tippecanoe in 1811 while Tecumseh was on a mission to the southeastern tribes. Although the battle that followed was actually a draw, it destroyed Tenskwatawa's credibility and the movement dissolved.

Id. at 631–632.

On Tecumseh and Tenskwatawa, *see generally* David Edmunds, *Tecumseh and the Quest for Indian Leadership* (1984); David Edmunds, *The Shawnee Prophet* (1983).

24. *Quoted in* W. C. Vanderwerth, *Indian Oratory* 64–65 (1971).

25. *Reprinted in The History and Culture of Iroquois Diplomacy* 137–153 (Francis Jennings, William N. Fenton, Mary A. Druke, & David Miller eds., 1985) [hereinafter *Iroquois Diplomacy*].

26. *See supra* Chapter 5, text accompanying notes 74–76.

27. *Iroquois Diplomacy, supra* note 25, at 141.

28. *Early American Indian Documents: Treaties and Laws, 1607–1789,* vol. 11, *Georgia Treaties, 1733–1763* 357 (John T. Juricek ed., 1989).

29. *See* Reginald Horsman, *Expansion and American Indian Policy, 1783–1812* 89–97 (1992).

30. 15 *National State Papers of the United States, 1789–1817,* pt. 2, *Texts of Documents, Administration of George Washington, 1789–1797: December 3, 1792–February 8, 1793* 65 (Eileen Daney Carzo ed., 1985).

31. *See supra* Chapter 5, text accompanying notes 52–57.

32. *Early American Indian Documents, Treaties and Laws, 1607–1789,* vol. 1, *Pennsylvania and Delaware Treaties, 1629–1737* 400 (Donald H. Kent ed., 1979).

33. *Early American Indian Documents: Treaties and Laws, 1607–1789,* vol. 2, *Pennsylvania Treaties, 1737–1756* 335–336 (Donald H. Kent ed., 1984).

34. Reginald Horsman, *Expansion and American Indian Policy, 1783–1812,* ix–x (1992). *See also supra* note 21.

35. *See supra* Chapter 1, text accompanying notes 1–30.

36. Horsman, *supra* note 34, at x.

37. *See supra* Introduction, text accompanying notes 28–29.

38. *See supra* Introduction, text accompanying notes 11–13.

39. *See id.* On Indian tribes' rights to a degree of measured separatism, *see* Charles F. Wilkinson, *American Indians, Time and the Law* 53–54, 121–122 (1987).

40. On the *Cherokee Cases, see* David H. Getches, Charles F. Wilkinson, & Robert A. Williams, Jr., *Federal Indian Law: Cases and Materials* 122–152 (3d ed. 1993).

41. *See id. See also* Robert Clinton, "Redressing the Legacy of Conquest: A

Vision Quest for a Decolonized Federal Indian Law," 46 *Ark. L. Rev.* 77, 129–132 (1993) (describing how the trust doctrine "conventionally is traced" to Chief Justice Marshall's decisions in the *Cherokee Cases, id.* at 130).

42. 30 U.S. (5 Pet.) 1 (1831).

43. *Id.* at 16.

44. *Id.* at 17. The United States' relationship to the Indians, Marshall declared in the patriarchal terminology that white Americans of his generation typically used in translating the language of Indian forest diplomacy, was that of a "guardian" to his "ward." *Id.*

45. 31 U.S. (6 Pet.) 515 (1832).

46. *Id.* at 555. Marshall was able to join this Indian understanding of the tribes' relationship with the United States to related principles found in the European Law of Nations. Citing to the Swiss international law scholar, Emmerich Vattel, Marshall wrote:

> A weak state, in order to provide for its safety, may place itself under the protection of one more powerful, without stripping itself of the right of government, and ceasing to be a state. Examples of this kind are not wanting in Europe. "Tributary and feudatory states," says Vattel, "do not thereby cease to be sovereign and independent states, so long as self-government and sovereign and independent authority are left in the administration of the state." At the present day, more than one state may be considered as holding its right of self-government under the guarantee and protection of one or more allies.

Id. at 561. On Vattel and the status of Indian tribes under the European Law of Nations, *see supra* Chapter 1, text accompanying notes 14–17.

47. As the Cherokees themselves declared in their 1830 memorial to Congress announcing the tribe's firm opposition to abandoning its treaty-guaranteed eastern homeland and removal to a newly created "Indian territory" west of the Mississippi:

> We wish to remain on the lands of our fathers. We have a perfect and original right to remain without interruption or molestation. The treaties with us, and the laws of the United States made in pursuance of treaties, guaranty our residence and privileges and secure us against intruders. Our only request is, that these treaties may be fulfilled, and these laws executed.

Reprinted in A. Guttman, *States' Rights and Indian Removal:* The Cherokee Nation v. Georgia 58 (1965).

48. *See supra* sources cited in note 41.

49. *Seminole Nation v. United States,* 316 U.S. 286, 297 (1942).

50. *See* Robert Clinton, "Redressing the Legacy of Conquest: A Vision Quest for a Decolonized Federal Indian Law," 46 *Ark. L. Rev.* 77, 107–108 (1993).

51. Charles F. Wilkinson, "To Feel the Summer in the Spring: The Treaty Fishing Rights of the Wisconsin Chippewa," 1991 *Wis. L. Rev.* 375, 378–379.

52. *See* Derrick A. Bell Jr., "*Brown v. Board of Education* and the Interest-Convergence Dilemma," 93 *Harv. L. Rev.* 518 (1980); Derrick A. Bell Jr., "Racial Realism," 24 *Conn. L. Rev.* 363 (1992).

53. Will Kymlicka, *Liberalism, Community and Culture* 13 (1989).

54. *Id.* at 153–154. *See also* N. Bruce Duthu, "Implicit Divestiture of Tribal

Powers: Locating Legitimate Sources of Authority in Indian Country," 19 *Am. Ind. L. Rev.* 353, 389–402 (1994) (arguing for a coherent theory of retained tribal powers that incorporates the insights of Kymlicka's *Liberalism, Community and Culture*).

55. *See supra* Introduction, text accompanying notes 20–22.

56. *See supra* notes 5–10.

57. *See* Baier, *supra* note 3, at 228.

58. Martha Minow, "When Difference Has Its Home: Group Homes for the Mentally Retarded, Equal Protection, and Legal Treatment of Difference," 22 *Harv. C.R.-C.L. L. Rev.* 111, 127 (1987).

59. *See supra* sources cited in note 6.

60. *See supra* Chapter 4, text accompanying notes 41–47.

61. *The Oxford Amnesty Lectures, supra* note 7, at 129.

62. On Unger, *see supra* note 8.

63. *See* Singer, *supra* note 9, at 751.

64. *See supra* text accompanying note 33.

Index